Busy People's Fun, Fast, Festive Christmas Cookbook

Dawn Hall

RUTLEDGE HILL PRESS
A Division of Thomas Nelson Publishers
Since 1798

www.thomasnelson.com

Published by Rutledge Hill Press, a Division of Thomas Nelson, Inc., P.O. Box 141000, Nashville, Tennessee, 37214.

Rutledge Hill Press books may be purchased in bulk for educational, business, fundraising, or sales promotional use. For information, please email SpecialMarkets@ThomasNelson.com.

Library of Congress Cataloging-in-Publication Data

Hall, Dawn.
  Busy people's fun, fast, festive Christmas cookbook / Dawn Hall.
     p. cm.
  ISBN 1-4016-0223-1 (hardcover)
  1. Christmas cookery. 2. Quick and easy cookery. 3. Low-fat diet—Recipes.
I. Title.
  TX739.2.C45H353 2005
  641.5'686—dc22   2005015189

Printed in China
05 06 07 08 09 — 5 4 3 2 1

It is with honor, admiration, and respect that I dedicate this book to Jo Anna Lund, the author of *Healthy Exchanges*. Jo Anna is a living example of a godly business woman who has taken the lemons in her life to make delicious lemon pie in order to bless others.

Contents

Menus at a Glance

Chapter Three: Christmas Day Dinners

Seafood Dinner
(Serves 6) 124

Spicy Seafood Soup
Seafood Topped Tossed Salad
Salmon Topped with Creamy Shrimp
Sauce
Bell Pepper Medley
Whole Wheat Buttermilk & Basil
Biscuits
Minty Angel Dessert Cups

Santa's Favorite Steak and Spinach
Roll Dinner (Serves 4) 133

Granny's Gourmet Tossed Salad
Steak & Spinach Roll (Santa's Favorite)
Garlic Smashed Red-Skin Potatoes
Holiday Broccoli
Christmas Tree Biscuits
Candy Cane Ice Cream Cups

Fancy Shmancy Sit-Down Dinner
(Serves 6) 142

Snow-Capped Icebergs
Filet Mignon Topped with Lobster
Dilled Smashed Potatoes
Asparagus with Crab & Blue Cheese
Cheese Filled Breadsticks
Virgin Cranberry Mimosa
Cranberry Sorbet

Yuletide Pork Roast Dinner
(Serves 6) 150

Cream of Spinach Soup
Yuletide Pork Roast with Lemon
Pepper and Rosemary
Savory Rice Stuffing
Broccoli Breakaway
Pumpkin Custard
Cut-Out Glazed Sugar Cookies

Homey-Ham Dinner
(Serves 6) 158

Tossed Salad with Smooth Cranberry
Salad Dressing
Christmas Skillet Ham Steaks
Sweet Potatoes with Caramelized
Onions
Onion Muffin Tops
Gingerbread & Eggnog Dessert Cups

Southern Country Ham Dinner
(Serves 8) 165

Mini-Ham with Sweet Sauce
Holiday Turnip Greens with Potatoes
Cranberry-Apple Warm, Sweet &
Spicy Chutney
Sweet Potato Mini-Muffins
Peachy Pumpkin Dish
Old-Fashioned Bread Pudding

Stuffed Cornish Hens
(Serves 6) 173

Stuffed Cornish Hens with Acorn
 Squash & Apples
Cucumber & Beet Salad
Cranberry-Nut Bread
Cranberry-Cinnamon Tapioca
 Pudding
Guiding Star Cookies

Turkey Buffet
(Serves 14) 181

Turkey Breast with Cloves & Warm
 Fruit Chutney
Green Beans & Potato Casserole
Sausage Stuffing
Punch Bowl Christmas Salad
Cran-Nutty Mini Biscuits
Pumpkin Trifle

Chapter Four: Kids' Birthday Party for Jesus (Ages 3 to 10)

Kids' Birthday Party
Menu 192

Grilled Cheese Christmas Puzzle
 Sandwiches
Snow-Covered Holiday Fruit Cups
Dill Dip with Assorted Vegetables
Snow-Topped Birthday Cupcakes
Kiddy Christmas Cocktails

With Special Thanks

First and foremost, I want to thank God for my gifts and talents to be able to create delicious-tasting, low-fat foods that are every bit as tasty (and often tastier) than the traditional high-fat, time-consuming foods we grew up loving. I would be a fool to take the credit for the amazing things God has done through me far and beyond my wildest hopes or dreams, and I will be forever grateful. To Him I give all praise and glory.

To Tina Wilkerson, I want to express my utmost appreciation and gratitude for her culinary education and expertise, which has been a total godsend. You were my right-hand man through this entire experience; and I am forever grateful for all of the long hours and double and triple testing of recipes you did to ensure our best efforts of providing the highest quality, best-tasting, low-fat, fast, and easy recipes made with seven or fewer easy-to-find ingredients. You were an asset that I cherish and value immensely. I don't know how I could have done this without you. Thank you with all my heart.

To Mary Shaffer, Josh Bialorucki, and Karen Schwanbeck-Lay: Thank you all for your help testing my recipes, proofreading, testing more recipe ideas, grocery shopping, retesting yet more of my recipe ideas, and all the other things that went into creating this book. Did I say "thank you" for testing my recipes?

To Larry Stone: Thank you for the vision of this book and for the freedom you have given me to expand on your literary insight and expertise.

Special thanks to my editor, Geoff Stone, for critiquing my work and helping me communicate more clearly.

I am very grateful to my literary agent, Coleen O'Shea, whose expertise guides and directs me with wise counsel.

Last, but surely not least, much appreciation to my family, who taste-tested more turkey, ham, and Christmas cookie recipes than they really cared to. No matter how good something tastes, too much of a good thing can be too much. I'll never forget that after three months of countless turkey and ham recipes, my daughter finally asked, "Mom, do we really have to eat another meal of turkey or ham tonight?" All I could do was smile.

Introduction

When my publisher asked if I would be interested in creating a Busy People's Christmas cookbook, I was immediately elated with the endless possibilities. What fun, I thought, as visions of festive holiday treats danced in my head.

Before I knew it, every waking—and sleeping—moment was filled with holiday recipe ideas. I was so excited I really was dreaming of recipes. I was so into it that my poor family had to live with a Christmas tree in our home for over two months to keep in the holiday spirit. The Christmas tree actually got cobwebs, and we had to dust the ornaments. My creative juices were flowing at times faster than I could write them on paper.

At one point while creating this book, I was on the road for a major book-signing in California and as a keynote speaker for a women's conference in Atlanta, Georgia. I literally had to tell myself when I was in my hotel, "Do not dream of recipes tonight. You have to get your sleep. You've got a big day ahead of you tomorrow."

Being able to literally dream up fast and easy, low-fat recipes is a gift from God, which I do not take for granted. It is to Him I give all the praise and glory for the tremendous success of the Busy People's cookbooks. It's not every day that more than a million copies of a person's cookbook series have sold. I am tremendously grateful and, to be quite honest, very humbled to be a part of this wonderful success journey. When asked how I thought of creating certain recipes, I simply reply with the truth, "It's a God thing."

Every single recipe has been tested in my very own home and sometimes retested numerous times. I personally require high standards for every recipe that is to be included in my books. At least seven people taste-tested each and every recipe in this book. After all, a recipe to be served at Christmas cannot simply be okay; it has to taste really good.

Not only do the recipes taste great, but all of us weight-conscious, heart-smart people can double count our blessings with this Christmas cookbook because we can eat guilt free because all of the recipes are low fat. Hold your horses; most are low in sugar too. Does this sound too good to be true? It isn't;

diabetics can enjoy most recipes in this cookbook too. Many people go through the holidays riddled with guilt over how they ate so many unhealthy foods, but not us. All of us cooking from this fantastic cookbook can eat totally guilt free because all of the food is good for your heart.

I tried to make this book as user friendly as possible. Instead of traditional chapters such as soups, salads, entrees, etc., I tried to super-simplify the entire Christmas meal-planning process for you. I honestly cannot think of anything I could have done to make this Christmas cookbook for busy people any easier or simpler except to actually do the grocery shopping for you. (Nice try, but that is not going to happen.) Each menu has a complete shopping list written for the entire meal; there's a time line to keep you on track; and there are beautiful centerpieces, many that are actually edible and part of your meal.

Nonetheless, no one needs to know how super-easy this is for you to put together. Just let your guests love every tender, juicy bite of succulent ham or turkey. Allow them to "ohhh" and "ahhh" at the beauty of your presentation and be captivated by your smooth ability to orchestrate such a lovely meal without a second thought. It'll be our little secret. Oh, yes, and no need to mention that every recipe is low-fat and made quickly and easily with seven easy-to-find grocery ingredients or less. I mean, why disappoint them? Some people feel more honored when they think someone has slaved over them by cooking all day or that they are eating fat-forbidden food. Do yourself a favor; don't burst their bubble. Just let them enjoy.

The serving sizes are based on the traditional American Heart and Diabetic Associations recommended serving sizes. Sometimes a recipe may have more servings than the menu states it will serve. Often people will eat more than one serving, thus we allowed extra servings. You can have comfort in knowing each menu will serve at least as many as the overall menu says it will.

Unless it is cooked in the slow cooker, every recipe in this entire book (except for four recipes) is totally prepared, cooked, and finished in thirty minutes or less. The four recipes in this book that are not cooked in fewer than thirty minutes are the Easy Oven-Roasted Turkey with Gravy (page 8), Traditional Baked Ham (page 10), Super Easy Lasagna (page 14), and Holiday Punch Bowl (page 31). These four recipes are easily prepared in about 20 minutes and are a cinch to do.

Icons are used throughout the book to notify the reader unique benefits of recipes. These icons represent the following benefits:

= Slow Cooker Recipe (Recipes that are prepared in a slow cooker.)

= Kid's Cooking Recipe (Recipes that are appropriate for older children to make with little adult supervision.)

= Pot Luck Recipe (Recipes that are a good choice to take to potluck dinners.)

Table and Buffet Decorating Tips

Think of the feeling you want your table to present when guests first see it. Do you want it to feel fancy, formal, casual, country, elegant, homey, fun, festive, or relaxed? Maybe you would like a little of two or three feelings, such as elegant yet comfortable and relaxing. Your table or buffet helps set the mood for the day.

- Keep it simple by keeping in mind one theme and stick with it. If you are using a Christmas tree seedling for a centerpiece, carry that theme throughout with the napkins and plates as well. If you are serving star cookies, use napkins and accessories with stars. Other fun and festive themes are:

Snowflakes	Stars
Snowballs	Log cabins
Snowmen	Happy birthday, Jesus
Santa	Nativity scene theme
Elves	

- Pick three or four colors and stick to the color scheme. Too much of a good thing can be just that—too much. When in doubt, go without. You want your table and buffet to enhance the beauty of your foods, not overpower them or fight for attention. The following are great color combinations:

Red and black	Plaids with greens,
White on white	reds, blacks, and whites
Cream and gold	Earth tones with country flair
Silver and blues	Earth tones with red
Whites and blues	Brown, red, and green
Green and red	Black, gold, and
(of course!)	cream or red
Red and white	

- Let the foods be the main attraction. You can feel confident that every single menu in this book is picture perfect for presentation. We worked diligently at making sure the color and flavor combinations were winning. After all, this isn't just any meal for goodness sake. This is Christmas!
- Make sure your table or buffet is set at least an hour before your guests arrive. Too often the hostess is not ready, her table is in disarray, and she has the panic-stricken look of a disaster waiting to happen. I know how crazy things can be. That is why being organized is key; and if you follow my easy step-by-step time line, you can't go wrong.

Sharing Christmas Responsibilities

In today's busy world, it can be exhausting for a working mom to work full time and, on top of that, have to do all the work of shopping for gifts, mailing Christmas cards, baking, wrapping gifts, grocery shopping, cleaning the house, cooking, setting the table, and then do all the cleanup alone as well, only to get up bright and early the next morning to go to work. Teamwork can be an extra special, needed blessing with the demands of Christmas traditions.

Have your children and spouse pitch in to help set up. There's no reason why one person should have to do everything. Some of our best conversations and times of bonding with my family and friends have been in the kitchen setting up or doing dishes.

Make cleanup a family and friends affair. Maybe some of you will disagree with me on this one, but I honestly think it's a good thing to let your guests help clean up. I'm not talking washing the floors and windows. I'm talking simple, basic kitchen maintenance. Delegate the work. One person wash, one person dry, one person put away dishes, one or two people divvy up leftovers to take home, another put refrigerated items in plastic zip-top bags, another help clear and wipe down the table.

Christmas Cards

Have everyone in your family write his or her own little paragraph updating his life. Everyone can sign the original letter and then make photocopies and mail. Have one person sign the card from the entire family. Have another person put the card and letter into an envelope. A family photo is especially appreciated by those who love you. If you have a favorite family photo taken sometime during the year, have multiples made and include that as well. Many people are doing this on their personal computers and printers, and it is quite impressive. Have another person put on the return address, stamp and seal the envelope. This is easiest to do with a wet sponge and saves the tongue big time.

Buying and Wrapping Presents

In order to stretch my Christmas dollars, I try to shop throughout the year. Have a folder with the list of people for whom you plan to purchase gifts. Whenever you see something you know a person on your list would really like, purchase it and write the gift next to the person's name. Sometimes, if I have time, I go so far as to wrap the gift before putting it away for safe keeping until Christmas. This means that some of my Christmas gifts are actually wrapped in July. Hey, it makes it easier for me.

I have found the investment of a few standard-size gift boxes worth their price in gold. It makes the entire gift-wrapping process go a lot faster. Standard sizes that can fit a multitude of assorted things are shirt boxes. Smart shoppers will purchase their gift boxes, wrapping paper, ribbons, gift bags, gift tags, bows, etc., the day after Christmas when they are on sale for a fraction of the price, and then save it all in the attic or closet where you store your decorations. Keep scissors and tape in plastic zip-top bags along with other zip-top bags with assorted colors of ribbon, bows, and gift tags.

This last year I was so swamped that I simply could not keep up. Instead of stressing myself out, I decided to lighten my load by delegating the wrapping of the gifts to my nephew. He wrapped the gifts and put the tags on them, and I did the fun part of decorating the packages with pretty ribbons and bows. Although he didn't wrap them as neatly as I would have, it wasn't important enough to get myself stressed out about it. He cut my wrapping time in half, and it was fun being together for the project. Ask your local high school or church if there is someone you can hire.

Last-Minute Gift Closet

Purchase gifts when there is a great sale. They will come in handy for last-minute Christmas gifts as well as gifts for other occasions. You can store the gifts in a large plastic container under your bed in this airtight, dust-proof manner, along with your already-purchased gift file, if you do not have a filing cabinet.

I hope these ideas are as helpful for you as they have been in my own life. What's most important to remember is not to get too busy to enjoy the holiday season.

Traditional Turkey

Helpful Turkey Tidbits:

- To thaw the turkey in the refrigerator, an 8 to 12-pound turkey will take 1 to 2 days. A 12 to 19-pound turkey will take 2 to 4 days and a 20 to 24-pound turkey will take 4 to 5 days.
- To thaw the turkey in cold water in its original packaging. Place the plug in the sink drain, put the turkey into the sink, and fill the sink with cold water. Changing the water every 30 minutes, leave the turkey in cold water for half an hour for every pound of turkey. So, if you have a 15-pound turkey, it will take $7\frac{1}{2}$ hours to thaw in the cold water. Do not use warm water.
- There is no need to add water to the pan when you are baking a turkey.
- Allowing the turkey to sit for 20 minutes after roasting will allow you to carve the turkey more easily.

Turkey Roasting Timetable	
Turkey Weight (pounds) Thawed and not stuffed	Roasting Time (hours) @ 350 degrees
8 to 12	$2\frac{1}{2}$ to $2\frac{3}{4}$
12 to 14	$2\frac{3}{4}$ to 3
14 to 18	3 to $3\frac{1}{2}$
18 to 20	$3\frac{1}{2}$ to $4\frac{1}{4}$
20 to 24	$4\frac{1}{4}$ to $4\frac{3}{4}$

Carving the Turkey

Helpful tidbit: Did you know Butterball has a staff to answer telephone calls about cooking turkeys? The toll-free number for the Butterball Turkey Talk-Line is 800-BUTTERBALL (800-288-8372).

I recommend removing and discarding the skin of the turkey before carving it, because the skin is full of unhealthy fat and cholesterol. Use a large, sharp knife with a pointed end for easier carving.

Sure, a beautifully roasted whole turkey on the throne of his platter decorated with all kinds of greenery and presented to the dining table looks stunning in photos for advertising; however, in my personal experience it has been a mess to carve the turkey at the table, especially with all the extra clutter placed on the platter. It looks picture-perfect, but in reality, it is perfectly a mess.

I suggest if you want to show off your masterpiece of Tom the Turkey, do so while he is resting. (Resting is the term used to let the turkey sit for approximately 20 minutes so it will help retain more of its juiciness and allow for easier carving.) Set him on the table so he can rest while you finish your last-minute meal preparations and bring the remaining foods to the table. Then after grace, take the turkey to the kitchen to quickly and easily carve it on a cutting board by following these simple steps:

1. Hold the end of the drumstick and cut through the meat where the drumstick is attached to the turkey.
2. Pull the drumstick out and back to separate it from the thigh. Use your knife to help cut through the joint.
3. Use a large fork to hold the turkey, and cut horizontally above the wing along the length of the turkey breast. If the wing comes off, that is okay.
4. At this point you can remove the entire breast in one piece by cutting along the side of the breastbone on top, removing the turkey breast, and placing it on a serving platter. Pull off the skin and cut the turkey breast into slices. Repeat with the other side.
5. Or you can slice the breast while it is still attached by placing your knife on top, close to the edge of the turkey, and cutting straight down.
6. Continue cutting until all of the meat is sliced. Turn the turkey around and do the other side. Be sure to remove the skin before serving the turkey to your guests.
7. Remove the thigh if desired.

Easy Oven-Roasted Turkey with Gravy

One of my assistants, Tina Wilkerson, who has her education in the culinary arts, took half of this turkey home for dinner. Now remember, her husband gets to eat the finest of foods. When he said, "This is the best turkey I've ever eaten," she didn't have the heart to tell him how super simple this was to make. I recommend not stuffing the turkey, because the turkey needs to cook longer when it is stuffed, and it will dry out.

1 (15-pound) whole turkey, thawed*	$2^1/_3$ cups reserved broth from the turkey (after the fat is removed)
1 tablespoon light soy sauce	Pinch of ground thyme
2 tablespoons cornstarch	Pinch of freshly ground black pepper
2 tablespoons water	

- Thaw a frozen turkey in the refrigerator for 2 days.
- Rinse the turkey in cold running water and place it in a 9 x 13-inch glass baking dish. I discard the neck and gizzards because they are high in fat.
- Cover the turkey completely with foil.
- Bake for 3 hours or until a meat thermometer reads 165 degrees. If it is available, buy a turkey that has a pop-up timer to let you know when it is done.
- After the turkey is cooked, uncover it, turn the oven to 500 degrees, and let it cook for 10 minutes to brown the skin. Sometimes ovens will have hot spots, so turn the turkey after 5 minutes to evenly brown the skin. Cook for another 5 minutes.
- Place the turkey on a serving platter and let it sit for 20 minutes for easier carving.
- Pour the turkey broth through a strainer into a bowl and discard any large pieces that are in the strainer.
- Remove the fat from the broth by skimming it off with a spoon. Or you can place one cold lettuce leaf at a time into the broth, pull it out, and discard it. The fat will stick to the lettuce leaf. Or you can place one bunched-up paper towel at a time on the top of the broth, remove it quickly, and discard it. The fat will stick to the paper towel and you can just throw it away.
- Pour the broth into a saucepan, add the soy sauce, and turn the heat on medium high.
- While the broth is cooking, in a small bowl stir together the cornstarch and water.

- When the broth is heated, pour in the cornstarch and water, stirring until thick and bubbly.
- Add the thyme and black pepper and stir.
- Pour the gravy into a gravy boat or small bowl.

Note: The pinch of thyme greatly enhances the flavor of the gravy and brings out the saltiness.

*See Helpful Turkey Tidbits on page 6 for information on thawing the turkey.

Yield: 15 (4-ounce) servings of turkey and 16 (2-tablespoon) servings of gravy

Preparation time: 10 minutes
Cooking time: 3 hours
Total time: 3 hours 10 minutes

Traditional Baked Ham

I see so many recipes that call for needless, painstaking efforts. Once you see how easy this recipe is, you'll agree. When I tested this recipe using presliced ham, the ham was too dry.

1 (8-pound) fully cooked, hickory smoked, boneless honey ham (Do not use presliced ham.)	1/2 teaspoon ground allspice
1 cup cherry cola soda	1 (20-ounce) can pineapple slices in pineapple juice
1/2 cup dark brown sugar	10 maraschino cherries

- Preheat the oven to 275 degrees.
- Place the ham in a 9 x 13-inch casserole.
- Pour the soda over the entire ham in the casserole dish.
- In a medium bowl stir together the dark brown sugar and allspice. Pat the sugar mixture on the ham.
- With toothpicks, secure the pineapple rings to the outside of the ham. (I use approximately three toothpicks per pineapple slice.)
- Using one toothpick per cherry, secure one cherry inside each ring of pineapple.
- Put two pieces of aluminum foil together lengthwise and seal to make a tent. Cover the casserole dish with the aluminum foil tent, securing it tightly around the casserole dish, but do not puncture the foil with the toothpicks.
- Bake for 4 to 5 hours or until a meat thermometer reads 160 degrees.
- Let the ham rest for about 10 minutes before cutting.
- Pour the ham juice into a small bowl so that guests can serve themselves juice for their ham if they wish.

Yield: 30 (4-ounce) servings

Preparation time: 10 minutes or less
Baking time: 4 to 5 hours
Total time: 5 hours 10 minutes or less

Chapter One

Christmas Eve Dinners

Christmas Eve for some families is their primary Christmas celebration. Food ranges from the traditional sit-down dinner to a vast array of assorted finger foods served buffet style to lighter fares as simple as soup and salad.

As blended families and large extended families try to find an attractive date everyone can attend, Christmas Eve is becoming almost as popular as Christmas Day itself. As the oldest of seven children with in-laws to take into consideration along with extended blended family situations, my parents started the tradition of having our family's Christmas celebration the Sunday before Christmas Day, which worked out great.

I have come to learn that what is most important isn't the actual date we gather to celebrate, but that we do take the time to celebrate together.

Christmas was celebrated on Thanksgiving Day this year because my husband's parents were going away for the winter months. We celebrated with my side of the family the Sunday before Christmas, and we celebrated with our children Christmas Eve and early Christmas morning. This gave me Christmas afternoon and evening free. It was absolutely wonderful to be able to travel the many hours on Christmas Day to visit my dear grandmother who didn't want to leave her nursing home. That was a first for me. Another first (because of that travel) was eating Chinese food on Christmas Day. Thank goodness that restaurant was open. I am especially grateful for a compassionate and caring husband who was gracious enough to set aside a relaxing holiday to be with his wife on a long drive to my grandmother's nursing home. That is love; that is what Christmas is all about.

Italian Christmas Eve Dinner

Serves 6

Italian Christmas Tossed Salads (page 16)
Busy Holiday Bruschetta (page 17)
Super Easy Lasagna (page 14)
Herbed Cauliflower (page 19)
Warm Spiced Cherries over Pears (page 18)

Edible Centerpiece

Place a plain green artificial wreath in the middle of the table and tuck fine European chocolates into the branches. (Foil-wrapped chocolate Santas and ornament balls would look nice.) Light a candle in the center of the wreath. Add a red Christmas ribbon bow to the wreath and you are done.

Supplies

9 x 13-inch casserole dish
6 dessert cups or
   tall-stemmed glasses

Plain green artificial wreath
Red ribbon bow
Food processor

Timeline

1. Set the table and make your centerpiece.
2. One and a half hours before serving time, make the Super Easy Lasagna and place it in the oven.
3. Forty-five minutes before serving time, make the Italian Christmas Tossed Salads and place them in the refrigerator. Do not put dressing on them until serving time.
4. Make the Bruschetta, but do not bake.
5. Set up everything to make the Warm Spiced Cherries over Pears. Put the pears in the dessert cups and the cherry cranberry mixture in the saucepan, but do not bake.

Last 15 minutes
6. Prepare the Herbed Cauliflower.
7. Bake the Busy Holiday Bruschetta.
8. Light the candle on the table.

9. Take the salads, bruschetta, lasagna, and cauliflower to the table.
10. After eating dinner, remove the plates. While clearing the table, heat the cherries.
11. Spoon the hot cherry mixture over the pears, top each dessert with 2 tablespoons dessert whipped topping, and then lightly top with nuts. Serve guests the warm desserts.

Grocery List

Frozen Foods
1 (8-ounce) container fat-free dessert whipped topping (only ¾ cup needed)
1 (16-ounce) bag frozen cauliflower
1 (12-ounce) bag sausage-flavored veggie crumbles or 1 pound low-fat turkey Italian sausage

Fresh Fruits and Vegetables
1 pound baby lettuces (spring mix)
3 Roma tomatoes
1 cucumber
1 yellow bell pepper

Staple Items
1 (29-ounce) can pears in light syrup
1 (14.5-ounce) can diced tomatoes with balsamic vinegar, basil, and olive oil
1 (16-ounce) box lasagna pasta (only 8 pieces needed)
2 (26-ounce) jars your favorite fat-free spaghetti sauce

Dairy
1 tablespoon light butter
6 teaspoons light margarine
1 (5-ounce) bag grated Parmesan cheese (only ½ cup needed)
1 (7-ounce) bag fancy shredded Parmesan cheese (only ¼ cup needed)
3 (8-ounce) packages fat-free shredded mozzarella cheese
1 (16-ounce) container fat-free cottage cheese
4 egg whites

Baking Items
2 tablespoons dried sweetened cranberries
1 (21-ounce) can lite cherry pie filling
1 tablespoon finely chopped walnuts
Nonfat cooking spray

Seasonings/Condiments
1 (8-ounce) bottle fat-free red wine vinaigrette salad dressing (only ¾ cup needed)
½ teaspoon ground cinnamon
2 teaspoons ranch salad dressing mix, dry
2 teaspoons dried parsley

Other
1 (17-ounce) loaf multigrain French bread (about ½ of a 17-ounce loaf is needed)
1 (8-ounce) package foil-wrapped fine European chocolates

☐ Super Easy Lasagna

I like this best when it sits for a day in the refrigerator before baking; however, it is good prepared and baked right away too. Although this recipe takes more than thirty minutes to bake and cool, it is so easy that I'm including it in this book. No pots and pans like the old-fashioned recipe, which used to be a real hassle to make. This recipe can be put together days in advance and refrigerated until you are ready to bake it. I promise you, you will get oodles of rave reviews. And if you don't tell anyone it is vegetarian, they'll never know.

1	(16-ounce) container fat-free cottage cheese	8	pieces lasagna pasta, uncooked
1/2	cup grated Parmesan cheese	1	(12-ounce) package sausage-flavored veggie crumbles* or 1 pound low-fat Italian turkey sausage, cooked, crumbled, and drained
4	eggs, separated		
2	(26-ounce) jars fat-free spaghetti sauce	2	(8-ounce) packages fat-free shredded mozzarella cheese

- Preheat the oven to 350 degrees.
- Spray a 9 x 13-inch casserole dish with nonfat cooking spray.
- In a food processor combine the cottage cheese, Parmesan cheese, and egg whites and process until well blended.
- Put 1 cup of the spaghetti sauce in the bottom of the prepared casserole dish.
- Put 4 strips of pasta on top of the sauce. (Put 3 strips down lengthwise and 1 strip across the end. You will need to break part of the end piece off so it will fit.)
- Layer with half of each of the following: cheese mixture, sausage-flavored crumbles, remaining spaghetti sauce, and mozzarella cheese. Repeat the layering again.
- Cover with aluminum foil and bake on the center rack in the oven for 1 hour.
- Remove the foil and bake for another 10 minutes on the top rack of the oven or until the cheese is bubbly.
- Let the lasagna sit for 10 minutes before cutting. Serve hot.

Yield: 9 servings

Note: Veggie crumbles are vegetarian meat substitutes made by Morning Star Farms. They are found in the frozen food section.

(with veggie crumbles)
Calories: 319 (7% fat); Total Fat: 3g; Cholesterol: 15mg; Carbohydrate: 36g; Dietary Fiber: 9g; Protein: 39g; Sodium: 1562mg; Diabetic Exchanges: 4½ very lean meat, 2 starch, 1 vegetable
(with turkey sausage)
Calories: 340 (10% fat); Total Fat: 4g; Cholesterol: 40mg; Carbohydrate: 34g; Dietary Fiber: 8g; Protein: 40g; Sodium: 1673mg; Diabetic Exchanges: 4½ very lean meat, 2 starch, 1 vegetable

Preparation time: 15 minutes
Baking time: 1 hour and 20 minutes
Total time: 1 hour and 35 minutes

A Gift She Gave Herself

At twelve years old, my daughter Ashley wanted to do something special to help those less fortunate during the holidays. She organized a food and clothing drive at her school during the month of December. The event was a huge success! Ashley originally planned this fundraiser to bless others, but she was the one who was blessed. Each day she came home from school even more in awe than the previous day of the outpouring of generosity. Often the greatest way to overcome feeling down is to count your blessings and do something for someone else. My hope is that whoever plans to help someone else will be blessed as much as my daughter. She thought she was helping others and in return by blessing them she received the gift of giving. It was a priceless gift she gave herself.

Italian Christmas Tossed Salads

These are just right for Italian-themed holiday dinners.

3	Roma tomatoes	1/4	cup fancy shredded Parmesan cheese
1/2	cucumber		
1	yellow bell pepper	3/4	cup fat-free red wine vinaigrette salad dressing
1	pound spring mix		

- Place six salad plates in the freezer while you prepare this salad. This will allow you to serve the salads on chilled plates.
- Slice the tomatoes into six slices per tomato so that you will have three slices for each plate.
- Run the prongs of a fork down the sides of the cucumber to make a pretty design in the green skin before slicing. Slice the cucumber into six slices.
- Slice the yellow bell pepper into six ringed slices.
- Divide the spring mix among the six chilled plates from the freezer.
- Place a cucumber slice in the middle of each salad, and place a bell pepper ring on each so that a cucumber is in the middle of each pepper ring.
- Arrange three tomato slices around the pepper and cucumber rings and sprinkle 2 teaspoons of cheese on each salad.
- Just before serving, drizzle 2 tablespoons of the dressing on each salad or serve the dressing on the side.

Yield: 6 servings

Calories: 81 (13% fat); Total Fat: 1g; Cholesterol: 2mg; Carbohydrate: 16g; Dietary Fiber: 2g; Protein: 3g; Sodium: 378mg; Diabetic Exchanges: 1½ vegetable, ½ other carbohydrate

Preparation time: 10 minutes

♒ Busy Holiday Bruschetta

This is perfect for when you're in a rush. The taste is fabulous, the aroma is inviting, and the colors complement any holiday meal.

12	teaspoons light butter		olive oil, drained and juices
12	(1/2-inch) slices multigrain French bread		discarded
1	(14.5-ounce) can diced tomatoes with balsamic vinegar, basil, and	1/2	cup shredded fat-free mozzarella

- Preheat the oven to 400 degrees.
- Spread ½ teaspoon butter on both sides of each slice of bread.
- Place the buttered slices on a cookie sheet.
- Top each slice of bread with the tomatoes, dividing them evenly among the slices.
- Sprinkle the cheese on the top of the tomatoes, dividing it evenly among the slices.
- Loosely cover the cookie sheet with foil, taking care not to let the foil touch the cheese or the cheese will stick to the foil.
- Bake on the lowest rack of the oven (to help the bottom of the bread to toast) for 3 minutes.
- Remove the foil, place the pan on the top shelf, and turn the oven to broil.
- Broil for 2 minutes or until the cheese is lightly golden.

Yield: 6 (2-piece) servings

Calories: 167 (14% fat); Total Fat: 3g; Cholesterol: 8mg; Carbohydrate: 28g; Dietary Fiber: 4g; Protein: 9g; Sodium: 496mg; Diabetic Exchanges: ½ lean meat, 1½ starch, 1 vegetable

Preparation time: 10 minutes or less
Cooking time: 5 minutes
Total time: 15 minutes or less

Warm Spiced Cherries over Pears

The presentation of this dessert is absolutely gorgeous, and the light, fruity taste of the warm cherries with bits of sweetened, dried cranberries oozing over the pears is awesome topped with the slight crunchiness of walnuts.

1	teaspoon ground cinnamon	1	(29-ounce) can pears in light syrup, drain and discard juice
1	(21-ounce) can lite cherry pie filling		
2	tablespoons finely chopped dried sweetened cranberries	3/4	cup fat-free dessert whipped topping
		1	tablespoon finely chopped walnuts

- In a medium-size, nonstick saucepan over medium heat, stir the cinnamon, pie filling, and cranberries until well mixed.
- Cover and cook for 4 to 5 minutes or until the mixture reaches a low boil.
- Place ½ cup pears in each of six dessert cups or glasses.
- Spoon the hot cherry mixture over the pears.
- Top each serving with 2 tablespoons whipped topping and then lightly sprinkle the nuts evenly over all the desserts.

Note: Six dessert cups or six stemmed tall glasses are needed. I think the stemmed glasses look prettier. If you don't have any, you can usually purchase them for about $1 each at most dollar stores.

Yield: 6 (1 dessert cup) servings

Calories: 141 (5% fat); Total Fat: 1g; Cholesterol: 0mg; Carbohydrate: 32g; Dietary Fiber: 2g; Protein: 1g; Sodium: 25mg; Diabetic Exchanges: 1 fruit, 1 other carbohydrate

Preparation time: 5 minutes or less
Cooking time: 5 minutes or less
Total time: 10 minutes or less

Herbed Cauliflower

1	tablespoon light butter	2	teaspoons dried parsley
2	teaspoons dry ranch salad dressing mix	1	(16-ounce) bag frozen cauliflower

- In a small bowl, microwave the butter for a few seconds until melted.
- Stir in the ranch dressing mix and the parsley.
- Microwave the cauliflower in a microwave-safe dish until fully heated, about 3 minutes.
- Drizzle the butter mixture over the cauliflower and gently toss.

Yield: 6 (½-cup) servings

Calories: 35 (26% fat); Total Fat: 1g; Cholesterol: 3mg; Carbohydrate: 4g; Dietary Fiber: 2g; Protein: 2g; Sodium: 172mg; Diabetic Exchanges: 1 vegetable

Preparation time: 3 minutes
Cooking time: 3 minutes
Total time: 6 minutes

Mexican Christmas Eve Dinner

Serves 8

In Mexico they celebrate Christmas with La Posada. For La Posada they re-create Mary and Joseph's search for shelter on the night that Jesus was born by walking from house to house pretending that they are seeking shelter.

After dinner on Christmas Day in Mexico the children get to try to break a piñata that is filled with candy. A rope is strung through the loop on the top of the piñata and two adults hold the ends of the ropes. Then they blindfold one child at a time, spin him or her around a few times, and let the child try to break the piñata with a stick.

Fiesta Chili Soup (page 26)
Southwestern Celebration Salad (page 26)
No-Cook Bean Dip (page 23)
Beefy Chili Enchilada Casserole (page 24)
Spicy Spanish Rice with Tomatoes and Green Chilies (page 25)
Virgin Cranberry Daiquiris (page 27)
Sweet Snowflake Tortillas (page 22)

Edible Centerpiece

Place a candy-filled piñata in the middle of the table. After dinner, hang it up, blindfold one child at a time, and let the child try to break the piñata open by hitting it with a stick or a bat.

Supplies

Large, round, microwave-safe casserole dish
Piñata
Stick to break the piñata (tie pretty ribbons around one end of the stick)
Dutch oven or soup pot

Timeline

1. Set your table and place a candy-filled piñata in the middle.
2. About 1¼ hours before dinner make the Sweet Snowflake Tortillas, but do not heat. Cover and set aside.
3. About 1 hour before serving time make the No-Cook Bean Dip, cover, and place in the refrigerator until serving time.
4. Assemble the Beefy Chili Enchilada Casserole and place in the refrigerator. You will cook this in a little while.

5. Thirty minutes before serving time, start the Spicy Spanish Rice with Tomatoes and Green Chiles.
6. Start cooking the Fiesta Chili Soup.
7. While the rice is simmering, put the Beefy Chili Enchilada Casserole into the microwave to heat.
8. Turn off the rice and keep it covered so it will stay hot.
9. Make the Southwestern Celebration Salad.

Last 15 minutes
10. Make the Virgin Cranberry Daiquiris. You will make this recipe twice, because it will not all fit in your blender at one time. Put the daiquiris into glasses and take them to the table.
11. Ladle the soup into bowls and take all of the food to the table except the tortillas.
12. After dinner, put the Sweet Snowflake Tortillas into the microwave to heat. Serve warm.

Grocery List

Fresh Fruits and Vegetables
2 pints grape or cherry tomatoes
1 bunch green onions (about 4 green onions needed for ½ cup)
2 (12-ounce) bags fresh cranberries (only 4 cups needed)
4 medium bananas
2 (16-ounce) bags iceberg salad

Staple Items
2 (12-ounce) cans roast beef
3 (15-ounce) cans 99% fat-free turkey chili without beans (I use Hormel)
1 (16-ounce) jar salsa (only 1½ cups needed)
1 (14.5-ounce) can diced tomatoes with green chilies
2 (14.5-ounce) cans Mexican-style stewed tomatoes with jalapeño peppers and spices
2 (10-ounce) cans enchilada sauce

2 (16-ounce) cans Mexican-style refried beans
1 (14.5-ounce) can fat-free, reduced-sodium chicken broth
1 (14-ounce) package enriched parboiled long grain rice (only 2 cups needed)
3 (14.5-ounce) cans beef broth (only 4 cups needed)
1 (12-ounce) jar fat-free savory beef gravy

Meats
1 pound ground eye of round (beef)

Dairy
3 (8-ounce) packages fat-free shredded cheddar cheese
1 (16-ounce) container plus ½ cup fat-free sour cream
1 (8-ounce) package fat-free cream cheese

2 (13.5-ounce) packages fat-free flour tortillas (10 in a pack)

Baking Items
1 (8-ounce) can nonfat cooking spray
1 pound confectioners' sugar (only ⅓ cup needed)
2 (1.9-ounce) boxes Splenda Granular

Seasonings/Condiments
1 (1-ounce) package taco seasoning mix (only 3 teaspoons needed)
1 teaspoon ground cinnamon

Other
1 large bag fat-free tortilla chips
1 (2-liter) bottle sugar-free lemon lime soda (only 4 cups needed)
1 (46-ounce) bottle vegetable juice (only ¼ cup needed)
1 (10.25-ounce) bag light Doritos (only 1 cup needed)
3 pounds candy to fill the piñata (This will vary depending on size.)

♦♦ Sweet Snowflake Tortillas

This is a tasty treat idea that came from paper snowflakes. Snowflakes never tasted so good.

⅓ cup Splenda Granular	I (13.5-ounce) package fat-free flour tortillas, 10 in a pack
⅓ cup confectioners' sugar	
I teaspoon ground cinnamon	Nonfat cooking spray

- In a small bowl stir together the Splenda, confectioners' sugar, and cinnamon. Follow the directions doing one snowflake at a time.
- Gently fold each tortilla into quarters (don't crease it, or it will tear) and cut pieces out of the folded flour tortilla with scissors to make cool snowflake designs when you open it up. (Do not unfold the tortilla while you are in the midst of cutting to see how you are doing, because if you try to refold it to make more cuts, the tortilla will break.)
- Unfold and spray both sides of the tortilla with nonfat cooking spray.
- Sprinkle both sides with the sugar mixture.
- Lay the snowflakes in a stack on a microwave-safe plate, placing a sheet of wax paper in between each tortilla snowflake.
- Microwave in a carousel microwave for about 1 minute or until all of the snowflakes are warmed. Serve immediately. These are pretty served on a plain, dark-colored plate.

Yield: 10 snowflakes

Calories: 111 (0% fat); Total Fat: 0g; Cholesterol: 0mg; Carbohydrate: 23g; Dietary Fiber: 2g; Protein: 3g; Sodium: 260mg; Diabetic Exchanges: 1½ starch

Preparation time: 10 minutes
Cooking time: 1 minute
Total time: 11 minutes

☐ No-Cook Bean Dip

This is so easy and so good. You will have extra for second helpings. For a fun, fiesta flair, serve this bean dip with red and green tortilla chips. They are usually popular during the holidays.

2 (16-ounce) cans Mexican-style refried beans	1 (8-ounce) package fat-free shredded Cheddar cheese, divided
1 (16-ounce) container fat-free sour cream	3 teaspoons taco seasoning mix
1 (8-ounce) package fat-free cream cheese	1 pint grape or cherry tomatoes, quartered
	½ cup chopped green onions

- With a spatula, spread the refried beans onto a cake plate.
- In a medium bowl stir together the sour cream, cream cheese, half the Cheddar cheese, and the taco seasoning.
- Spread the cream cheese mixture on top of the refried beans.
- Place the tomatoes and green onions on top.
- Sprinkle the remaining Cheddar cheese on top.
- Cover and keep chilled until ready to serve.
- Serve with fat-free tortilla chips.

Yield: 16 (½-cup) servings

Calories: 126 (5% fat); Total Fat: 1g; Cholesterol: 10mg; Carbohydrate: 18g; Dietary Fiber: 3g; Protein: 11g; Sodium: 499mg; Diabetic Exchanges: 1 very lean meat, 1 starch

Preparation time: 20 minutes

Beefy Chili Enchilada Casserole

This is very meaty and so good.

2	(12-ounce) cans roast beef, shredded	1	(8-ounce) package fat-free, shredded Cheddar cheese
2	(15-ounce) cans 99% fat-free turkey chili without beans	1	(13.5-ounce) package fat-free flour tortillas
1	(10-ounce) can enchilada sauce		

- Place the roast beef in a large bowl, and with two forks shred the beef into small pieces.
- Stir in the chili, enchilada sauce, and cheese until well mixed.
- Spray a large round microwave-safe casserole dish with nonfat cooking spray.
- Put 1½ cups of the beef mixture into the bottom of the prepared casserole dish.
- Put 2 tortillas over the mixture. If your dish is smaller than the tortillas, just cut off some of the excess so that the tortillas will lie flat. If your dish is larger than the tortillas, tear one of the tortillas and place it over the beef mixture so that the beef mixture is completely covered by the tortillas.
- Continue alternating layers of beef mixture with tortillas, ending with the beef mixture. You should have 2 tortillas left that you could use for the Sweet Snowflake Tortilla recipe in this menu.
- Take a sharp knife and puncture slits all the way through the casserole in at least five places.
- Cover and cook in a carousel microwave on high for 10 to 15 minutes or until completely heated through. Check the temperature of the casserole after 10 minutes.
- Let it sit for 2 to 3 minutes before serving. Cut into eight pieces.

Yield: 8 servings

Calories: 315 (10% fat); Total Fat: 4g; Cholesterol: 78mg; Carbohydrate: 31g; Dietary Fiber: 3g; Protein: 38g; Sodium: 1712mg; Diabetic Exchanges: 4 very lean meat, 2 starch

Preparation time: 10 minutes
Cooking time: 18 minutes or less
Total time: 28 minutes or less

Spicy Spanish Rice with Tomatoes and Green Chilies

My friends and family think this tastes like it came from a fancy Mexican restaurant, and that is a great compliment.

1	(10-ounce) can enchilada sauce	1	(14.5-ounce) can diced tomatoes with green chilies, not drained
1	(14.5-ounce) can fat-free, reduced-sodium chicken broth	2	cups enriched, parboiled long grain rice (I use Uncle Ben's)

- In a medium-size, nonstick saucepan over medium-high heat, stir together and bring the enchilada sauce, chicken broth, and tomatoes to a boil.
- Stir in the rice. Reduce the heat to medium, cover, and simmer for 20 minutes.
- Remove from the heat. If all of the liquid is not absorbed, let the rice stand, covered, for 5 minutes.
- Fluff with a fork and serve.

Yield: 16 (½-cup) servings

Calories: 97 (0% fat); Total Fat: 0g; Cholesterol: 0mg; Carbohydrate: 21g; Dietary Fiber: 1g; Protein: 3g; Sodium: 222mg; Diabetic Exchanges: 1½ starch

Preparation time: 2 minutes
Cooking and resting time: 25 minutes
Total time: 27 minutes

Fiesta Chili Soup

Here's a great way to start off any holiday fiesta.

1 pound ground eye of round	1 (12-ounce) jar fat-free savory beef gravy
4 cups beef broth (made with bouillon is okay)	1 (15-ounce) can 99% fat-free turkey chili without beans (I use Hormel)
1 cup mild salsa	12 fat-free tortilla chips
2 (14.5-ounce) cans Mexican-style stewed tomatoes with jalapeño peppers and spices	

- Brown the beef in a large Dutch oven or soup pot over medium heat.
- Add the beef broth, salsa, stewed tomatoes, gravy, and chili and continue cooking to a low boil.
- Place a 1-cup serving in each bowl and top the soup with 1 crushed tortilla chip.
- Serve hot.

Yield: 13 (1-cup) servings

Calories: 115 (14% fat); Total Fat: 2g; Cholesterol: 27mg; Carbohydrate: 11g; Dietary Fiber: 2g; Protein: 12g; Sodium: 893mg; Diabetic Exchanges: 1½ very lean meat, ½ starch, 1 vegetable

Preparation time: 2 to 3 minutes
Cooking time: 15 minutes
Total time: 17 to 18 minutes

☖ Southwestern Celebration Salad

You can assemble the dressing ahead of time; however, do not combine the salad dressing with the entire salad until right before you are ready to serve, because the salad and Doritos will get soggy.

½ cup fat-free sour cream	2 (16-ounce) bags iceberg salad
¼ cup vegetable juice	1 cup cherry tomatoes
½ cup salsa	1 cup crushed light Doritos
½ cup fat-free shredded Cheddar cheese	

- In a medium-size mixing bowl stir together the sour cream, vegetable juice, salsa, and Cheddar cheese until well mixed. Cover and keep chilled until ready to assemble the entire salad.
- Place the salad in a large bowl. Top with the tomatoes. Cover and keep chilled until ready to serve.
- When ready to eat, toss the salad with the salad dressing and sprinkle the crushed Doritos on top.

Yield: 10 (1½-cup) servings

Calories: 63 (0% fat); Total Fat: 0g; Cholesterol: 3mg; Carbohydrate: 11g; Dietary Fiber: 2g; Protein: 4g; Sodium: 195mg; Diabetic Exchanges: ½ starch, 1 vegetable

🕐 **Preparation time:** 10 minutes or less

Virgin Cranberry Daiquiris

You will need to make this recipe two times. Even though there is no citrus, this has a citrusy flavor.

2	cups frozen cranberries	4	cups ice cubes
2	cups Splenda Granular	2	medium bananas
2	cups sugar-free lemon-lime soda		

- Place the cranberries, Splenda, lemon-lime soda, and ice cubes in a blender and process on high for 2 minutes.
- Add the bananas and process for 1 minute or until all the ice is smooth.
- Pour the mixture into glasses.

Yield: 5 (1-cup) servings

Calories: 98 (0% fat); Total Fat: 0g; Cholesterol: 0mg; Carbohydrate: 25g; Dietary Fiber: 3g; Protein: 1g; Sodium: 15mg; Diabetic Exchanges: 1 fruit, ½ other carbohydrate

🕐 **Preparation time:** 5 minutes

Christmas Eve Appetizer and Dessert Buffet

Serves 14

Christmas Wreath-Shaped Vegetable Tray with Dip (page 33)
Cranberry Cocktail Spread (page 35)
Corned Beef Appetizer Roll-Ups (page 37)
Chipped Beef & Swiss Cheese Pastry Roll-Ups (page 39)
Snowman Cheese Spread (page 36)
Merry Cherry Pizza (page 38)
Old-Fashioned Baked Custard (page 32)
Holiday Punch Bowl (page 31)
Pistachio Cream Mini Tarts (page 34)

Edible Centerpiece

Use the Christmas Wreath-Shaped Vegetable Tray with Dip as a centerpiece for the buffet table.

Supplies

2 ice-cube trays	Electric mixer
Ice cream scoop	Pedestal cake plate (optional)
Punch bowl and ladle	Food processor
1-inch Star and bell shaped	10 x 15-inch jelly-roll pan
cookie cutters	14 ramekins (5-ounce porcelain cups)

Timeline

1. The night before the party or at least $2\frac{3}{4}$ hours before serving time, make the cherry ice cubes for the Holiday Punch Bowl.
2. Set up the buffet table. Be sure to put out plates, napkins, and silverware at one end of the table. Put out the punch bowl and ladle. Put the cups around it. Do not fill until serving time.
3. Two hours before serving time, make the Old-Fashioned Baked Custard and place it in the refrigerator until serving time.
4. While the custard is baking, assemble the Christmas Wreath-Shaped Vegetable Tray and make dip. Cover and place in the refrigerator until serving time. Put 1 cup fat-free dressing into a small serving bowl, cover, and place in the refrigerator.
5. Make the Pistachio Cream Mini-Tarts, place on a serving tray, cover, and refrigerate.

6. Make the Cranberry Cocktail Spread, cover, and refrigerate.
7. Make the Snowman Cheese Spread, cover, and refrigerate. Do not put crackers with the spread.
8. Prepare the Corned Beef Appetizer Roll-Ups, but do not cook. Cover and refrigerate.
9. Bake the crust for the Merry Cherry Pizza. While the crust is baking, get the toppings ready for the pizza.
10. Twenty-five minutes before serving time, make the Chipped Beef and Swiss Cheese Pastry Roll-Ups.

Last 15 minutes
11. While the roll-ups are baking, place the cherry ice cubes into the punch bowl and make the Holiday Punch.
12. Remove the Corned Beef Appetizer Roll-Ups from the refrigerator, microwave, and place the pimientos over the tops.
13. Remove all foods to be served from the refrigerator and place them on the buffet table. Put reduced-fat crackers out with the Snowman Cheese Spread and the Cranberry Cocktail Spread.

Grocery List

Frozen Foods
1 (16-ounce) box phyllo (filo) dough
    (only 10 sheets needed)
1 quart raspberry sherbet, frozen
2 (2.1-ounce) boxes mini phyllo (filo)
    dough shells (15 shells per box)

Fresh Fruits and Vegetables
4 small heads broccoli
1 large cucumber
12 grape tomatoes
1 orange or red bell pepper
1 cup fresh cranberries
1 bunch fresh green onion tops
    (only 1 tablespoon needed)
1 large navel orange
1 small navel orange for decorating,
    optional

To decorate Snowman Cheese Spread, optional
1 mini carrot (for nose)
5 black olives (for eyes and
    buttons)
1 cherry tomato (for mouth)
3 green onions (for arms and
    scarf)
1 orange bell pepper (for hat)

Staple Items
1 (8-ounce) can jellied cranberry sauce
    (only 3 tablespoons needed)
2 (14.5-ounce) boxes reduced-fat,
    butter-flavored crackers

Meats
10 (1½-ounce) slices extra-lean corned
    beef

1 (2.5-ounce) package dried chipped beef

Dairy

1 (8-ounce) package fat-free shredded mozzarella cheese (only 1¾ cups needed)

1 (8-ounce) package fat-free Swiss cheese slices (only 7½ slices needed)

4 (8-ounce) packages fat-free cream cheese

1 (8-ounce) roll reduced-fat crescent roll dough (in the refrigerator aisle)

1 (2-quart) container fat-free low-carb milk (only ½ cup needed)

2 pints fat-free half-and-half

1 (8-ounce) container liquid egg substitute

Baking Items

2 (1.9-ounce) boxes Splenda Granular

1 (1-ounce) package fat-free sugar-free instant pistachio pudding mix

1 (1.3-ounce) envelope Dream Whip (there are 4 envelopes per box)

1 (2.25-ounce) bag slivered almonds, toasted (only 1 tablespoon)

1 (2.25-ounce) bag finely chopped pecans (only 4 tablespoons needed)

1 (8-ounce) can nonfat cooking spray

Seasonings/Condiments

1 (8-ounce) bottle of your favorite fat-free dressing

1 teaspoon dried parsley

1 teaspoon almond extract

3 teaspoons vanilla extract

Ground nutmeg, optional

Other

3 teaspoons prepared horseradish

1 (13-ounce) package whole wheat low-carb/low-fat garlic and herb tortillas

1 (4-ounce) jar diced pimentos, packed in water (only 2 tablespoons needed)

2 (6-ounce) jars maraschino cherries (1 red and 1 green, if available)

1 (10-ounce) jar red maraschino cherries

1 (10-ounce) jar green maraschino cherries

1 (2-liter) bottle sugar-free lemon lime soda

1 (2-liter) bottle sugar-free red raspberry soda

1 (64-ounce) container light cranberry juice cocktail (⅔ less sugar)

Holiday Punch Bowl

What's unique about this punch is the way I use ordinary ingredients in extraordinary ways to make this special for the holidays. I've never seen another punch like it.

2 empty ice cube trays	$^1/_2$ (2-liter) sugar-free red raspberry soda, chilled
24 red maraschino cherries	
24 green maraschino cherries	1 (64-ounce) container light cranberry juice cocktail ($^2/_3$ less sugar), chilled
$^1/_2$ (2-liter) sugar-free lemon-lime soda, chilled, plus enough for the ice cube trays	
	1 quart frozen raspberry sherbet

- Put 1 red cherry and 1 green cherry into every empty mold in the ice cube tray. Usually there are about 12 ice cube molds per tray.
- Pour just enough lemon-lime soda into every ice cube mold to fill it. The cherries may rise and that is okay.
- Freeze for about 2 hours or until ice cubes are completely frozen. To save time, I freeze these ahead of time and store in a zip-top plastic bag.
- Once you are ready to assemble your punch, place the ice cubes in the bottom of the punch bowl.
- Pour $^1/_2$ a 2-liter bottle of sugar-free lemon-lime soda, $^1/_2$ a 2-liter bottle of sugar-free red raspberry soda, and the cranberry juice into the punch bowl.
- Using an ice cream scoop, make balls of sherbet and place them into the punch bowl.
- Place the ladle in the punch bowl and the cups around the bowl. Serve immediately.

Yield: 20 (1-cup) servings

Calories: 88 (0% fat); Total Fat: 0g; Cholesterol: 0mg; Carbohydrate: 20g; Dietary Fiber: 0g; Protein: 0g; Sodium: 59mg; Diabetic Exchanges: 1$^1/_2$ other carbohydrate

Preparation time: 10 minutes
Freezing time: 2 hours
Total time: 2 hours 10 minutes

Old-Fashioned Baked Custard

It doesn't get any more old-fashioned than this, folks. Nutmeg is one of the oldest known spices. It tastes just like Grandma used to make (and no one will miss all the fat or extra calories).

4	cups fat-free half-and-half	1	cup Splenda Granular
2	teaspoons vanilla extract		Ground nutmeg
1	cup liquid egg substitute		

- Preheat the oven to 325 degrees.
- Fill a roasting pan with ½ inch very hot water and place it in the oven.
- With an electric mixer on medium speed, beat together the half-and-half, vanilla, egg substitute, and Splenda until well blended.
- Pour into fourteen ramekins (small, 5-ounce, porcelain cups).
- Place the ramekins in the hot water.
- Sprinkle the top of each with a dash of nutmeg.
- Bake for 25 minutes or until the centers are almost set, but not fully. You want the center to be a tad bit wobbly.
- Remove from the oven and refrigerate. As the custard cools, it will set more.
- Serve chilled.

Yield: 14 servings

Calories: 63 (0% fat); Total Fat: 0g; Cholesterol: 0mg; Carbohydrate: 11g; Dietary Fiber: 0g; Protein: 6g; Sodium: 104mg; Diabetic Exchanges: 1 very lean meat, 1 other carbohydrate

Preparation time: 5 minutes
Baking time: 25 minutes
Total time: 30 minutes or less

🍲 Christmas Wreath-Shaped Vegetable Tray with Dip

4	small heads broccoli	12	grape tomatoes
1	large cucumber, sliced	1	cup your favorite fat-free dressing for a dip
1	orange or red bell pepper		

- Cut off the stems of the broccoli and discard. Cut or break the broccoli into florets.
- Starting from the outside perimeter of a cake plate, place the cucumber slices (save a few slices to decorate the top of the wreath) and all the broccoli florets into a pretty wreath design. (See photo.)
- Using a small (1-inch) star and bell-shaped cookie cutter, cut stars and bells out of the bell pepper.
- Cut stars and bells out of the middle of a few of the cucumber slices.
- Garnish the wreath by placing the bell pepper and cucumber shapes on the top of the broccoli.
- Also garnish the wreath with four groupings of 3 small grape tomatoes each.
- Serve the fat-free salad dressing on the side.

Yield: 16 (½-cup) servings of vegetables and (1-tablespoon) servings of dip

Calories: 68 (8% fat); Total Fat: 1g; Cholesterol: 0mg; Carbohydrate: 14g; Dietary Fiber: 3g; Protein: 4g; Sodium: 217mg; Diabetic Exchanges: 1½ vegetable, ½ other carbohydrate

🕐 **Preparation time:** 20 minutes or less

🍲 Pistachio Cream Mini Tarts

The color of these is great for Christmas. The size is just right for buffet finger foods.

1 (1-ounce) package fat-free, sugar-free instant pistachio pudding mix	½ cup fat-free, low-carb milk
1 (1.3-ounce) envelope Dream Whip (there are 4 envelopes per box)	2 plus 2 tablespoons finely chopped pecans
1 cup cold water	2 (2.1-ounce) boxes mini phyllo (fillo) dough shells (15 shells per box)*

- With an electric mixer in a deep medium-size mixing bowl, combine the pudding mix, Dream Whip, water, and milk on low speed for 1 minute and then for 4 minutes on high speed, scraping the bowl often.
- Stir 2 tablespoons chopped pecans into the cream mixture.
- Spoon 1 tablespoon of the cream mixture into each mini phyllo shell. Top very lightly with the remaining 2 tablespoons pecans, dividing them evenly among the tarts.
- Place on a pretty pedestal cake plate for added height in your buffet.

Note: Phyllo dough is super easy to work with and is found in the dessert freezer aisle. It is very thin layers of pastry. It comes in either full sheets of 9 x 26 inches or half sheets of 9 x 13 inches. The 9 x 13-inch size is perfect for this recipe. If needed, full sheets can be cut in half.

Yield: 15 (2-tart) servings

Calories: 62 (32% fat); Total Fat: 2g; Cholesterol: 0mg; Carbohydrate: 9g; Dietary Fiber: 0g; Protein: 1g; Sodium: 117mg; Diabetic Exchanges: ½ starch, ½ fat

🕐 **Preparation time:** 15 minutes or less

☐ ✦ Cranberry Cocktail Spread

My hat goes off to my talented daughter, Ashley. She created this delicious, festive holiday appetizer. I am quite impressed and I know your guests will be too. It's the right combination of slightly sweet and tart. Have the children help by spreading the cream cheese onto a plate.

1 cup fresh cranberries	1 cup Splenda granular
1 large navel orange, peel included, cut into eighths*	1 (8-ounce) package fat-free cream cheese
1 tablespoon fresh green onion tops	1 small navel orange for decorating (optional)
3 tablespoons jellied cranberry sauce	

- Put the cranberries, orange sections with the peel, and green onion into a food processor, and process for 1 minute or until finely chopped.
- Put the cranberry mixture into a medium-size bowl and with a spatula stir in the jellied cranberry sauce and Splenda until well mixed.
- With a knife spread the cream cheese onto a 12-inch plate with a ½-inch lip around the perimeter (so juices won't run off).
- With a spatula completely cover the cream cheese with the cranberry mixture.
- This is all set to eat as is or keep chilled until ready to serve.
- Serve with reduced-fat, butter-flavored crackers on the side in a separate container. Make sure the crackers do not touch this appetizer or the crackers will become soggy.
- Cut the small orange into thin slices and lay the slices overlapping each other along the outer rim around part of the plate.

Note: Remove any dark spots from the skin and also the spot on the orange where the branch of the tree used to connect to the orange. Make sure there are no seeds in the orange. Seeds can cause a bitter flavor.

Yield: 16 (2-tablespoon) servings

Calories: 34 (0% fat); Total Fat: 0g; Cholesterol: 2mg; Carbohydrate: 6g; Dietary Fiber: 1g; Protein: 2g; Sodium: 71mg; Diabetic Exchanges: ½ other carbohydrate

🕐 **Preparation time:** 15 minutes or less

⌂ ♔ Snowman Cheese Spread

The recipe only takes less than five minutes to prepare; however, assembling this adorable little guy and getting him dressed for the party takes about ten minutes. He's well worth the effort and time though; his flavor is a hit with everybody.

1	(8-ounce) package fat-free cream cheese		with seeds removed and discarded (for mouth)
3	teaspoons prepared horseradish	3	green onions (for arms and scarf)
1³/₄ cups shredded fat-free mozzarella cheese		1	orange bell pepper (cut a piece shaped as a hat)
For decorating:		5	black olives, use only the ends (for eyes and buttons)
1	mini carrot (for nose)		
1	cherry tomato cut into a sliver		

- In a medium-size mixing bowl stir together the cream cheese, horseradish, and mozzarella cheese.
- Divide the cheese mixture into three balls with one of the balls smaller than the other two. Place them on a serving plate and shape into a snowman, using the smaller ball for the head. The snowman will be lying down on the plate, not standing up.
- Use the vegetable pieces and black olives for eyes for decorating the snowman.
- Serve with reduced-fat crackers.

Variation: **Snowball Cheese Ball.** Not as adorable as the snowman, this is an easier variation. Place the cheese spread on a small serving plate and shape into a ball, patting the sides to make it look like a snowball. Garnish with a small sprig of silk pine and serve with reduced-fat crackers.

Yield: 16 (2-tablespoon) servings

Calories: 35 (0% fat); Total Fat: 0g; Cholesterol: 5mg; Carbohydrate: 2g; Dietary Fiber: 0g; Protein: 6g; Sodium: 222mg; Diabetic Exchanges: 1 very lean meat

🕐 **Preparation time:** 20 minutes or less

Corned Beef Appetizer Roll-Ups

The little bit of diced pimiento on top of each roll really dresses these up for the holidays.

10	tablespoons fat-free cream cheese	10	large (1.5-ounce) slices extra-lean corned beef
1	(13-ounce) package whole wheat low-carb, low-fat garlic and herb tortillas (10 in a package)	2	tablespoons diced pimientos, packed in water

- Spread 1 tablespoon cream cheese on each tortilla.
- Lay 1 slice corned beef on top of the cream cheese and roll the tortilla.
- Cut each roll into six pieces and lay the rolls cut side up on a microwave-safe plate. You will need more than one plate.
- Microwave each plate for 1 minute and sprinkle the diced pimientos over all the rolls.
- Serve warm.

Yield: 15 (4-piece) servings

Calories: 106 (34% fat); Total Fat: 4g; Cholesterol: 21mg; Carbohydrate: 8g; Dietary Fiber: 2g; Protein: 11g; Sodium: 650mg; Diabetic Exchanges: 1½ lean meat, ½ starch

Preparation time: 10 minutes
Cooking time: 3 minutes or less
Total time: 13 minutes or less

Merry Cherry Pizza

Cute, colorful, and cheerful describes this tasty finger-food dessert to a T.

2	(6-ounce) jars maraschino cherries (preferably 1 red and 1 green)	1	teaspoon almond extract
1	(8-ounce) package reduced-fat crescent roll dough (in the refrigerator aisle)	1	teaspoon vanilla extract
		4	tablespoons Splenda Granular
1	(8-ounce) package fat-free cream cheese	1	tablespoon finely chopped, toasted slivered almonds

- Preheat the oven to 375 degrees.
- Spray a 10 x 15-inch jelly-roll pan with nonfat cooking spray.
- Drain the maraschino cherries and set them on a paper towel to dry. (Keep the red and green cherries on separate paper towels.)
- With your hands, press the dough into the prepared jelly-roll pan. With your fingers, pinch the seams of the dough together.
- Bake for 9 to 10 minutes.
- While the crust is baking, finely chop the cherries in a food processor. If you are using red and green cherries, chop them separately. The colors of the cherries are prettier if the red and green are not chopped together.
- With a spatula stir the cream cheese, almond extract, vanilla, and Splenda in a separate bowl until well mixed.
- Once the crust has finished baking, let it cool for a few minutes.
- Spread the warm crust with the cream cheese mixture.
- Top with the chopped cherries.
- Sprinkle the top lightly with the chopped almonds.
- Cut into 2-inch squares.

Yield: 24 servings

Calories: 76 (22% fat); Total Fat: 2g; Cholesterol: 2mg; Carbohydrate: 11g; Dietary Fiber: 0g; Protein: 2g; Sodium: 124mg; Diabetic Exchanges: ½ other carbohydrate, ½ fat

Preparation time: 10 minutes
Baking time: 9 to 10 minutes
Total time: 20 minutes

Chipped Beef & Swiss Cheese Pastry Roll-Ups

It's hard to believe we can eat such a super flaky and crispy pastry crust and still have it be so low in fat and calories.

10 (9 x 13-inch) sheets phyllo (filo) dough*	into quarters
7 1/2 slices fat-free Swiss cheese, cut	2 1/2 ounces dried chipped beef
	1 teaspoon dried parsley

- Preheat the oven to 350 degrees.
- Spray a cookie sheet with nonfat cooking spray.
- Use two sheets phyllo dough at a time.
- Cover the remaining sheets to be used with a slightly damp cloth so they won't dry out.
- Place 5 quartered pieces of cheese along the edge of the 9-inch side of the phyllo dough.
- Place 4 slices dried chipped beef on top of the cheese.
- Very tightly roll up the phyllo dough sheet like a jelly roll, starting at the end with the cheese and beef.
- Spray the outside of the roll with nonfat cooking spray to help seal the crust closed.
- Sprinkle the top of the roll lightly with dried parsley.
- With a very sharp knife cut the roll into four pieces.
- Place the rolls on the prepared cookie sheet seam side down. Rolls can be set close together; however, do not let them touch each other.
- Bake for 7 minutes or until golden brown.

Note: A 16-ounce box of phyllo (filo) dough either has 2 (8-ounce) packages in it that measure 9 x 13 inches each or one (16-ounce) package that measures 9 x 26 inches. If you have the large size, simply cut the entire package of phyllo dough in half to obtain two 9 x 13-inch stacks of phyllo dough and save the extra sheets for later use.

Yield: 20 (1-piece) servings

Calories: 52 (10% fat); Total Fat: 1g; Cholesterol: 3mg; Carbohydrate: 8g; Dietary Fiber: 0g; Protein: 4g; Sodium: 155mg; Diabetic Exchanges: 1/2 very lean meat, 1/2 starch

Preparation time: 10 minutes
Baking time: 7 minutes
Total time: 17 minutes

Christmas Eve Sweets, Treats, and Hors D'oeuvres Buffet

Serves 16

Cranberry Salsa (page 42)
Reuben Roll-Ups (page 50)
Smoked Salmon Rolls (page 47)
Bacon, Onion & Pineapple Spread (page 43)
Cucumber & Ham Dip (page 48)
Cherry-Berry Kiwi Trifle (page 44)
Creamiest Old-Fashioned Rice Pudding (page 45)
Maraschino Cherry-Chocolate Chip Muffin Tops (page 46)
Warm Peppermint Candy Cane Dessert Beverage (page 49)

Edible Centerpiece

Place appetizers on displays of different heights for a centerpiece with added dimensions. If you don't have access to a three-tier display, simply make your own by placing stacked books or boxes of assorted heights on the counter. Cover the boxes with a large piece of material. A tablecloth or plain colored bed sheet works well. Once books or boxes are completely covered with material place plates of appetizers on the varied boxes of different heights.

Clockwise from top: Cucumber & Ham Dip, Reuben Roll-ups, and Smoked Salmon Rolls

Supplies

Food processor
Electric mixer
Two muffin tins
Trifle bowl

Tapered candle
Holiday bowl
Slow cooker
Baking sheets

Timeline

1. Set up the buffet table, placing plates, napkins, and silverware at one end of the table.
2. Two hours before serving time, prepare the Cranberry Salsa, cover, and place in the refrigerator.
3. Make the Bacon, Onion, and Pineapple Spread, cover, and place in the refrigerator.
4. Prepare the Cherry-Berry Kiwi Trifle, cover, and place in the refrigerator.

5. Make the Creamiest Old-Fashioned Rice Pudding, cover, and refrigerate.
6. Make the Maraschino Cherry-Chocolate Chip Muffin Tops and place in the oven.
7. While the muffin tops are baking, make the Smoked Salmon Rolls, cover, and place in the refrigerator.
8. Take the muffin tops out of the oven. Prepare the Cucumber and Ham Dip, cover, and refrigerate. Hollow out the bread bowl, cover, and set aside.
9. Start the Warm Peppermint Candy Cane Dessert Beverage.
10. While the beverage is heating up, start the Reuben Roll-Ups.

Last 15 minutes
11. While the roll-ups are baking put chips with the salsa, crackers with the spread, and the Cucumber and Ham Dip in the bread bowl. Take these to the buffet.
12. Place the beverage in a slow cooker and place the cups and garnishes next to it for the guests to serve themselves.
13. Set the food out on the buffet.

Grocery List

Frozen Foods
1 (16-ounce) bag dark, sweet, pitted frozen cherries
1 (16-ounce) bag frozen whole strawberries
4 (8-ounce) containers fat-free dessert whipped topping
1 (16-ounce) box phyllo (filo) dough (only ½ of a 16-ounce box needed)

Fresh Fruits and Vegetables
1 (12-ounce) bag fresh cranberries (only 1 cup needed)
6 kiwi
1 bunch green onion tops (only 6 tablespoons needed)
1 medium cucumber
1 small white onion (only ¼ cup needed)

Staple Items
1 (20-ounce) can crushed pineapple
1 (23-ounce) jar no-sugar-added applesauce (only 1 cup needed)

Meats
2 (8-ounce) packages smoked salmon, pre-sliced
1 (4-ounce) package lean ham, finely chopped
1 pound extra-lean corned beef, sliced thin

Dairy
6 (8-ounce) containers fat-free cream cheese
1½ gallons fat-free, low-carb milk (need 1 gallon and 3 cups total)
1 (8-ounce) container fat-free sour cream (only 2 tablespoons needed)

1 pint fat-free, low-carb French vanilla liquid creamer
1 (8-ounce) package fat-free mozzarella cheese, shredded (only 1¼ cups needed)

Baking Items
¾ cup raisins
3 (1-ounce) packages sugar-free fat-free instant vanilla pudding mix
1 (12-ounce) bag mini-chocolate chips (only 2 tablespoons needed)
1 (5-pound) bag whole wheat flour (only 3 cups needed)
1 (9.7-ounce) bag Splenda Granular
2 teaspoons baking soda
1 (8-ounce) can nonfat cooking spray

Seasonings/Condiments
1 (1-ounce) bottle almond extract (only ½ teaspoons needed)
1 (1-ounce) bottle mint extract (only 3 teaspoons needed)
½ teaspoon lemon-pepper seasoning
Dried parsley
Ground cinnamon

½ cup fat-free mayonnaise
1 (0.59-ounce) package ranch salad dressing mix (only 2 teaspoons needed)
1 (8-ounce) bottle fat-free Thousand Island dressing, optional

Other
1 (15.5-ounce) jar sugar-free strawberry preserves (only ½ cup needed)
1 (3-ounce) jar 30%-less-fat-bacon pieces (only ⅓ cup needed)
1 (12-ounce) angel food cake
1 (14-ounce) box enriched white rice (3 cups cooked needed)
1 (10-ounce jar) maraschino cherries (only ⅔ of a 10-ounce jar needed)
1 round loaf pumpernickel bread
20 mini peppermint candy canes
1 (14.5-ounce) box reduced-fat, butter-flavored crackers
1 (10.25-ounce) bag baked tortilla chips
1 small container of 250 toothpicks

🍲 Cranberry Salsa

Yum! You'll be the talk of the town when you serve this at your party. This multi-purpose recipe is so diversified. It is great with baked tortilla chips; reduced-fat, butter-flavored crackers; angel food cake; cottage cheese; and turkey or lean pork roast.

1 cup whole fresh cranberries	½ cup Splenda Granular
½ cup sugar-free strawberry preserves	½ cup crushed pineapple

■ Put the cranberries in a food processor and process for 30 seconds or until cranberries are finely chopped.

- Add the strawberry preserves and Splenda and process for 30 seconds.
- Place the cranberry mixture into a small mixing bowl and stir in the pineapple.

Yield: 12 (2-tablespoon) servings

Calories: 20 (0% fat); Total Fat: 0g; Cholesterol: 0mg; Carbohydrate: 7g; Dietary Fiber: 0g;
Protein: 0g; Sodium: 1mg; Diabetic Exchanges: ½ fruit

Preparation time: 5 minutes or less

Bacon, Onion & Pineapple Spread

This smooth flavor combination has just a hint of pineapple for a one-of-a-kind taste that everyone at my holiday party enjoyed with butter-flavored crackers.

2 (8-ounce) containers fat-free cream cheese	1 tablespoon Splenda Granular
1 (8-ounce) can crushed pineapple in its own juice, drained, juice discarded	⅓ cup 30%-less-fat-bacon pieces
	¼ cup chopped green onion tops
½ teaspoon almond extract	½ teaspoon lemon pepper seasoning

- In a medium bowl with a spatula stir together the cream cheese, pineapple, almond extract, Splenda, bacon, green onions, and lemon pepper seasoning.
- Ready to eat or cover and keep chilled until ready to eat.
- I think this is best served with reduced-fat butter-flavored crackers.

Yield: 20 (2-tablespoon) servings

Calories: 37 (0% fat); Total Fat: 0g; Cholesterol: 7mg; Carbohydrate: 3g; Dietary Fiber: 0g;
Protein: 4g; Sodium: 169mg; Diabetic Exchanges: ½ very lean meat

Preparation time: 10 minutes

▭ ♔ Cherry-Berry Kiwi Trifle

I love this dessert. I even like it when the strawberries are still slightly frozen. To save time: Make this while the berries and cherries are still frozen. The frozen fruit will thaw within 15 to 20 minutes for a cool and refreshing dessert beautiful for any holiday dinner edible centerpiece.

1	(16-ounce) bag dark, sweet, pitted, frozen cherries	1	(8-ounce) container fat-free dessert whipped topping
1	(16-ounce) bag frozen whole strawberries	1	(12-ounce) angel food cake, torn into bite-size pieces
1	plus ¼ cups Splenda Granular	6	kiwis, peeled and sliced (2 cups)
1	(8-ounce) package fat-free cream cheese		

- In a medium bowl toss the cherries and strawberries with ¼ cup Splenda.
- In a large bowl with an electric mixer beat together the remaining 1 cup Splenda, cream cheese, and whipped dessert topping until smooth and creamy. Takes about a minute or two.
- With a spatula stir the angel food cake pieces into the cream mixture.
- Spoon half the angel food cake mixture into the trifle bowl.
- Spoon half the berry mixture over the cake.
- Arrange the entire kiwi on top of the berries, making sure you can see the pretty green layer of kiwi through the glass trifle bowl.
- Spread the remaining angel food cake mixture on top of the kiwi.
- Top with the remaining berries.
- If not serving within a half hour, cover and keep refrigerated.

Yield: 16 (½-cup) servings

Calories: 145 (0% fat); Total Fat: 0g; Cholesterol: 2mg ; Carbohydrate: 31g; Dietary Fiber: 2g; Protein: 4g; Sodium: 222mg; Diabetic Exchanges: 1 fruit, 1 other carbohydrate

🕐 **Preparation time:** 20 minutes or less

🍲 Creamiest Old-Fashioned Rice Pudding

To make this old-time holiday favorite dessert even quicker, I bring home leftover rice after going out for Chinese because restaurants usually give you too much rice to eat anyway.

³/₄ cup raisins	4¹/₂ cups fat-free dessert whipped topping
3 cups water	
3 (1-ounce) packages sugar-free, fat-free instant vanilla pudding mix	3 cups cold cooked rice*
	Ground cinnamon
3 cups fat-free, low-carb milk	

- In a microwave-safe bowl cook the raisins in the water for 1 minute. Then let the raisins sit in the water until you are finished preparing this dessert. This will help soften the raisins and make them tender and less chewy.
- In a large bowl beat with an electric mixer the pudding mix with the milk until the pudding mix is completely dissolved, well blended, and thick.
- With a spatula stir in the dessert whipped topping until well blended.
- Drain and discard the water from the raisins. Pat the raisins dry with a towel.
- Stir the raisins and rice (make sure the rice isn't clumpy) into the creamy mixture until well mixed.
- Put into a serving bowl or individual dessert cups and sprinkle the top of the rice pudding lightly with cinnamon.

*Note: Rice from a restaurant has a harder texture than homemade rice.

Yield: 18 (¹/₂-cup) servings

Calories: 111 (0% fat); Total Fat: 0g; Cholesterol: 1mg; Carbohydrate: 23g; Dietary Fiber: 0g; Protein: 3g; Sodium: 242mg; Diabetic Exchanges: 1 starch, ¹/₂ fruit

🕐 **Preparation time:** 10 minutes
Cooking time: 1 minute
Total time: 11 minutes

☐ Maraschino Cherry-Chocolate Chip Muffin Tops

If you like the tops of muffins, you will love these. They are moist and delicious.

20 maraschino cherries (two-thirds of a 10-ounce jar), cut up	1 cup no-sugar-added applesauce
2¹/₂ cups Homemade Whole Wheat, Sweet Baking Mix (page 220)	1 teaspoon almond extract
¹/₂ cup fat-free mayonnaise	2 tablespoons mini chocolate chips

- Preheat the oven to 350 degrees.
- Spray 16 cups of two muffin tins with nonfat cooking spray.
- Drain the cherries and pat dry with paper towels. Cut the cherries into eighths.
- In a medium-size mixing bowl combine the sweet baking mix, mayonnaise, applesauce, almond extract, and maraschino cherries. Stir until well combined.
- Place a heaping tablespoon into each muffin tin.
- Sprinkle each muffin lightly with mini chocolate chips (no more than 15 per muffin).
- Bake for 12 to 14 minutes.

Yield: 16 (1-muffin top) servings

Calories: 81 (9% fat); Total Fat: 1g; Cholesterol: 1mg; Carbohydrate: 17g; Dietary Fiber: 2g; Protein: 2g; Sodium: 149mg; Diabetic Exchanges: 1 starch

🕐 **Preparation time:** 10 minutes or less
Baking time: 12 to 14 minutes
Total time: 24 minutes or less

☐ Smoked Salmon Rolls

This is very elegant and sophisticated for the adult palate.

2	(8-ounce) packages fat-free cream cheese	Dried parsley
2	tablespoons green onion tops, chopped	Reduced-fat, butter-flavored crackers (optional)
2	(8-ounce) packages smoked salmon, presliced	

- In a medium bowl with a fork stir the cream cheese and green onions until well mixed.
- Lightly spread some of the cream cheese mixture over each slice of smoked salmon.
- Roll each piece of salmon with the cream cheese jelly-roll style and cut into ½-inch lengths.
- Sprinkle with parsley and place a toothpick into each salmon roll. Place on a pretty serving plate.
- Cover and keep chilled until ready to serve.

Note: If you prefer, you can place each roll on a cracker, not using any tooth-picks, and place the crackers on a serving plate. Serve immediately. Do not put on crackers too far in advance or the crackers will become soggy.

Yield: 32 (2-piece) servings

Calories: 32 (20% fat); Total Fat: 1g; Cholesterol: 6mg; Carbohydrate: 1g; Dietary Fiber: 0g; Protein: 5g; Sodium: 354mg; Diabetic Exchanges: 1 very lean meat

⊘ **Preparation time:** 15 minutes

🍲 Cucumber & Ham Dip

I	medium cucumber	2	tablespoons fat-free sour cream
2	teaspoons dry ranch salad dressing mix	I	(4-ounce) package lean ham, finely chopped
$1/4$	cup finely chopped white onion	I	round loaf pumpernickel bread
$1/2$	(8-ounce) package fat-free cream cheese		

- Cut the cucumber in half lengthwise. With a spoon remove all the seeds. Do not peel the cucumber; finely chop it.
- In a medium bowl, stir the salad dressing mix, onion, cream cheese, and sour cream together until well blended.
- Stir in the ham and cucumber until well mixed.
- Cut off the top of the round loaf and hollow out the bread leaving 1 inch of bread on the sides to form a bread bowl.
- Cut the bread that you scooped out and the top into 1-inch pieces and place around the bread bowl on a cake plate. Keep the pieces in a zip-top bag until serving time.
- At serving time, place the dip in the hollowed out bread bowl.

Yield: 16 (2-tablespoon) servings

(with bread)
Calories: 94 (11% fat); Total Fat: 1g; Cholesterol: 5mg; Carbohydrate: 16g; Dietary Fiber: 2g; Protein: 5g; Sodium: 364mg; Diabetic Exchanges: $1/2$ very lean meat, 1 starch
(without bread)
Calories: 23 (0% fat); Total Fat: 0g; Cholesterol: 5mg; Carbohydrate: 2g; Dietary Fiber: 0g; Protein: 3g; Sodium: 173mg; Diabetic Exchanges: $1/2$ very lean meat

🕐 **Preparation time:** 15 minutes or less

Warm Peppermint Candy Cane Dessert Beverage

Whenever I serve this I get plenty of "oohs" and "ahhs" because it is so lovely and festive.

16	cups fat-free, low-carb milk (two 1/2-gallon containers)	2	cups fat-free dessert whipped topping
2	cups fat-free, low-carb French vanilla liquid creamer	8	teaspoons crushed peppermint candy cane
3/4	cup Splenda Granular	16	mini peppermint candy canes
3	teaspoons mint extract		

- In a large saucepan or Dutch oven, heat the milk and creamer over medium heat until hot, about 15 minutes.
- Stir in the Splenda and mint extract.
- Taste the dessert beverage. If you would like it sweeter, add 1/4 cup more of the Splenda. Or, if you would like it to have more mint flavor, you can add 1 teaspoon of the mint extract.
- Pour into a large slow cooker to keep warm, or ladle into mugs and put 2 tablespoons of fat-free dessert whipped topping on top of each serving.
- Sprinkle lightly with 1/2 teaspoon crushed peppermint candy. Garnish each serving with a mini candy cane sticking out of the dessert whipped topping, letting it rest on the rim of the mug.
- Serve immediately.

Note: For this recipe I prefer to use the dessert whipped topping in a can because it dresses this up prettier than a scoop or dab of dessert whipped topping. However, dessert whipped topping from a container works fine as well.

Yield: 16 (1¼-cup) servings

Calories: 119 (0% fat); Total Fat: 0g; Cholesterol: 6mg; Carbohydrate: 12g; Dietary Fiber: 0g; Protein: 14g; Sodium: 241mg; Diabetic Exchanges: 1 very lean meat, 1 skim milk

Preparation time: 5 minutes or less
Cooking time: 15 minutes or less
Total time: 20 minutes or less

Reuben Roll-Ups

20 sheets phyllo (filo) dough, 9 x 13 inches (half a 16-ounce box)	**1¼** cups fat-free mozzarella cheese, shredded
1 pound extra-lean corned beef, thinly sliced	Fat-free Thousand Island dressing (optional)

- Spray two baking sheets with nonfat cooking spray.
- Preheat the oven to 400 degrees.
- Lay one sheet of phyllo dough on a cutting board and spray with nonfat cooking spray.
- Dividing the corned beef evenly among the 20 sheets of phyllo (¾ ounce per roll-up), place the corned beef on the 9-inch side of the phyllo about 2 inches up and then sprinkle with 1 tablespoon mozzarella cheese.
- Starting at the end with the corned beef, tightly roll the phyllo around the corned beef and cheese.
- Cut the roll into four pieces. Place the cut rolls on the prepared baking sheet seam side down. Repeat until all of the phyllo is used.
- Spray the tops of the rolls with nonfat cooking spray.
- Bake for 6 minutes.
- If desired, serve with the Thousand Island dressing on the side to dip the rolls.

Yield: 20 (4-piece) servings

Calories: 79 (21% fat); Total Fat: 2g; Cholesterol: 17mg; Carbohydrate: 8g; Dietary Fiber: 0g; Protein: 8g; Sodium: 444mg; Diabetic Exchanges: 1 very lean meat, 1 starch

Preparation time: 15 minutes
Cooking time: 6 minutes
Total time: 21 minutes

Chapter Two

Breakfasts & Brunches

Whether your Christmas morning is for one or many, it is nice to have it special. After all, it is Christmas.

I very vividly remember the great anticipation I had as a child counting down the days and awaiting with enormous eagerness our traditional Christmas morning feast that my dad would have waiting for us: Dunkin' Donuts. To me those sugary, fatty-filled doughnuts were love at first sight. They were a highlight of my Christmas morning. As I think of it now, I smile, feeling all happy inside. With seven children in our family, money was tight and these doughnuts were a very rare treat.

Some people eat to live. Our family lived to eat. Pigging out on foods we normally didn't have had been an unhealthy habit our parents let us do on special occasions. I treasured the way Dad brought home dozens of those scrumptious doughnuts and would let us kids eat till our hearts' content. I remember feeling kind of "woozy" from too much sugar. You can bet we children didn't eat a doughnut or two. For us kids, this doughnut feast was a dream come true. Looking back I now have no doubt why I used to feel like I had the flu for the rest of the day.

For many families Christmas morning is as much a tradition as Christmas Eve for some and Christmas Day for others. No matter what your level of celebration is for Christmas morning, one thing I am sure of: You will find a breakfast in this chapter guaranteed to fulfill your desires, unless of course you want nothing more than Dunkin' Donuts. If that is the direction you are headed, all I can say is, these delicious breakfasts won't have you feeling "woozy" the rest of the day like those doughnuts do, and these meals taste so good that you won't even miss Dunkin' Donuts.

Breakfast for One

Just because you are by yourself doesn't mean you shouldn't have something special to start your Christmas morning. This simply delicious and delightfully light breakfast is just the special treat.

Cranberries & Cream Smoothie (page 53)
Christmas Mixed Berries Breakfast Sandwich (page 54)
Turkey Breakfast Sausage Links
Coffee

Supplies
Blender
Toaster

Timeline
1. Turn on some Christmas music and set the table.
2. Fifteen minutes before serving time, brew the coffee.
3. Prepare the Cranberries & Cream Smoothie
4. Prepare the Christmas Mixed Berries Breakfast Sandwich
5. Heat the sausage in the microwave.

Grocery List

Frozen Foods
1 pint low-fat frozen vanilla yogurt (only ½ cup needed)
1 (10-count) package fat-free waffles (only 2 needed)
1 (16-ounce) bag frozen mixed berries (only ½ cup needed)
1 (8-ounce) container fat-free dessert whipped topping (only 1 tablespoon needed)
1 (5.2-ounce) package low-fat fully-cooked turkey breakfast sausage links (only 2 needed)

Fresh Fruits and Vegetables
1 (12-ounce) bag frozen cranberries (only ⅛ cup needed)

Staple Items
Coffee

Dairy
1 (2-quart) container fat-free, low-carb milk (only ½ cup needed)

Baking Items
1 (1.9-ounce) box Splenda granular (only 4½ tablespoons needed)

Other
1 small bottle lite blueberry syrup (only 1 tablespoon needed)

Cranberries & Cream Smoothie

What a terrific way to add holiday splendor to an all-time favorite breakfast beverage.

$^1/_8$ cup frozen cranberries	$2^1/_2$ tablespoons Splenda Granular
$^1/_2$ cup fat-free, low-carb milk	$^1/_2$ cup low-fat frozen vanilla yogurt

- Put the cranberries in a blender with the milk and Splenda and process on high until finely chopped, about 1 minute.
- Add the frozen yogurt and process until smooth and creamy.

Yield: 1 (1-cup) serving

Calories: 157 (8% fat); Total Fat: 1g; Cholesterol: 8mg; Carbohydrate: 25g; Dietary Fiber: 1g; Protein: 10g; Sodium: 164mg; Diabetic Exchanges: 1½ skim milk

Preparation time: 5 minutes

Easiest Gift Wrapping Ever

It was 8:00 A.M. on Christmas morning and my entire family needed to get ready for church before we opened gifts. We have to leave for church at ten., so that meant we had an hour to get ready and an hour to open gifts. On the way to her bedroom my daughter, Whitney, shouted out, "I still have to wrap my gifts." Talk about waiting until the last minute. An hour later everyone gathered as planned around the tree, and there was Whitney surrounded some uniquely wrapped gifts. Each gift was in the bag from the store it was purchased from. The top of the bag was rolled shut and stapled with a bow. With a permanent marker she'd written on the bag the name of the person for whom the gift was for. We all laughed. Her stress-free gift-giving idea definitely was unconventional and I admired the fact that she felt free to be unique. Many of us could learn a thing or two from her.

☃ Christmas Mixed Berries Breakfast Sandwich

Any of Santa's helpers would be thrilled to enjoy this special breakfast treat.

2 fat-free waffles (found in frozen breakfast foods aisle)	1 tablespoon light blueberry syrup
1/2 cup frozen mixed berries, thawed	1 tablespoon fat-free dessert whipped topping
2 tablespoons Splenda Granular	

- Toast the waffles in a toaster until golden brown.
- Warm the berries in the microwave for 30 to 45 seconds or until fully heated. Set aside three berries to use later and spread the remaining berries on top of one waffle.
- Sprinkle the Splenda over the berries.
- Put the second waffle on top.
- Microwave the syrup for about 5 seconds, just enough to fully heat it. Drizzle the warm syrup over the top of the sandwich, allowing the syrup to run over the edges.
- Top with the dessert whipped topping and the 3 remaining berries.
- Serve immediately.

Yield: 1 serving

Calories: 198 (0% fat); Total Fat: 0g; Cholesterol: 0mg; Carbohydrate: 44g; Dietary Fiber: 3g; Protein: 6g; Sodium: 279mg; Diabetic Exchanges: 2 starch, 1 fruit

Preparation time: 10 minutes

Romantic Breakfast in Bed

Serves 2

Wear something extra-romantic to deliver this Christmas breakfast in bed to the love of your life. Think of how special your loved one will feel when surprised with this thoughtful gift of love to start the Christmas Day. It's very simple to put together so you can enjoy it too.

Puffy Seafood Omelet (page 57)
Christmas Cinnamon Toast (page 58)
Chocolate Almond Steamer (page 58)
Virgin Mimosa (page 59)

Supplies

Blender
2 Champagne flutes
Christmas tree cookie cutter
Toaster

Breakfast tray
Red rose
Love note or a small gift

Timeline

1. Twenty minutes before you are ready to serve, place a single red rose, a love note, and, if you have one, a small gift on a breakfast tray.
2. Prepare the Puffy Seafood Omelet.
3. While the omelet is cooking, start the Christmas Cinnamon Toast and put the water in the microwave for the Chocolate Almond Steamer.
4. Put the butter and cinnamon mixture on the toast.
5. Finish the Chocolate Almond Steamer.
6. Make the Mimosa.
7. Divide the omelet and place it on two plates.
8. Turn on soft romantic Christmas music.
9. Place food and beverages on breakfast tray.
10. Deliver with a smile and a sweet kiss.

Grocery List

Staple Items
1 loaf light bread

Meats
1 (8-ounce) package imitation crabmeat (only ½ cup needed)
1 (8-ounce) package cooked, peeled, and cleaned shrimp (only ¼ cup needed)

Dairy
1 (8-ounce) container liquid egg substitute
2 tablespoons fat-free, low-carb milk
1 (8-ounce) fat-free shredded mozzarella cheese (only 3 tablespoons needed)
1 pound light butter (only 4 teaspoons needed)
1 pint nonfat dairy liquid creamer (only 4 tablespoons needed)
1 (2-quart) container light orange juice beverage (only 1 cup needed)

Baking Items
1 (1.9-ounce) box Splenda Granular (only 4 teaspoons needed)
1 (1.75-ounce) box Splenda Packets (only 2 individual packets needed)
1 (8-ounce) can nonfat cooking spray

Seasonings/Condiments
3 tablespoons fat-free mayonnaise
1 teaspoon ground cinnamon
1 (1-ounce) bottle almond extract (only ½ teaspoon needed)

Other
1 (2.32-ounce) box sugar-free hot chocolate packets (only 2 packets needed)
1 (25.4-ounce) bottle sparkling white grape juice (only 4 tablespoons needed)
Fresh parsley sprigs, optional

Puffy Seafood Omelet

You'll never have to worry about being puffy eating this low-cal and extra-special omelet.

1	cup liquid egg substitute	3	tablespoons fat-free mayonnaise
2	tablespoons fat-free, low-carb milk	3	tablespoons shredded fat-free mozzarella cheese
1/2	cup finely chopped imitation crab-meat		Parsley
1/4	cup firmly packed, chopped cooked shrimp		Salt and pepper

- In a small mixing bowl stir the egg substitute and the milk together.
- Spray a small nonstick skillet with nonfat cooking spray.
- Place the skillet on the stove on medium heat.
- Pour the egg mixture in the skillet, cover, and let cook for 2 to 3 minutes.
- Turn the eggs over in one big round piece when the edges are dry.
- Place the chopped crabmeat on the eggs, cover, turn off the heat, and let it cook for 2 minutes or until the eggs are completely cooked.
- Place the omelet on a plate, folding it in half so that the crabmeat is in the center like a filling.
- Return the skillet to the stove, turn the heat to medium, and add the shrimp, mayonnaise, and cheese.
- Cover and let cook for 1 minute or until thoroughly heated, stirring once.
- Pour the shrimp sauce over the omelet, cut it in half, and serve on two plates.
- Garnish with parsley and add salt and pepper to taste.

Yield: 2 servings

Calories: 145 (7% fat); Total Fat: 1g; Cholesterol: 46mg; Carbohydrate: 9g; Dietary Fiber: 1g; Protein: 23g; Sodium: 620mg; Diabetic Exchanges: 3 very lean meat, 1/2 other carbohydrate

Preparation time: 5 minutes
Cooking time: 6 minutes
Total time: 11 minutes

✦✦ Christmas Cinnamon Toast

This is just taking a simple recipe and making it more special for the holidays by creating fun shapes.

1	teaspoon ground cinnamon	4	pieces light bread
4	teaspoons Splenda Granular	4	teaspoons light butter

- In a small bowl combine the cinnamon and Splenda. Stir until well mixed.
- Place the bread in a toaster and toast lightly.
- Remove the bread from the toaster and place on a cutting board. Cut the toast with a medium-size cookie cutter no bigger than the piece of bread and discard the scraps.
- Spread the butter on the shaped toast.
- Sprinkle 1¼ teaspoons of the cinnamon-Splenda mixture over each buttered toast.

Yield: 2 (2-piece) servings

Calories: 105 (35% fat); Total Fat: 4g; Cholesterol: 13mg; Carbohydrate: 16g; Dietary Fiber: 6g; Protein: 4g; Sodium: 248mg; Diabetic Exchanges: 1 starch, 1 fat

Preparation time: 1 minute or less
Toasting time: 2 minutes
Total time: 3 minutes

Chocolate Almond Steamer

Oh, man! I thought I'd died and gone to heaven. It's hard to believe something this soothing and delicious is fat-free and sugar-free too.

2	cups water	4	tablespoons nonfat dairy liquid creamer
2	packets dry fat-free, sugar-free hot chocolate mix*	2	individual packets Splenda
		½	teaspoon almond extract

- Heat the water in a microwave for 2 minutes.

- Put the water, hot chocolate mix, creamer, Splenda, and almond extract in a blender. Cover the blender, leaving a slight space between the lid and the blender to let steam escape.
- Process in the blender on highest speed for 20 to 30 seconds, or until the mix has a nice frothy top when the blender is turned off.
- Pour into two mugs and serve immediately.

Note: There are 10 packets per box.

Yield: 2 (9-ounce) servings

Calories: 50 (0% fat); Total Fat: 0g; Cholesterol: 0mg; Carbohydrate: 11g; Dietary Fiber: 1g; Protein: 1g; Sodium: 95mg; Diabetic Exchanges: 1 other carbohydrate

Preparation time: 1 minute
Cooking time: 2 minutes
Total time: 3 minutes

🏃 Virgin Mimosa

This is normally an alcoholic beverage made with champagne and orange juice; however, I wanted an alcohol-free version so our children could enjoy it with us also.

¹/₂ cup light orange juice	2 tablespoons nonalcoholic sparkling white grape juice

- Pour the orange juice into a champagne flute.
- Add the grape juice and stir.

Note: Keep the juices chilled in the refrigerator so the ingredients are ready.

Yield: 1 serving

Calories: 47 (0% fat); Total Fat: 0g; Cholesterol: 0mg; Carbohydrate: 11g; Dietary Fiber: 0g; Protein: 1g; Sodium: 2mg; Diabetic Exchanges: 1 fruit

Preparation time: 2 minutes

Remembering Christmases Past Breakfast

Serves 4

Festive Frittata (page 63)
Eggnog French Toast (page 65)
Creamy Fruit Salad (page 62)
Pumpkin Cider (page 64)

Edible Centerpiece

Place a pretty teapot with a ribbon tied around the handle on a ceramic trivet in the middle of the table. You will be putting the Pumpkin Cider in the teapot later. Take family photos of Christmases past, put them into small frames, and place them around the teapot. At each place setting, put a small Christmas photo in a frame that the guest can take home.

Supplies

Teapot	Glass serving bowl
Small picture frames	Electric mixer
Old family Christmas photos	Cast-iron skillet

Timeline

1. Set the table before you begin cooking and don't forget to put out pretty teacups or holiday mugs for everyone. If you are serving sugar-free syrup or confectioners' sugar with the Eggnog French Toast, you can put that on the table too.
2. About 45 minutes before serving time, make the Creamy Fruit Salad, cover, and put it in the refrigerator.
3. About 40 minutes before serving time, start the Festive Frittata.
4. Remove the frittata from the oven. Keep the frittata warm by turning the oven off and opening the oven door to let the oven cool for a few minutes. Then cover the cooked frittata and place it in the warm oven.
5. Make the Pumpkin Cider.

Last 15 minutes
6. Make the French toast and pour the cider into the teapot.
7. Put the fruit salad, frittata, and French toast on the table.

Grocery List

Fresh Fruits and Vegetables
1 small onion (½ cup needed)
1 small zucchini (1 cup needed)
1 small red pepper (½ cup needed)

Staple Items
1 (30-ounce) can tropical fruit salad in light syrup
1 loaf light wheat bread
1 small bottle sugar-free maple syrup or powdered sugar, optional

Meats
½ pound extra-lean ham

Dairy
6 eggs
1 (8-ounce) container liquid egg substitute or 8 eggs
1 (2-quart) container fat-free low-carb milk (only ¾ cup needed)
1 (8-ounce) package fat-free Swiss cheese slices (only 2 slices needed)

Baking Items
1 (21-ounce) can lemon crème pie filling (or lemon pie filling) (only ½ cup needed)
1 (14-ounce) bag shredded coconut (only 1 tablespoon needed)
1 (1.9-ounce) box Splenda Granular (only ⅔ cup needed)
1 (20-ounce) can pumpkin pie mix (only 1¼ cups needed)
1 (8-ounce) can nonfat cooking spray

Seasonings/Condiments
½ teaspoon vanilla extract
½ teaspoon rum extract
¼ teaspoon ground nutmeg

Other
1 (1.8-ounce) box sugar-free lemonade drink mix

☐ ☗ Creamy Fruit Salad

To save time making the pudding, I use canned lemon crème pudding from the grocery store already made and with no fat. This salad tastes best chilled, so store your ingredients in the refrigerator as soon as you get home from the grocery store.

I	(30-ounce) can tropical fruit salad in light syrup, juice drained and discarded	¹/₂	cup lemon crème pie filling* (or lemon pie filling)
		I	tablespoon shredded coconut

- Gently stir into a pretty, small to medium-size, serving bowl the fruit and lemon pie filling. I like to use glass because the colors of the fruit are so pretty to see through the bowl.
- Sprinkle the top of the salad lightly with the shredded coconut.
- Eat as is or cover and keep refrigerated until ready to eat.

*Note: Lemon crème pie filling comes in a 21-ounce can and is found with either pie fillings or in the pudding aisle. Use only ½ cup and save the rest for later use.

Yield: 6 (½-cup) servings

Calories: 113 (6% fat); Total Fat: 1g; Cholesterol: 0mg; Carbohydrate: 27g; Dietary Fiber: 1g; Protein: 0g; Sodium: 42mg; Diabetic Exchanges: 1 fruit, 1 other carbohydrate

⊘ **Preparation time:** 5 minutes or less

Festive Frittata

The red and green colors complement this very impressive puffy egg entrée.

6	eggs, separated (save two yolks)	$^1/_3$	red pepper, diced (about $^1/_2$ cup)
$^1/_2$	cup chopped onion	$^1/_2$	pound extra-lean ham, chopped
I	small zucchini, cut into $^1/_2$-inch pieces (about I cup)	2	slices fat-free Swiss cheese, cut in quarters

- Preheat the oven to 400 degrees.
- In a medium to large glass bowl with an electric mixer beat the egg whites on high until soft peaks form. Add the 2 egg yolks, reducing the speed to low and continuing to mix until well blended.
- Spray a 12-inch nonstick skillet with nonfat cooking spray. Do not use a skillet with a plastic handle because this recipe will eventually go in the oven.
- Over high heat cook the onion for 2 to 3 minutes until lightly browned.
- Stir in the zucchini and red pepper and cook over high heat for an additional 2 minutes with the lid on, stirring occasionally.
- Stir in the ham, cover, and cook for 1 minute.
- With a spatula gently stir the eggs into the skillet just enough to mix.
- Cook, covered, for 2 to 3 minutes until edges are dry but center is wet.
- Take the lid off the skillet, put the skillet on the top shelf of the oven, and cook until lightly browned, about 2 to 3 minutes.
- Remove from the oven. Increase the heat to 500 degrees. Arrange the cheese in a pretty pattern on top and bake for 1 minute or until the cheese is melted. Cut into 4 pieces.

Note: Give the extra four egg yolks to your cats, dogs, or horses in their food to help their coats shine more.

Yield: 4 servings

Calories: 153 (32% fat); Total Fat: 5g; Cholesterol: 128mg; Carbohydrate: 4g; Dietary Fiber: 1g; Protein: 21g; Sodium: 888mg; Diabetic Exchanges: 3 lean meat, 1 vegetable

Preparation time: 10 minutes or less
Cooking time: 13 minutes or less
Total time: 23 minutes or less

Pumpkin Cider

*I know the way these ingredients are used sounds unusual, but trust me—this is deli-
cious, smooth, and comforting; it's a very relaxing and satisfying warm beverage.*

---

6   cups sugar-free lemonade $^1/_3$ cup Splenda Granular
1$^1/_4$ cups pumpkin pie mix*

- Put the lemonade in a medium-size saucepan and heat until piping hot.
- Add the pumpkin pie mix and the Splenda and stir until dissolved.
- Serve immediately in the teapot in the center of the table or in holiday
  mugs or teacups.

*Note: I used the pumpkin pie mix I had left over from the Pumpkin Trifle
recipe.

Yield: 7 (1-cup) servings

Calories: 58 (0% fat); Total Fat: 0g; Cholesterol: 0mg; Carbohydrate: 12g; Dietary Fiber: 1g;
Protein: 1g; Sodium: 62mg; Diabetic Exchanges: 1 other carbohydrate

Preparation time: 4 minutes
Cooking time: 5 to 6 minutes
Total time: 10 minutes or less

Eggnog French Toast

This is delicious just how it is. It doesn't need any syrup. If you want, you can sprinkle a little confectioners' sugar on each slice.

1 cup liquid egg substitute or 8 egg whites and a few drops of yellow food coloring	$3/4$ cup fat-free, low-carb milk
	$1/2$ teaspoon rum extract
	$1/4$ teaspoon ground nutmeg
$1/3$ cup Splenda Granular	12 slices light whole wheat bread
$1/2$ teaspoon vanilla extract	

- Preheat a large skillet or griddle on medium-high heat.
- Spray it with nonfat cooking spray.
- In a large bowl beat with a whisk the egg substitute, Splenda, vanilla, milk, rum extract, and nutmeg until well blended.
- Dip the bread into the batter and place it in a hot skillet or griddle.
- Cook 1 to 2 minutes on each side or until golden brown.

Yield: 6 (2-piece) servings

Calories: 117 (4% fat); Total Fat: 1g; Cholesterol: 1mg; Carbohydrate: 21g; Dietary Fiber: 7g; Protein: 10g; Sodium: 340mg; Diabetic Exchanges: 1 very lean meat, 1½ starch

Preparation time: 5 minutes
Cooking time: 10 minutes
Total time: 15 minutes

Southern-Style Breakfast

Serves 5

Country Skillet Scramble (page 72)
Sausage Gravy (page 70)
Chocolate Gravy (page 71)
Snowman Biscuits (page 69)
Frosted Grapes (page 68)
Warm Mint Milk (page 73)

Edible Centerpiece

Surround a white pillar candle on a small plate with frosted grapes, and place the plate on a stemmed glass upside down in the middle of the table. Use a glass that is slightly wide for added stability. (See photo on page 68.)

Supplies

White pillar candle   Food processor
Baking sheet   Medium nonstick saucepans

Timeline

1. Set the table. Put mugs out for the Warm Mint Milk.
2. Prepare the Frosted Grapes and make your centerpiece.
3. Forty-five minutes before serving time, prepare the Snowman Biscuits. Do not bake. Set aside.
4. Make the Sausage Gravy.
5. While the Sausage Gravy is cooking, start the Chocolate Gravy, making sure you stir it constantly. As soon as it comes to a low boil, remove the saucepan from the heat and turn off the burner.
6. Once the Sausage Gravy is fully cooked, turn off the heat and cover to keep it warm.
7. Make the Country Skillet Scramble.

Last 15 minutes

8. Bake the Snowman Biscuits
9. While the scramble is cooking, make the Warm Mint Milk.
10. Ladle ½-cup servings of the Sausage Gravy into individual small bowls and place a Snowman Biscuit, standing up, in the bowl. Repeat with the Chocolate Gravy.
11. Take everything to the table while it is piping hot.

Grocery List

Frozen Foods
2 (5.2 ounce) boxes low-fat fully-cooked breakfast sausage links (found in frozen meat aisle)
1 (9-ounce) package frozen turnip greens

Fresh Fruits and Vegetables
1 pound green grapes
1 small red bell pepper (only ½ cup needed)
1 small onion (only ½ cup needed)

Dairy
2 (12-ounce) rolls low-fat buttermilk biscuits (10 per roll)
1 (2-quart) container fat-free, low-carb milk (only 7 cups needed)
1 quart fat-free half-and-half (only 3½ cups needed)
3 (4-ounce) containers liquid egg substitute
1 (8-ounce) package fat-free shredded mild cheddar cheese (only 1 cup needed)
1 pint fat-free, low-carb French vanilla liquid creamer (only ½ cup plus 2 tablespoons needed)

Baking Items
1 (1.75-ounce) box individual packets Splenda (only 10 packets needed)
1 (1.9-ounce) box Splenda Granular (only ½ cup needed)
1 (16-ounce) box cornstarch (only 2 tablespoons needed)
1 (2-ounce) box sugar-free cook and serve chocolate pudding mix
1 (8-ounce) can nonfat cooking spray

Seasonings/Condiments
1 (2.5-ounce) package butter-flavored sprinkles, such as Butter Buds (only 2 tablespoons needed)
Ground black pepper
1 teaspoon lemon pepper
1 (1-ounce) bottle mint extract (only 1¼ teaspoons needed)

Other
5 mini candy canes, optional

♀♂ Frosted Grapes

This is the best way to eat grapes. I love the burst of fruit flavor that pops in your mouth.

¹/₂ cup Splenda Granular	I pound green seedless grapes

- Place the Splenda in a medium-size bowl.
- Leave the grapes in a bunch and rinse the grapes under cold running water. Gently shake the grapes to remove the excess water.
- Hold the bunch of grapes by the stem and roll them in the Splenda until they are completely coated.
- Place the grapes on a small, pretty plate and place a candle in the middle of the plate if you wish. Sprinkle the extra Splenda from the bowl over the grapes.

Yield: 5 servings

Calories: 72 (0% fat); Total Fat: 0g; Cholesterol: 0mg; Carbohydrate: 19g; Dietary Fiber: 1g; Protein: 1g; Sodium: 2mg; Diabetic Exchanges: 1 fruit

⏱ **Preparation time:** 5 minutes

✝✝ Snowman Biscuits

These are the most adorable biscuits, and they're so easy to make.

> **2   (12-ounce) cans low-fat buttermilk biscuits, divided**

- Preheat the oven to 400 degrees.
- Spray two baking sheets with nonfat cooking spray.
- Place 13 biscuits on the baking sheet.
- Take 7 biscuits, cut them in half, and roll each half biscuit into a ball. Place a ball directly next to a whole biscuit on the baking sheets to make a head for the snowman. Make sure they are touching so that they will stay together after baking. You can discard the 1 remaining half-biscuit.
- Bake for 10 minutes.

Note: There are 10 biscuits per can.

Yield: 13 (1-snowman) servings

Calories: 258 (16% fat); Total Fat: 5g; Cholesterol: 0mg; Carbohydrate: 48g; Dietary Fiber: 2g; Protein: 7g; Sodium: 1252mg; Diabetic Exchanges: 3 starch

Preparation time: 5 minutes
Baking time: 10 minutes
Total time: 15 minutes

Sausage Gravy

Is there any breakfast recipe that says old-fashioned, country-Christmas-goodness better than this stick-to-your-ribs (but not your hips or thighs) all-time favorite? I think not.

2	(5.2 ounce) boxes low-fat, fully-cooked, breakfast sausage links	2	tablespoons butter-flavored sprinkles
2	tablespoons cornstarch		Dash of freshly ground black pepper
2	cups fat-free, low-carb milk		

- Grind the sausage links in a food processor until finely chopped.
- In a medium nonstick saucepan with a whisk stir together the cornstarch and milk until the cornstarch is completely dissolved.
- After the cornstarch is dissolved, turn the heat to medium and stir in the butter-flavored sprinkles and the sausage.
- Cook, stirring frequently, until the mixture is thick, creamy, and fully heated. If desired, you can add freshly ground black pepper. However, taste first, because some sausage crumbles can be pretty flavorful.
- Serve hot with Snowman Biscuits (page 69).

Yield: 5 (½-cup) servings

Calories: 147 (17% fat); Total Fat: 2g; Cholesterol: 41mg; Carbohydrate: 8g; Dietary Fiber: 0g; Protein: 17g; Sodium: 687mg; Diabetic Exchanges: 2 very lean meat, ½ starch

Preparation time: 3 to 5 minutes
Cooking time: 20 minutes
Total time: 23 to 25 minutes

Chocolate Gravy

This southern favorite is definitely a hit with people of all ages.

1 (2-ounce) box dry, sugar-free, cook-and-serve chocolate pudding mix	3½ cups fat-free half-and-half

- In a medium-size nonstick saucepan over medium heat with a whisk, stir together constantly the pudding mix and milk until completely dissolved, thoroughly heated, and beginning to thicken.
- As soon as the mixture comes to a low boil, turn the heat off, remove the saucepan from the burner, and let the gravy cool for 10 minutes. This is very important. The gravy will thicken as it cools.
- Serve warm with Snowman Biscuits (page 69).

Yield: 7 (½-cup) servings

Calories: 147 (0% fat); Total Fat: 0g; Cholesterol: 0mg; Carbohydrate: 31g; Dietary Fiber: 0g; Protein: 11g; Sodium: 636mg; Diabetic Exchanges: 2 other carbohydrate

Preparation time: 15 minutes
Cooking time: 10 minutes
Total time: 25 minutes

※ ※ ※

A Visit from Santa

When our children were little, my husband and I would take our children for a drive after church on Christmas Eve to see the pretty lights on homes in our neighborhood. Every year I would come up with an excuse for my husband to stop by the house. I'd scurry around putting the children's wrapped presents under the tree. I'd come out to the car and in total amazement say, "You're not going to believe this. Santa was here!" The children would always be elated.

Country Skillet Scramble

Scrambles such as this are fantastic for serving large groups.

1	(9-ounce) package frozen turnip greens, still frozen	1	teaspoon lemon pepper
1/2	cup chopped red bell pepper	3	(4-ounce) containers liquid egg substitute
1/2	cup chopped onion	1	cup fat-free mild Cheddar cheese, shredded

- Spray a 12-inch nonstick skillet with nonfat cooking spray.
- Cook the turnip greens, red bell pepper, onion, and lemon pepper together over medium heat with the lid on, stirring occasionally for 3 to 4 minutes or until all of the vegetables are tender. (No need for added liquid; the frozen turnip greens and moisture from the vegetables are enough to keep them moist while cooking.)
- Once the vegetables are tender, drain the excess liquid from the skillet and discard.
- Pour the egg substitute into the skillet. With a pancake turner, stir constantly, scraping the sides and bottom of the skillet and mixing all of the ingredients together until fully cooked. You can tell the eggs are fully cooked when they no longer look wet.
- Sprinkle the top with the cheese and stir. Turn off the heat. Cover and let sit for 3 to 4 minutes or until the cheese is melted.
- Serve hot.

Yield: 5 (¾-cup) servings

Calories: 86 (0% fat); Total Fat: 0g; Cholesterol: 4mg; Carbohydrate: 6g; Dietary Fiber: 2g; Protein: 15g; Sodium: 426mg; Diabetic Exchanges: 2 very lean meat, 1 vegetable

Preparation time: 5 minutes
Cooking time: 15 minutes
Total time: 20 minutes

Warm Mint Milk

This is a terrific nutritious and delicious way to begin your day, or to have as a midday snack to help you relax, or as a soothing hot beverage to gently take you to the end of your day. The aroma of the mint has relaxing qualities about it as well.

5	cups fat-free, low-carb milk	1¹/₄	teaspoons mint extract
¹/₂	cup plus 2 tablespoons fat-free, low-carb French vanilla liquid creamer	10	individual packets Splenda
		5	mini candy canes (optional)

■ In a medium-size saucepan stir the milk, creamer, mint extract, and Splenda together until well mixed.

■ Place over medium-low heat until hot, stirring occassionally.

■ Serve in individual cups. If desired, lay a mini candy cane on the rim of the cup for an easy holiday touch.

Yield: 5 (9-ounce) servings

Calories: 90 (0% fat); Total Fat: 0g; Cholesterol: 6mg; Carbohydrate: 6g; Dietary Fiber: 0g; Protein: 14g; Sodium: 236mg; Diabetic Exchanges: 1¹/₂ very lean meat, ¹/₂ skim milk

Preparation time: 1 minute
Cooking time: 10 minutes
Total time: 11 minutes

Everyone's Happy Breakfast

Serves 6

Usually I don't serve pancakes and French toast together. However, to make everyone in the family happy, I made both. The family felt quite special being served both of these at the same time. (And the picky eater had something to eat.)

Cinnamon & Spice and Everything Nice French Toast **(page 78)**
Cranberry & Walnut Pancakes **(page 77)**
Strawberry Christmas Tree **(page 76)**
Snowy Fruit Dip **(page 76)**
Apple Cinnamon Topping **(page 79)**
Turkey Bacon
Coffee or Tea

Edible Centerpiece
The Strawberry Christmas Tree will be your centerpiece for this breakfast.

Supplies
1 Styrofoam cone (14½ inches tall by 4 inches wide on bottom)
Nonstick griddle

Timeline
1. Set the table. Leave a place in the middle of the table for the Strawberry Christmas Tree and Snowy Fruit Dip.
2. One and a quarter hours before serving time, make the Strawberry Christmas Tree and place it in the middle of the table.
3. Make the Snowy Fruit Dip and keep refrigerated until ready to eat.
4. Brew fresh coffee or tea and keep it warm.
5. Lay the slices of turkey bacon on a jelly-roll pan and bake in a 400-degree oven until crispy.
6. Make the Cranberry and Walnut Pancakes. Check to see if the bacon is finished.
7. When the bacon and pancakes are done, store each of them in a 9 x 13-inch casserole dish and cover with foil. Keep in the oven on the lowest temperature to keep warm.
8. Prepare the French toast.

Last 10 minutes

9. Prepare the Apple Cinnamon Topping
10. Take the Snowy Fruit Dip, bacon, pancakes, French toast, apple topping, and coffee or tea to the table.

Grocery List

Frozen Foods
1 (8-ounce) container fat-free dessert whipped topping (only ¾ cup needed)

Fresh Fruits and Vegetables
2½ pounds fresh strawberries
1 Granny Smith apple

Staple Items
1 (25-ounce) jar cinnamon applesauce (only 1 cup needed)
1 (16-ounce) can whole cranberry sauce (only ¾ cup needed)
1 (64-ounce) bottle light cranberry juice cocktail (only 1¼ cups needed)
1 loaf light whole-grain bread
Coffee or tea

Meats
½ pound turkey bacon

Dairy
1 (8-ounce) package fat-free cream cheese
2 eggs
2 (4-ounce) containers liquid egg substitute (or 8 eggs)
1 pint fat-free, low-carb French vanilla nondairy liquid creamer (only ⅔ cup needed)
Butter spray, optional

Baking Items
1 (1.9-ounce) box Splenda Granular (only 1 cup plus 5 tablespoons needed)
1 pound confectioners' sugar (only ⅓ cup needed)
1 (14-ounce) bag shredded coconut (only 1 tablespoon needed)
1 (2.25-ounce) bag chopped walnuts (only 3 tablespoons needed)
1 (2-pound) bag all-purpose flour (only 3 cups needed)
2 teaspoons baking soda
1 (8-ounce) can nonfat cooking spray

Seasonings/Condiments
1 (1-ounce) bottle coconut extract (only 1 teaspoon needed)
½ teaspoon allspice
¼ teaspoon ground cloves
½ teaspoon ground cinnamon

Other
Red toothpicks, if available
1 small bottle sugar-free syrup of your favorite flavor, optional (only 6 tablespoons needed)

🍲 👫 Strawberry Christmas Tree

Here's an impressive Christmas tree-shaped centerpiece that is every bit as tasty as it is beautiful. This serves more than we need; however, it will stay fresh and is a great healthy snack to nibble on until dinner is served.

1 Styrofoam cone (14¹/₂ inches tall by 4 inches wide on bottom) Toothpicks, red if available	2¹/₂ pounds fresh strawberries with stems on

- Cover the cone with aluminum foil.
- Put a toothpick into the green part of the strawberry. Gently press the strawberry and toothpick into the foam cone, starting at the bottom and working your way up until all the strawberries are used. There will be spots where the foil is showing. This is okay.
- Place the strawberry-covered cone on a pretty dinner plate and put it in the middle of your table for a lovely holiday centerpiece.
- Place the Snowy Fruit Dip (see below) next to the tree in the middle of your table for dipping the strawberries.

Yield: 1 tree with 10 servings

Calories: 36 (0% fat); Total Fat: 0g; Cholestérol: 0mg; Carbohydrate: 9g; Dietary Fiber: 2g; Protein: 1g; Sodium: 1mg; Diabetic Exchanges: ¹/₂ fruit

🕐 **Preparation time:** 30 minutes

🍲 👫 Snowy Fruit Dip

This is fabulous with fresh fruit (and pretzel sticks too).

1 (8-ounce) package fat-free cream cheese ¹/₂ cup Splenda Granular ¹/₃ cup confectioners' sugar	1 teaspoon coconut extract 1 tablespoon finely chopped shredded coconut

- In a small mixing bowl stir together with a fork the cream cheese, Splenda, confectioners' sugar, and coconut extract.
- Pour the dip into a small pretty serving bowl and sprinkle the coconut over the top.

Yield: 8 (2-tablespoon) servings

Calories: 61 (0% fat); Total Fat: 0g; Cholesterol: 5mg; Carbohydrate: 9g; Dietary Fiber: 0g; Protein: 4g; Sodium: 142mg; Diabetic Exchanges: ½ very lean meat, ½ other carbohydrate

🕐 **Preparation time:** 5 minutes or less

Cranberry & Walnut Pancakes

Here's a terrific and unique way to use cranberry sauce from the holidays.

2 egg whites	2 plus I tablespoons very finely chopped walnuts
1¼ cups light cranberry juice cocktail	³/₄ cup whole cranberry sauce (from a can is fine)
2 cups Homemade Baking Mix (page 000)	³/₄ cup fat-free dessert whipped topping

- Preheat a nonstick griddle to 400 degrees or a nonstick skillet over high heat.
- Combine the egg whites and cranberry juice in a mixing bowl and beat until well blended.
- Stir in the baking mix and the 2 tablespoons walnuts. The batter may be lumpy.
- Spray the griddle or skillet with nonfat cooking spray.
- Pour ¼ cup batter for each pancake onto the prepared griddle.
- Cook until bubbles appear on the surface and the underside is golden.
- Flip each pancake and cook until the other side is golden.
- Microwave the cranberry sauce for 1 minute or until heated thoroughly.
- Top each pancake with 1 tablespoon of the cranberry sauce.
- Then top each pancake with 1 tablespoon dessert whipped topping.
- Sprinkle each very lightly with the remaining chopped walnuts, about ¼ teaspoon for each pancake.

Yield: 6 (2-pancake) servings

Calories: 238 (11% fat); Total Fat: 3g; Cholesterol: 0mg; Carbohydrate: 47g; Dietary Fiber: 2g; Protein: 5g; Sodium: 287mg; Diabetic Exchanges: 2 starch, 1 other carbohydrate

🕐 **Preparation time:** 5 minutes or less
Cooking time: 12 minutes or less
Total time: 17 minutes or less

Cinnamon & Spice and Everything Nice French Toast

This French toast is a zesty twist to an old-time favorite.

2 (4-ounce) containers liquid egg substitute (or 8 egg whites)	1/2 teaspoon ground cinnamon
2/3 cup fat-free, low-carb French vanilla nondairy liquid creamer	12 slices light whole-grain bread
2 tablespoons Splenda Granular	6 tablespoons sugar-free syrup (optional)
1/4 teaspoon ground cloves	Butter spray (optional)

- Preheat a nonstick skillet or griddle over medium-high heat.
- Coat with nonfat cooking spray.
- Beat the egg substitute, nondairy creamer, Splenda, cloves, and cinnamon in a bowl briskly with a fork until well mixed. The spices will float to the top. That is fine.
- Dip the bread slices into the egg mixture one at a time.
- Arrange the dipped bread slices into the prepared skillet, making sure the edges of the bread do not touch each other.
- Cook the French toast until the bottoms are golden brown.
- Turn the bread slices and cook the other side until golden brown.
- Top each serving with 1 tablespoon sugar-free syrup and up to 10 sprays of fat-free butter spray, or use the Apple Cinnamon Topping on next page.
- These can be made ahead of time and stored in zip-top bags in the freezer. Just put them in the microwave or the toaster to heat.

Yield: 6 (2-slice) servings

Calories: 109 (4% fat); Total Fat: 1g; Cholesterol: 1mg; Carbohydrate: 20g; Dietary Fiber: 7g; Protein: 9g; Sodium: 331mg; Diabetic Exchanges: 1 very lean meat, 1½ starch

Preparation time: 3 minutes
Cooking time: 12 minutes
Total time: 15 minutes

Apple Cinnamon Topping

This is great with the Cinnamon & Spice and Everything Nice French Toast. It would also be good with pancakes. It is made with allspice, which is the dried berry of the pimiento tree. It has the flavor combination of cinnamon, nutmeg, and cloves, which is why it is called allspice.

1	Granny Smith apple with peel on, finely chopped (about 1¼ cups chopped apple)	3	tablespoons Splenda Granular
		¹/2	teaspoon allspice
1	cup cinnamon applesauce		

- Place the chopped apples, applesauce, Splenda, and allspice in a small saucepan and stir together over medium-high heat.
- Cook for 8 minutes, stirring frequently.
- Serve warm or cover and put in the refrigerator to use later.

Yield: 7 (¼-cup) servings

Calories: 28 (0% fat); Total Fat: 0g; Cholesterol: 0mg; Carbohydrate: 7g; Dietary Fiber: 1g; Protein: 0g; Sodium: 1mg; Diabetic Exchanges: ½ fruit

Preparation time: 5 minutes
Cooking time: 8 minutes
Total time: 13 minutes

Serves 16

For Helpful Ideas for large gatherings, see the Turkey Buffet Menu on page 181.

Breakfast Scramble (page 89)
Christmas Tree French Toast (page 88)
Ham & Cheddar Biscuits (page 86)
Pumpkin Crumb Squares (page 85)
Crispy Christmas Breakfast Wreath (page 84)
Red & Green Grape Salad (page 83)
Broccoli & Tomato Trifle (page 90)
Eggnog Cappuccino (page 87)
Carved Watermelon

Edible Centerpiece

What a cute, clever, and creative idea. This is excellent for a breakfast centerpiece in a warm climate. Cut the stem end off your watermelon to make a flat bottom, so it will stand upright. With a small knife, draw a Christmas tree shape on three sides of the watermelon. Do not cut all the way through; just do an outline first.

Once you have the outline then cut through the watermelon rind following the outline of the Christmas trees. Pull out the pieces of the rind. (You can cut them into smaller pieces and pull out each piece.) With your hands, reach through the Christmas tree shaped holes and scoop out the red part of the watermelon and set it aside.

Cut the watermelon that was scooped out into chunks and carefully place the chunks back into the hollowed out watermelon using your carved watermelon as a very decorative red and green serving bowl.

Supplies

Christmas tree-shaped cookie cutter   2 trifle bowls
Electric mixer   Slow cooker
10 x 15-inch jelly-roll pan

Timeline

1. Set the table, leaving a place in the middle of the table for the carved watermelon.
2. About 3 hours before serving time, make the Red & Green Grape Salad, cover, and place it in the refrigerator until serving time.
3. Make the Crispy Christmas Breakfast Wreath and let it cool.
4. While the breakfast wreath is baking, make the Pumpkin Crumb Squares.
5. Take the wreath out of the oven, increase the heat to 375 degrees, and put the Pumpkin Crumb Squares into the oven.
6. Make the carved watermelon.
7. Make the Ham & Cheddar Biscuits. Be sure to remove the Pumpkin Crumb Squares when they are finished and set aside until serving time.
8. While the biscuits are baking, make the Eggnog Cappuccino and place it in a slow cooker to keep warm. You can place a ladle on a small plate next to the cappuccino for guests to serve themselves. Remove the biscuits from the oven and set aside until serving time.

Forty-five minutes before serving
9. Start the Christmas Tree French Toast and place it in the oven on warm until serving time. Make sure your oven heat is either turned off (still warm from a previous baking) or on the lowest heat.
10. Start the Breakfast Scramble.
11. While the scramble is cooking, start the Broccoli & Tomato Trifle.

Last 15 minutes
12. Place the carved watermelon in the middle of the table.
13. Finish the Broccoli & Tomato Trifle.
14. Cut the Pumpkin Crumb Squares into pieces.
15. Place all of the food on the table. Don't forget to get the Red & Green Grape Salad out of the refrigerator.

Grocery List

Frozen Foods
2 (16-ounce) bags frozen broccoli cuts
1 (16-ounce) bag frozen bell pepper
    stir-fry mixture

Fresh Fruits and Vegetables
5 cups red seedless grapes
5 cups green seedless grapes
½ cup green onion tops
1 watermelon, medium size, seedless
    would be best
1 pint cherry or grape tomatoes

Staple Items
4½ cups unsweetened whole-grain
    cereal flakes
16 cups fresh-brewed coffee
2 loaves white lite bread
Sugar-free maple syrup, optional

Meats
1 cup extra-lean ham (Lunchmeat
    is fine)
2 cups Canadian bacon, sliced

Dairy
18 eggs
1 pound light margarine (only
    3 tablespoons needed) (half the
    fat of regular)
4 (16-ounce) containers liquid egg
    substitute
1 (2 quart) carton fat-free, low-carb
    milk
1 pint fat-free, low-carb French vanilla
    liquid creamer (only 1 cup
    needed)
2 (8-ounce) packages fat-free shred-
    ded mild Cheddar cheese

Baking Items
1 (39-ounce) can pumpkin pie mix
1 (7-ounce) package cherry crumb
    topping mix
1 (9.7-ounce) Splenda Granular
    (5 cups needed)
1 (2-pound) bag all-purpose flour
    (only 3 cups needed)
1 (12-ounce) box baking soda (only
    4 teaspoons needed)
1 (5-pound) bag whole wheat flour
    (only 3 cups needed)
1 (8-ounce) can nonfat cooking spray

Seasonings/Condiments
1 quart fat-free whipped salad
    dressing (only ½ cup needed)
1 pint light whipped salad dressing
    (only ½ cup needed)
3 teaspoons vanilla extract
1 small bottle green food coloring
1 teaspoon rum extract
1 (2.5-ounce) imitation butter-flavored
    sprinkles (I use Butter Buds) (only
    3 tablespoons needed)
½ teaspoon dried chives
1 (8-ounce) bottle fat-free Italian
    salad dressing (only ½ cup
    needed)

Other
1 (3-ounce) package reduced-fat
    bacon crumbles (only 4 table-
    spoons needed)
1 (12-ounce) bag cinnamon candies,
    such as Red Hots (only 48 pieces
    needed)

🍲 👫 Red & Green Grape Salad

The color combination of this unique fruit salad is lovely for the holidays.

1/4 cup fat-free whipped salad dressing	10 cups seedless grapes, firmly packed (5 cups red and 5 cups green)
1/4 cup light whipped salad dressing	1/2 cup chopped green onion tops
2 tablespoons Splenda Granular	
3 plus 1 tablespoons reduced-fat bacon crumbles	

- In a medium mixing bowl with a spatula stir the fat-free whipped salad dressing, light whipped salad dressing, Splenda, 3 tablespoons crumbled bacon, and onions until well mixed.
- Using a large glass serving bowl or trifle bowl place 2½ cups green grapes, then 2½ cups red grapes and repeat.
- Spread the salad dressing mixture on top and sprinkle the remaining 1 tablespoon crumbled bacon on top.

Yield: 20 (½-cup) servings

Calories: 72 (12% fat); Total Fat: 1g; Cholesterol: 3mg; Carbohydrate: 16g; Dietary Fiber: 1g; Protein: 1g; Sodium: 89mg; Diabetic Exchanges: 1 fruit

🕐 **Preparation time:** 15 to 20 minutes

Crispy Christmas Breakfast Wreath

Although this is not our centerpiece for this menu, it could make a lovely centerpiece for your holiday breakfast table. It has the sweet nutty flavor of a breakfast bar.

3	egg whites	4 1/2 cups unsweetened whole-grain cereal flakes*	
1	cup Splenda Granular		
2	teaspoons vanilla extract	48 cinnamon candies	
20	drops green liquid food coloring		

- Preheat the oven to 350 degrees.
- Spray 1 large cookie sheet with nonfat cooking spray.
- In a large glass bowl with an electric mixer beat the egg whites until soft peaks form.
- Slowly add the Splenda, vanilla, and green food coloring.
- Gently stir in the cereal.
- Spray your hands with nonfat cooking spray. Place the cereal mixture on the cookie sheet and form it into a wreath 10 inches across, making the wreath 2½ inches wide all the way around.
- Place the cinnamon candies on the wreath in groups of three to look like holly berries.
- Bake for 10 to 12 minutes.
- Cool while on the cookie sheet.
- Place on a cake plate, add a red ribbon bow, and press into the wreath with a wire. When you are ready to serve, cut the wreath into twenty pieces.

Note: I tested this recipe twice, each time using a different cereal. The cereals I used were Honey Bunches of Oats and then Whole-Grain Total. Our favorite was the Honey Bunches of Oats.

Yield: 20 servings

Calories: 44 (0% fat); Total Fat: 0g; Cholesterol: 0mg; Carbohydrate: 10g; Dietary Fiber: 1g; Protein: 1g; Sodium: 66mg; Diabetic Exchanges: ½ starch

Preparation time: 10 minutes
Cooking time: 10 minutes
Total time: 20 minutes

⬚ Pumpkin Crumb Squares

The first day this tastes like moist pumpkin bread with a light crumb topping and mellow spice flavor. The next day it tastes a lot like pumpkin sponge cake.

1	(39-ounce) can pumpkin pie mix	1	(7-ounce) package dry cherry crumb topping mix
2¼	cups Homemade Whole Wheat Sweet Baking Mix (page 220)	3	tablespoons light margarine, melted
2	egg whites		

- Preheat the oven to 375 degrees.
- Spray a 10 x 15-inch jelly-roll pan with nonfat cooking spray.
- In a large mixing bowl combine the pumpkin pie mix, baking mix, and the egg whites until well mixed.
- Spread the pumpkin mixture into the prepared jelly-roll pan.
- Stir the cherry crumb topping mix and the margarine with a fork until crumbly.
- Sprinkle the crumb mixture on top of the pumpkin mixture and gently press together.
- Bake for 17 minutes.
- Let it sit for a few minutes to cool before cutting into 24 pieces.

Yield: 24 (1-piece) servings

Calories: 112 (9% fat); Total Fat: 1g; Cholesterol: 0mg; Carbohydrate: 23g; Dietary Fiber: 2g; Protein: 2g; Sodium: 164mg; Diabetic Exchanges: 1½ other carbohydrate

⏱ **Preparation time:** 10 minutes
Cooking time: 17 minutes
Total time: 27 minutes

⛫ Ham & Cheddar Biscuits

These babies are out-of-this-world delicious. My family gobbled them up so fast.

2	cups Homemade Baking Mix (page 219)	I	cup extra-lean ham, chopped into small pieces
I	tablespoon imitation butter-flavored sprinkles	I	cup fat-free shredded Cheddar cheese
3/4	cup fat-free, low-carb milk		

- Preheat the oven to 400 degrees.
- Spray two cookie sheets with nonfat cooking spray.
- In a large mixing bowl, combine the baking mix, butter sprinkles, and milk and stir with a fork until well blended.
- Add the chopped ham and Cheddar cheese and stir until combined.
- Drop by the rounded tablespoon onto the prepared pan.
- Bake for 8 to 9 minutes.

Yield: 16 (1-biscuit) servings

Calories: 75 (7% fat); Total Fat: 1g; Cholesterol: 5mg; Carbohydrate: 11g; Dietary Fiber: 0g; Protein: 6g; Sodium: 300mg; Diabetic Exchanges: 1/2 very lean meat, 1 starch

🕐 **Preparation time:** 10 minutes
Cooking time: 8 to 9 minutes
Total time: 19 minutes or less

Eggnog Cappuccino

This is a wonderful union of two favorite beverages (coffee and eggnog) for a marvelous, warm, holiday beverage that's sweet, smooth, and creamy. It's very versatile for the holidays. It makes a terrific dessert beverage, is good to warm up with after Christmas caroling with appetizers or cookies, and is a good source of fat-free protein as a breakfast beverage as well.

1¹/₂ cups pasteurized liquid egg substitute*	6¹/₂ cups fat-free, low-carb milk
1 cup Splenda Granular	1 teaspoon rum extract
1 teaspoon vanilla extract	16 cups fresh-brewed coffee

- In a large saucepan or Dutch oven whisk together quickly the egg substitute, Splenda, vanilla, milk, and rum extract until the Splenda is dissolved.
- Place the saucepan on the stove and turn the heat to medium.
- Slowly pour the hot coffee into the eggnog mixture while constantly stirring with the whisk.
- Once the beverage looks like it is about to begin a low boil, turn the heat down to medium low.
- Put 3 cups of the Eggnog Cappuccino into the blender. Put the lid on the blender, but leave a small opening between the lid and the blender so the heat can escape.
- Process for about 30 seconds to 1 minute on high speed until frothy on top. Pour the cappuccino back into the saucepan. If you want more froth, you can repeat this step with more cappuccino.
- Serve immediately while hot in cups or mugs. If you wish, you can put it in a slow cooker on low to keep warm until ready to serve. You can have the guests serve themselves by placing a pretty ladle on a holiday plate next to the slow cooker.

*Note: Do not use raw eggs since they are not pasteurized and could cause food-borne illness.

Yield: 24 (1-cup) servings

Calories: 33 (0% fat); Total Fat: 0g; Cholesterol: 1mg; Carbohydrate: 2g; Dietary Fiber: 0g; Protein: 5g; Sodium: 91mg; Diabetic Exchanges: 1 very lean meat

Preparation time: 10 minutes or less

⚐ Christmas Tree French Toast

My children got a real kick out of the fun Christmas tree color and shape. The flavor was a huge hit too. Have the children cut the Christmas tree shapes to save time.

2	loaves light white bread	I	cup fat-free, low-carb French vanilla liquid creamer
8	egg whites		
4	whole eggs	¹/₄	cup Splenda Granular
		14	drops green food coloring

- Using a Christmas tree-shaped cookie cutter, cut each slice of bread into a tree shape. Discard the crusts of bread and do not use end pieces of the loaf.*
- In a medium-size mixing bowl stir with a whisk the egg whites, whole eggs, French vanilla creamer, Splenda, and green food coloring.
- Preheat a skillet or griddle to medium heat.
- Spray the preheated skillet or griddle with nonfat cooking spray immediately before placing the dipped bread on the prepared cooking surface. Do not spray it too far in advance or the spray may get too hot and darken the French toast.
- Dip each piece of bread into the egg mixture and place in the prepared skillet or griddle. Turn when the bottom of the French toast is lightly browned.
- Remove from the skillet when each tree is lightly browned on both sides.

Note: Crust and end pieces of bread are good to use for bread pudding. Look on page 168 in this book for a delicious bread pudding recipe.

Yield: 21 (2-piece) servings

Calories: 105 (11% fat); Total Fat: 1g; Cholesterol: 41mg; Carbohydrate: 19g; Dietary Fiber: 7g; Protein: 7g; Sodium: 274mg; Diabetic Exchanges: ¹/₂ very lean meat, 1¹/₂ starch

Preparation time: 10 minutes or less
Cooking time: 15 minutes or less
Total time: 25 minutes or less

Breakfast Scramble

This flavor combination is excellent.

1	(16-ounce) bag frozen bell pepper stir-fry mixture	3	(16-ounce) containers liquid egg substitute
1/2	cup fat-free Italian salad dressing	1	(8-ounce) package fat-free mild Cheddar cheese, shredded
2	cups Canadian bacon, sliced		

- In a large nonstick skillet with the lid on, cook over medium to medium-high heat the pepper mixture and salad dressing until the vegetables are tender. Cook for 5 to 7 minutes, stirring occassionally.
- While the peppers are cooking, cut the Canadian bacon slices into sixths.
- Remove the lid and drain the excess liquid. Stir in the bacon and egg substitute and continue cooking, stirring frequently, until the eggs are no longer wet looking.
- Sprinkle with the cheese and stir. Turn off the heat and let sit with the lid on for 2 to 3 minutes or until the cheese is melted.

Yield: 16 (½-cup) servings

Calories: 92 (6% fat); Total Fat: 1g; Cholesterol: 11mg; Carbohydrate: 4g; Dietary Fiber: 0g; Protein: 16g; Sodium: 616mg; Diabetic Exchanges: 2 very lean meat

Preparation time: 5 minutes
Cooking time: 15 minutes
Total time: 20 minutes

Broccoli & Tomato Trifle

Displaying this pretty red, green, and white layered vegetable dish, along with the added height of the glass trifle bowl, adds a touch of Christmas celebration to any table.

2	(16-ounce) bags frozen broccoli cuts	2	teaspoons Splenda Granular
I	pint cherry or grape tomatoes	2	tablespoons imitation butter-flavored sprinkles
1/4	cup light whipped salad dressing	1/2	teaspoon dried chives
1/4	cup fat-free whipped salad dressing		

- In a microwave-safe bowl covered with wax paper (to help retain moisture), cook the broccoli in the microwave for 10 to 11 minutes, stirring occasionally.
- Put the tomatoes in a medium-size skillet sprayed with nonfat cooking spray. Spray the tomatoes with nonfat cooking spray also. Heat the tomatoes over medium heat for about 2 to 3 minutes, just enough to warm them. Some areas of the tomatoes may get browned a little. That is okay. Once the tomatoes are fully heated, turn off the heat and cover to keep them warm.
- While the broccoli and tomatoes are cooking, stir together the light salad dressing, the fat-free salad dressing, and the Splenda in a medium bowl until well mixed.
- Stir the broccoli with the butter-flavored sprinkles. Put the broccoli in the bottom of the trifle bowl.
- Place the cooked tomatoes on top of the broccoli.
- Spread the salad dressing mixture over the tomatoes.
- Sprinkle the top with the chives.
- Serve immediately.

Yield: 16 (½-cup) servings

Calories: 36 (23% fat); Total Fat: 1g; Cholesterol: 1mg; Carbohydrate: 6g; Dietary Fiber: 2g; Protein: 2g; Sodium: 125mg; Diabetic Exchanges: 1 vegetable

Preparation time: 5 minutes
Cooking time: 12 minutes
Total time: 17 minutes

Chapter Three

Christmas Day Dinners

As a little girl I vividly remember thinking my grandma's basement was huge, and the Ping-Pong table we all ate around was enormous. I felt like royalty at a grand banquet hall and my grandma was the queen. (Grandpa died when I was very young.) I loved feeling like a "big girl" when my grandma and Dad let me stand on a chair in between them to do dishes after dinner.

Now I am the hostess and our Ping-Pong table doesn't feel so big. Now I'm in my mid-forties. My young nieces and nephews think I am so old. I feel so young, until the day after Christmas after I have played a game of Twister with them (all for the sake of making fun memories) and my legs are so sore I can barely walk.

When I was a teen, my grandma remarried a wonderful man, and I loved seeing my grandparents kiss after Grandpa prayed before every meal. Their kisses symbolized their unity in this teenager's eyes. Although it seemed they never had a cross word, they did have hard times. Without their realizing it, their influence has inspired and encouraged me in my times of trouble.

When I was about ten years old we had Christmas dinner at my great aunt's; to me it was like eating in a fancy restaurant. I always felt so special when I ate with her fine china, good silverware, and cloth napkins. Now I am the aunt and hostess. My nephew, Daren, once asked his mother, "Why does Aunt Dawn have to make things so special?" Because I am making memories, and I want these memories to be special, positive influences just like my grandparents and my aunt made for me without even realizing it.

Whether we realize it or not our actions influence the lives around us. What kind of Christmas memories are you making? I hope they are special.

Traditional Christmas Dinner

Serves 12

I don't normally recommend having two potato side dishes at one meal; however, this is Christmas and this traditional meal is sure to please both white-potato and sweet-potato lovers. After all, Christmas only comes once a year.

Herbed Turkey (page 96)
Homemade Gravy (page 103)
Savory Stuffing (page 101)
Candied Yam Mini Casserole (page 102)
Whipped Mashed Potatoes (page 100)
Green Beans & Ham (page 95)
Spiced Cranberry Sauce (page 97)
Biscuits or Rolls
Gingerbread (page 98)
Eggnog (page 99)

Edible Centerpiece

Place six or seven red and green apples (all apples should be about the same size) on a dinner plate. Place a salad plate of the same pattern on top of the apples and place about five apples on that plate. Place a saucer of the same pattern on top of the five apples, place three apples on that plate, and place one apple on top of that to form an apple Christmas tree. Place silk green leaves and baby's breath in between the pieces of fruit.

Supplies

Large and small slow cooker
Food processor (not a mini one)
10 x 15-inch jelly-roll pan
Electric mixer

9-inch round or square pan
Baby's breath
Silk green leaves

Helpful Ideas: It seems like when you are serving a large crowd, there are often leftovers. To keep leftover food from going to your waist and also not going to waste, either divvy up the leftovers in plastic zip-top bags to send home with guests, or freeze them in individual containers you can pop into the microwave for a quickie meal.

Timeline

1. Set the table and make the centerpiece.
2. About 5 hours before serving time, start the Green Beans & Ham.
3. About 4 hours 30 minutes before serving time, start the Herbed Turkey.
4. About 2 hours before serving time, prepare the Spiced Cranberry Sauce, let it cool, and then refrigerate.
5. Make and bake the Gingerbread.
6. While the Gingerbread is baking, make the Eggnog and place it in a one-gallon pitcher. Cover and refrigerate the Eggnog until serving time.
7. Start the Whipped Mashed Potatoes.
8. While the potatoes are cooking, start the Savory Stuffing.
9. About 45 minutes before mealtime, finish the Whipped Mashed Potatoes and keep them warm until serving time.
10. Finish the stuffing, remove the pan from the heat, cover, and keep the stuffing warm in the saucepan.
11. Make the Candied Yam Mini Casserole.

Last 15 minutes

12. Put your favorite store-bought rolls in the oven. Set the timer so you won't forget and accidentally burn your biscuits.
13. Remove the turkey from the slow-cooker and place it on a platter. Place the turkey on the table to rest.
14. Make the Homemade Gravy and place it in a bowl with a small ladle or a gravy boat.
15. Put all the side dishes into serving bowls and take them to the table. If needed, place the Candied Yam Mini Casserole in the microwave for 2 minutes.
16. Take all of the food to the table, including the rolls from the oven.
17. Take the turkey back into the kitchen to carve it easily on a cutting board (see page 7). Cut the meat off both sides in two large pieces and cut them into twelve pieces.
18. Have someone pour the Eggnog into glasses and serve them.
19. After everyone has finished eating, remove the dinner dishes and serve the Gingerbread.

Grocery List

Frozen Foods
2 (1-pound) bags frozen green beans
1 (7½-pound) whole turkey breast
  (on the bone)
2 (30-ounce) bags frozen fat-free
  shredded hash browns
1 (10-ounce) bag frozen chopped
  onion (only 1 cup needed)
1 (12-ounce) bag sausage-flavored
  veggie crumbles or 1 pound
  low-fat turkey Italian sausage
1 (8-ounce) container fat-free dessert
  whipped topping

Fresh Fruits and Vegetables
2 (12-ounce) bags fresh or frozen
  cranberries
1 heart of celery (only ¾ cup needed)
16 apples

Staple Items
1 (8-ounce) can water chestnuts
1 (23-ounce) jar no-sugar-added
  applesauce (only ½ cup needed)
4 (14.5-ounce) cans fat-free chicken
  broth
1 loaf seedless sliced rye bread
2 (40-ounce) cans cut yams

Meats
½ pound extra-lean ham

Dairy
5 eggs
1 pound light margarine (only ½ cup
  needed)
5 (4-ounce) containers pasteurized
  liquid egg substitute (only 2¼
  cups needed)
2 (2-quart) containers fat-free, low-
  carb milk (only 10 cups needed)

Baking Items
1 pound sugar (only 2 cups needed)
1 (5-pound) bag whole wheat flour
  (only 3 cups needed)
2 (1.9-ounce) boxes Splenda Granular
  (only 3½ cups needed)
2 teaspoons baking soda
1 (12-ounce) jar molasses (only ¾ cup
  needed)
1 (12-ounce) can fat-free evaporated
  milk
1 (7-ounce) jar marshmallow crème
  (only 1 cup needed)
1 (8-ounce) can nonfat cooking spray

Seasonings/Condiments
1 (8-ounce) bottle fat-free zesty
  Italian salad dressing
½ teaspoon dried thyme
1 teaspoon dried sage
1 teaspoon Cajun seasoning (not
  Cajun powder)
1 teaspoon paprika
1 teaspoon black pepper
1⅛ teaspoons ground cinnamon
2 teaspoons ground allspice
Ground nutmeg, optional
4 teaspoons ground ginger
1½ teaspoons vanilla extract
1½ teaspoons rum extract
2 (2.5-ounce) bottles imitation
  butter-flavored sprinkles, such as
  Butter Buds (1 cup needed)

🍲 🍲 Green Beans & Ham

This smells and tastes wonderful. The Italian dressing really dresses up the green beans.

2 (1-pound) bags frozen green beans	¹/₂ cup fat-free zesty Italian salad dressing
1 (8-ounce) can water chestnuts, finely chopped and drained	¹/₂ pound extra-lean ham, finely chopped

- Spray a slow cooker with nonfat cooking spray.
- Put the green beans, water chestnuts, Italian dressing, and ham into the slow-cooker.
- Gently stir, cover, and cook on low for 5 hours.
- Do not put into a serving bowl until ready to serve.

Yield: 16 (¹/₂-cup) servings

Calories: 44 (15% fat); Total Fat: 1g; Cholesterol: 7mg; Carbohydrate: 5g; Dietary Fiber: 2g; Protein: 4g; Sodium: 353mg; Diabetic Exchanges: ¹/₂ very lean meat, 1 vegetable

Preparation time: 5 minutes
Cooking time: 5 hours
Total time: 5 hours 5 minutes

Vacations for Christmas Gifts

Teenagers tend to dislike long family vacations because they hate to leave their friends for longer than a week. I have found a way to compromise by taking mini vacations and as a Christmas gift I give each of my girls money to be used during the vacation—enough to cover all their meals and entertainment. If they have money left over, they get to keep it. This is a great way to teach them financial responsibility, and at the same time I get my family-bonding-time fix that I want. It's a real win/win thing! Now that's what I call a great two-for-one Christmas gift.

🍲 🍽 Herbed Turkey

This is probably one of the most moist turkeys you will ever eat. The spices are wonderful. I will be making my turkey like this from now on.

7¹/₂ -pound whole turkey breast (on the bone)	1 teaspoon paprika
	1 teaspoon black pepper
¹/₂ teaspoon rubbed thyme	¹/₂ cup fat-free zesty Italian salad dressing
1 teaspoon Cajun seasoning	

- Spray a large slow cooker with nonfat cooking spray.
- Place the turkey on a cutting board and remove the skin by pulling it off with your hands. Discard the skin.
- In a small mixing bowl stir together the thyme, Cajun seasoning, paprika, and black pepper.
- With your hands, press the spices onto the outside of the turkey until they lightly cover the whole turkey breast.
- Place the turkey in the slow cooker.
- Lightly drizzle the Italian dressing over the top and into the bottom of the slow cooker. If you pour slowly, the spices will stay on the outside of the turkey breast.
- Cover and cook on high for 3½ to 4 hours or until the meat is completely white and reaches 165 degrees on a meat thermometer.
- When the turkey is completely cooked, place it on a platter.
- To make gravy with the remaining juices see the Homemade Gravy recipe in this menu on page 103.

Note: The nutritional information will remain the same per each serving of 4 ounces of meat; however, the total number of servings will vary depending on the size of the turkey breast.

Yield: 16 (4-ounce) servings

Calories: 166 (8% fat); Total Fat: 1g; Cholesterol: 100mg; Carbohydrate: 1g; Dietary Fiber: 0g; Protein: 35g; Sodium: 152mg; Diabetic Exchanges: 4 very lean meat

🕐 **Preparation time:** 15 minutes
Cooking time: 3½ to 4 hours
Total time: 4 hours 15 minutes or less

Spiced Cranberry Sauce

The cranberry plant is an evergreen that is native to North America. The color of this cranberry sauce is gorgeous. This would be great served warm over ice cream.

2	cups sugar	2	(12-ounce) bags fresh or frozen cranberries
2	teaspoons ground allspice		
2	cups water		

- Put the sugar, allspice, water, and cranberries in a nonstick medium-size saucepan over medium heat until the mixture comes to a low boil.
- Reduce the heat, cover, and cook at a low boil for 10 minutes, stirring occasionally.
- Cool completely before refrigerating.
- Serve chilled.

Yield: 20 ($\frac{1}{4}$-cup) servings

Calories: 94 (0% fat); Total Fat: 0g; Cholesterol: 0mg; Carbohydrate: 24g; Dietary Fiber: 2g; Protein: 0g; Sodium: 1mg; Diabetic Exchanges: 1$\frac{1}{2}$ other carbohydrate

Preparation time: 3 minutes
Cooking time: 10 minutes
Total time: 13 minutes or less

♨ Gingerbread

America has more variations of gingerbread than any other country. This is a wonderful gingerbread by itself, or you can serve it with whipped cream.

4	cups Homemade Whole Wheat, Sweet Baking Mix (page 220)	3/4	cup molasses
4	teaspoons ground ginger	1/2	cup (1 stick) light margarine, melted
5	egg whites	1	cup boiling water
		1/2	cup no-sugar-added applesauce

- Preheat the oven to 350 degrees.
- Spray a 10 x 15-inch jelly-roll pan with nonfat cooking spray.
- In a large mixing bowl stir together the whole wheat baking mix, ginger, egg whites, molasses, margarine, boiling water, and applesauce.
- Pour the mixture into the prepared pan.
- Bake for 12 minutes.
- Let the gingerbread cool for a few minutes and cut into 20 pieces.

Yield: 20 (1-piece) servings

Calories: 127 (17% fat); Total Fat: 3g; Cholesterol: 0mg; Carbohydrate: 24g; Dietary Fiber: 2g; Protein: 3g; Sodium: 161mg; Diabetic Exchanges: 1 starch, 1/2 other carbohydrate, 1/2 fat

⏱ **Preparation time:** 15 minutes
Cooking time: 12 minutes
Total time: 27 minutes

Eggnog

This is not as thick as regular eggnog, but is every bit as delicious and has the smooth consistency of the high-fat version. With this new low-fat recipe, I can't see why anyone would even want to waste calories on the old high-fat, high-sugar eggnog.

2¼ cups pasteurized liquid egg substitute*	10 cups fat-free, low-carb milk
1 cup Splenda Granular	1½ teaspoons rum extract
1½ teaspoons vanilla extract	Ground nutmeg

- In a large bowl combine the egg substitute, Splenda, vanilla, milk, and rum extract, and beat with an electric mixer on medium speed until well blended.
- The eggnog is ready to drink; or pour it into a pitcher, cover, and keep chilled until ready to serve.
- Sprinkle each serving with a dash of nutmeg just before serving.

*Note: Do not use raw eggs since they are not pasteurized and could cause food-borne illness.

Yield: 16 (¾-cup) servings

Calories: 69 (0% fat); Total Fat: 0g; Cholesterol: 3mg; Carbohydrate: 4g; Dietary Fiber: 0g; Protein: 11g; Sodium: 202mg; Diabetic Exchanges: 1 very lean meat, ½ skim milk

Preparation time: 5 minutes or less

Whipped Mashed Potatoes

These are too light and creamy to be called mashed. There are small pieces of potato in each bite. No one will ever know you didn't have to peel potatoes. It seems like too many servings of potatoes, but they are so good you will want to have extra for second helpings.

2	(30-ounce) bags frozen fat-free shredded hash browns	$^1/_4$	cup imitation butter-flavored sprinkles
2	(14.5-ounce) cans fat-free chicken broth	1	cup fat-free evaporated milk

- In a large saucepan or Dutch oven place the hash browns and the chicken broth.
- Cover and heat on high until it comes to a full boil.
- Remove the pan from the heat and let sit, covered for 5 minutes.
- Drain the potatoes and discard the chicken broth.
- Place the potatoes back into the pan and stir in the butter-flavored sprinkles and the milk until well mixed.
- In a food processor, whip half of the potato mixture at a time for 3 to 4 minutes and place into a large serving bowl. These may seem too runny, but they will thicken as they sit for a minute.
- Cover bowl with plastic wrap and wrap bowl in a large bath towel to keep warm until dinner is served.

Yield: 22 ($^1/_2$-cup) servings

Calories: 74 (0% fat); Total Fat: 0g; Cholesterol: 0mg; Carbohydrate: 16g; Dietary Fiber: 1g; Protein: 3g; Sodium: 155mg; Diabetic Exchanges: 1 starch

Preparation time: 10 minutes
Cooking time: 20 minutes
Total time: 30 minutes

🍲 Savory Stuffing

My assistants, friends, and family went nuts over this stuffing recipe. With great enthu-siasm one friend said, "Next year you'll have to taste my homemade dressing, Dawn. It's going to taste very familiar."

"Really?" I asked, puzzled that my original recipe tasted like hers. "How can that be?"

"Yeah, it's going to be this recipe," she said with a grin from ear to ear as she licked her spoon.

$3/4$	cup chopped celery	I	(I2-ounce) bag vegetarian sausage-flavored crumbles * or I pound low-fat Italian turkey sausage cooked, drained, and crumbled
I	cup frozen chopped onion		
I	(14.5 ounce) can chicken broth		
$3/4$	teaspoon rubbed sage or $1/2$ tea-spoon ground sage	14	slices seedless rye bread, toasted and cubed into $1/2$-inch pieces
$1/4$	cup imitation butter-flavored sprinkles		

- In a large saucepan bring the celery, onion, chicken broth, sage, butter-flavored sprinkles, and sausage-flavored crumbles to a boil.
- Once to a full boil, stir in the toasted bread cubes.
- Turn off the heat. Cover and let the stuffing sit for 5 to 10 minutes.
- Keep the stuffing warm until ready to serve. Fluff with a fork before serving.

Note: Veggie crumbles are vegetarian meat substitutes made by Morning Star Farms. They are found in the frozen food section.

Yield: 14 ($1/2$-cup) servings

(with vegetarian sausage crumbles)
Calories: 132 (16% fat); Total Fat: 2g; Cholesterol: 0mg; Carbohydrate: 20g; Dietary Fiber: 3g; Protein: 8g; Sodium: 530mg; Diabetic Exchanges: $1/2$ very lean meat, $1 1/2$ starch
(with turkey sausage)
Calories: 134 (15% fat); Total Fat: 2g; Cholesterol: 16gmg; Carbohydrate: 18g; Dietary Fiber: 2g; Protein: 8g; Sodium: 554mg; Diabetic Exchanges: $1/2$ very lean meat, 1 starch

Preparation time: 15 minutes
Cooking time: 10 minutes
Total time: 25 minutes

Candied Yam Mini Casserole

Unlike sickeningly sweet candied yams layered with oodles of fat and calories, this light version is every bit as tasty and satisfying even though it is made in a fraction of the time.

2 (40-ounce) cans cut yams, drain and discard juice	1 plus $^1/_8$ teaspoon ground cinnamon
$^1/_3$ cup imitation butter-flavored sprinkles	$^1/_2$ cup Splenda Granular
	1 cup marshmallow crème

- Place an oven rack on the highest level closest to the heating element.
- Preheat the oven to 500 degrees. If your oven has a "broil" knob, turn the knob to broil.
- Spray a 9-inch-round or 9-inch-square ovenproof pan with nonfat cooking spray.
- In a medium-size nonstick saucepan over medium-low heat stir the yams, butter-flavored sprinkles, 1 teaspoon cinnamon, and Splenda until well mixed. Some of the yams will become mashed and most will remain in chunks.
- Cover and heat for 5 to 8 minutes or until fully heated.
- Spread the yams into the prepared pan.
- Spread the marshmallow crème over the top of the yams.
- Place the yams on the top rack and broil for 45 seconds to 1 minute or until the marshmallow crème is partially toasted.
- Sprinkle the remaining $^1/_8$ teaspoon cinnamon on top of the marshmallow crème.
- Serve immediately.

Yield: 12 ($^1/_2$-cup) servings

Calories: 198 (0% fat); Total Fat: 0g; Cholesterol: 0mg; Carbohydrate: 48g; Dietary Fiber: 4g; Protein: 2g; Sodium: 239mg; Diabetic Exchanges: 1 starch, 2 other carbohydrate

Preparation time: 2 minutes
Cooking time: 10 minutes or less
Total time: 12 minutes or less

Homemade Gravy

3 cups juice remaining from Herbed Turkey (Use canned if neccessary.)	3 tablespoons cornstarch $^1/_4$ cup cold water

- Pour the juice from the slow cooker into a saucepan and heat on high. (If you don't have 3 cups broth, add canned chicken broth to the juice from the slow cooker to make 3 cups.)
- While the juice is cooking, place the cornstarch in a small bowl. Add the water and stir with a whisk.
- Pour the cornstarch mixture into the hot broth, stirring constantly.
- Cook until thick, about 1 to 2 minutes.
- Remove from the heat and let the broth sit for a couple of minutes to thicken.

Note: This is not your ordinary gravy; it has the spices and the zesty Italian dressing, which give it a unique flavor.

Yield: 12 ($^1/_4$-cup) servings

Calories: 14 (0% fat); Total Fat: 0g; Cholesterol: 0mg; Carbohydrate: 3g; Dietary Fiber: 0; Protein: 1g; Sodium: 78mg; Diabetic Exchanges: Free

Preparation time: 5 minutes
Cooking and cooling time: 5 minutes
Total preparation time: 10 minutes

Roasted Turkey Breast Dinner

Serves 8

Crimson & Emerald Spinach Salad (page 110)
Roasted Turkey Breast with Potatoes
& Onion Gravy (page 106)
Christmas Cauliflower (page 111)
Basil & Garlic Biscuits (page 112)
Pumpkin Mousse (page 109)
Snowman Cookies (page 108)

Edible Centerpiece

Place one to three large candles approximately 6 inches in diameter in the center of your table. Place them in three candle holders of different heights. Set the Snowman Cookies around the candles for a super snowman theme. Use snowman flatware, napkins, cups, etc., to complete the snowman theme. (See photo on page 109.)

Supplies

Large candles	9 x13-inch casserole dish
Candle holders of different heights	Baking sheets
Large oblong slow cooker	Electric mixer

Timeline

1. Set the table.
2. Place the candles in the candleholders in the middle of the table.
3. About 5½ hours before serving time, start the roasted turkey breast.
4. Bake the Snowman Cookies. Keep in an airtight container until dinner is ready to be served. Then place the Snowman Cookies around the candles in the middle of the table.
5. Prepare the Pumpkin Mousse, cover, and refrigerate until ready to serve.
6. Make the spinach salad, but do not put on the salad dressing. Cover and refrigerate the salad and dressing until serving time.
7. Make the Christmas Cauliflower 30 minutes before serving time.
8. While the cauliflower is cooking, bake the Basil and Garlic Biscuits.
9. Finish the centerpiece. You can set extra cookies on a plate for your guests.

Last 15 minutes

10. Take the Roasted Turkey Breast and Potatoes out of the slow cooker and place them on a serving platter.
11. Make the Onion Gravy.
12. Finish the cauliflower.
13. Take the salad and dressing, biscuits, cauliflower, turkey and potatoes, onion gravy, and pumpkin mousse to the table.
14. Light the candles.
15. If desired, for easier carving take the turkey breast into the kitchen to carve on a cutting board.

Grocery List

Frozen Foods
1 (8-ounce) container fat-free dessert whipped topping
1 (2-quart) container fat-free frozen vanilla yogurt (only 2½ cups needed)

Fresh Fruits and Vegetables
2 pounds potatoes
1 large onion
1 pound carrots
2 (11-ounce) bags pre-washed baby spinach
1 large head cauliflower
1 (1-ounce) package fresh basil (⅓ cup needed)
1 (4.5-ounce) jar minced garlic (only 2 teaspoons needed)
Small bunch fresh parsley sprigs, optional

Staple Items
2 (1-ounce) envelopes onion soup mix
1 (37-ounce or smaller) box pancake mix (only 1¼ cups needed)
1 (15.5-ounce) can sliced beets

1 (14.5-ounce) can fat-free chicken broth

Meats
7½ pounds turkey breast (on the bone)

Dairy
2 eggs
1 (4-ounce) package fat-free feta cheese crumbles (only ¼ cup needed)
1 (8-ounce) container fat-free French onion dip

Baking Items
1 (16-ounce) box cornstarch (only 4 tablespoons needed)
1 (18.25-ounce) box of white cake mix
1 (12-ounce) bag mini chocolate chips (only 1 tablespoon needed)
1 (30-ounce) can pumpkin pie mix (only 2 cups needed)
1 (1.7 ounce) box fat-free, sugar-free instant vanilla pudding mix
1 (2-pound) bag all-purpose flour (only 3 cups needed)

1 (1.9-ounce) box Splenda Granular
(only ½ cup plus 1 tablespoon
needed)
1 (12-ounce) box baking soda (only
2 teaspoons needed)
1 (8-ounce) can nonfat cooking spray

Seasonings/Condiments
½ teaspoon cream of tartar
1 (8-ounce) bottle fat-free red wine
vinaigrette salad dressing (only
½ cup needed)
1 (12-ounce) bottle cocktail sauce
(only ⅓ cup needed)
⅓ cup fat-free whipped salad
dressing

1 (3-ounce) container garlic salt (only
1 tablespoon plus 1 teaspoon
needed)
1 teaspoon dried sweet basil

Other
1 (3-ounce) jar reduced-fat real bacon
pieces (only 5 tablespoons
needed)

☐ Roasted Turkey Breast with Potatoes & Onion Gravy

Here's a super easy way to cook (your favorite part of) the turkey without heating up the entire house with a hot oven. Warm climate environments will especially appreciate this benefit.

1	(7.5-pound) turkey breast (on the bone)	2	envelopes onion soup mix (1 ounce each)
2	pounds potatoes, quartered (about 9 cups)	¼	plus ¼ cup cold water
1	large onion, peeled and quartered		Fresh parsley sprigs (optional)
1	pound carrots, peeled and cut into 2-inch lengths	4	tablespoons cornstarch

- Spray a large, oblong slow cooker with nonfat cooking spray.
- Rinse the turkey breast under cold running water and place it in the prepared slow cooker.
- Place the potatoes, onions, and carrots on and around the turkey breast.
- In a small bowl stir together 1 onion soup mix and ¼ cup water.
- Pour the soup mix over the turkey and vegetables.

- Cover the slow cooker and cook on high for 4½ to 5 hours or until it is no longer pink in the middle. If the lid won't fit tight on the slow cooker, put the lid on and then cover the lid with aluminum foil, wrapping the foil around the top edge of the slow cooker so that no steam can escape while the turkey is cooking.
- When the turkey is done, place it on a large platter, and with a slotted spoon remove the vegetables from the slow cooker and place them around the turkey breast. Place fresh sprigs of parsley around the turkey. For a prettier presentation you can sprinkle paprika on the turkey to give it a browned look. You will be removing the skin before you slice the turkey.
- Pour the juice from the slow cooker (we had 3½ cups juice) into a medium-size saucepan and add the remaining envelope onion soup mix. Turn the heat on medium high. (If you do not have 3½ cups of juice from the slow cooker, add canned chicken broth to the juice to make 3½ cups.)
- In a small bowl stir together the cornstarch and the remaining ¼ cup cold water.
- Pour the cornstarch mixture into the saucepan, stirring constantly until it is thick. Serve the gravy on the side.
- Remove the skin and discard. (Turkey skin is loaded with unhealthy cholesterol.)

Note: For a crispy, golden brown skin, put the poultry in a 9 x 13-inch casserole dish and bake it in the oven at 500 degrees for 5 to 10 minutes. Let it rest for at least 15 to 20 minutes to help it retain more of its juices before cutting.

Yield: 16 (4-ounce) servings of turkey without skin

(4 ounces of turkey)
Calories: 162 (8% fat); Total Fat: 1g; Cholesterol: 100mg; Carbohydrate: 0g; Dietary Fiber: 0g; Protein: 35g; Sodium: 65mg; Diabetic Exchanges: 4 very lean meat
(½ cup potatoes)
Calories: 49 (0% fat); Total Fat: 0g; Cholesterol: 0mg; Carbohydrate: 12g; Dietary Fiber: 2g; Protein: 2g; Sodium: 18mg; Diabetic Exchanges: ½ starch, 1 vegetable
(¼ cup onion gravy)
Calories: 18 (0% fat); Total Fat: 0g; Cholesterol: 0mg; Carbohydrate: 4g; Dietary Fiber: 0g; Protein: 0g; Sodium: 230mg; Diabetic Exchanges: Free

Preparation time: 20 minutes
Cooking time: 4½ to 5 hours
Total time: 5 hours 20 minutes or less

⌂ ⛄ Snowman Cookies

These freeze and store well. See the photo on the next page.

1	(8-ounce) container fat-free dessert whipped topping	1¹/4	cups dry pancake mix
2	egg whites	¹/2	teaspoon cream of tartar
1	(18.25-ounce) box dry white cake mix	1	tablespoon mini chocolate chips

- Preheat the oven to 350 degrees.
- Spray two cookie sheets with nonfat cooking spray.
- Mix the dessert whipped topping and the egg whites in a large mixing bowl until completely blended.
- Add the cake mix and stir until combined.
- Stir in the pancake mix and cream of tartar. The dough will be stiff but still sticky to the touch.
- Spray your hands with nonfat cooking spray. Roll 1 teaspoon of the dough in your hands to form a ball. Place the ball on the prepared cookie sheet. This will be the head of the snowman.
- Then roll 1 tablespoon of the dough in your hands to form a ball. This will be the body of the snowman. Place the ball on the prepared cookie sheet so that the head and body are touching. Continue until all of the dough is used.
- This dough will spread; leave enough room in between each snowman so that they do not touch when they are baking. I suggest no more than eight snowman cookies per baking sheet.
- Place 2 mini chocolate chips on the head to make eyes. Then place 2 chocolate chips on the body to form buttons.
- Bake for 7 to 9 minutes.

Yield: 30 cookies

Calories: 109 (17% fat); Total Fat: 2g; Cholesterol: 0mg; Carbohydrate: 20g; Dietary Fiber: 0g; Protein: 1g; Sodium: 189mg; Diabetic Exchanges: 1¹/2 other carbohydrate, ¹/2 fat

🕐 **Preparation time:** 10 minutes
Cooking time: 7 to 9 minutes per two baking sheets
(You'll need to bake twice for all 30 cookies.)
Total time: 30 minutes or less

♔♕ Pumpkin Mousse

The most difficult part of this recipe is not eating too much, because it tastes so good. It's smooth, creamy, and delicious to the last bite.

2¹/2 cups fat-free frozen vanilla yogurt, softened

1 (1.7 ounce) box dry fat-free, sugar-free instant vanilla pudding mix

2 cups pumpkin pie mix

- In a large bowl with an electric mixer on medium speed mix the yogurt, pudding mix, and pumpkin pie mix until well blended.
- Put into a pretty serving bowl or individual dessert cups.
- The mousse is ready to eat or keep refrigerated until ready to serve.

Yield: 8 (¹/2-cup) servings

Calories: 149 (0% fat); Total Fat: 0g; Cholesterol: 0mg; Carbohydrate: 34g; Dietary Fiber: 2g; Protein: 3g; Sodium: 376mg; Diabetic Exchanges: 2¹/2 other carbohydrate

⏱ **Total preparation time:** 10 minutes or less

Snowman Cookies

☕ Crimson & Emerald Spinach Salad

The rich holiday colors in this gorgeous salad match up with its delicious flavor that adults especially enjoy and appreciate.

1 (15.5-ounce) can sliced beets, chilled*	2 (11-ounce) bags prewashed baby spinach (or 14 cups)
1 tablespoon Splenda Granular	1/4 cup fat-free feta cheese crumbles
1/2 cup fat-free red wine vinaigrette salad dressing	2 tablespoons reduced-fat real bacon pieces

- Drain the juice from the beets. Keep 1/2 cup juice and discard the rest.
- In a medium bowl stir together the 1/2 cup juice from the beets, Splenda, and salad dressing until well blended. Cover and keep refrigerated until ready to use.
- Place the spinach in a large serving bowl. Arrange the beets in a pretty design on top of the spinach.
- Sprinkle the top of the salad with the feta cheese and bacon.
- Cover and keep refrigerated until ready to eat.
- Just before serving pour the prepared dressing over the salad, or serve the dressing on the side and let guests put on the salad dressing.

Note: To save time, have the beets already chilling and ready to use by storing them in the refrigerator as soon as you arrive home from the store.

Yield: 8 (1¾-cup) servings

Calories: 65 (9% fat); Total Fat: 1g; Cholesterol: 3mg; Carbohydrate: 12g; Dietary Fiber: 2g; Protein: 4g; Sodium: 343mg; Diabetic Exchanges: 2½ vegetable

🕐 **Total preparation time:** 10 minutes or less

Christmas Cauliflower

The colors and flavors of this vegetable dish complement holiday fare.

I tablespoon garlic salt	$^1/_3$ cup fat-free whipped salad dressing
I large head cauliflower	2 plus I tablespoons reduced-fat, real
$^1/_3$ cup fresh basil, chopped	crumbled bacon
$^1/_3$ cup cocktail sauce	Salt and pepper (optional)

- In a large saucepan or Dutch oven put $1^1/_2$ to 2 inches of water and the garlic salt. If you have a steamer basket, put it in the pan; if you don't have one, don't worry about it.
- Cover and turn the water on high heat.
- Separate the cauliflower into large florets. One floret could be about half the size of your fist, about 2 to 3 inches. Remove any dark spots that are on the cauliflower.
- Place the florets in the steamer basket or directly in the water, and place the chopped basil directly on the cauliflower in the pan and cover.
- When the water comes to a full boil, turn off the heat and let the pan sit, covered, for 15 minutes.
- Stir together with a whisk the cocktail sauce, salad dressing, and 2 tablespoons bacon until all lumps are gone. Microwave for 1 minute and stir again.
- With a slotted spoon or ladle remove the basil and cauliflower from the pan, and arrange in a large serving bowl so that the pretty parts of the florets are facing up. Place any basil that has fallen on top of the florets.
- With a spatula or a wooden spoon spread the cocktail sauce mixture over the top of the cauliflower.
- Sprinkle 1 tablespoon crumbled bacon on top. Add salt and pepper to taste, if desired.
- Serve immediately.

Yield: 12 ($^1/_2$-cup) servings

Calories: 36 (13% fat); Total Fat: 1g; Cholesterol: 3mg; Carbohydrate: 6g; Dietary Fiber: 2g; Protein: 2g; Sodium: 407mg; Diabetic Exchanges: 1 vegetable

Preparation time: 15 minutes
Cooking time: 15 minutes
Total time: 30 minutes

Basil & Garlic Biscuits

Even though these are very easy to make, they are pretty and dress up a table nicely.

1¹/₃	cups Homemade Baking Mix (page 219)	2	teaspoons minced garlic
³/₄	cup fat-free French onion dip	1	teaspoon dried sweet basil
			Garlic salt

- Preheat the oven to 350 degrees.
- Spray a baking sheet with nonfat cooking spray.
- In a medium mixing bowl stir together the Homemade Baking Mix, French onion dip, minced garlic, and dried basil.
- Drop by the rounded tablespoon onto the prepared baking sheet.
- Sprinkle the garlic salt on the tops of the biscuits.
- Bake for 10 minutes.

Yield: 10 (1-biscuit) servings

Calories: 70 (0% fat); Total Fat: 0g; Cholesterol: 3mg; Carbohydrate: 14g; Dietary Fiber: 0g; Protein: 3g; Sodium: 252mg; Diabetic Exchanges: 1 starch

Preparation time: 5 minutes
Baking time: 10 minutes
Total time: 15 minutes

Turkey Breast Roast with Cinnamon Sweet Potatoes

Serves 8

Cranberry Chutney (page 123)
Turkey Breast Roast with Cinnamon Sweet Potatoes (page 116)
Broccoli Casserole (page 117)
Christmas-Style Waldorf Salad (page 120)
Banana-Nut Bread (page 122)
Strawberry-Banana Christmas Parfaits (page 121)
Edible Ornament Cookies (page 118)

Edible Centerpiece

Use an artificial Christmas tree seedling (18 inches or smaller) as a centerpiece, decorate the tree with the Edible Ornament Cookies along with bows. It will not only look festive, it'll serve as a tasty dessert as well. Have the children help sprinkle on the colored sugar, cut out cookies, and thread the ribbon through the baked cookies to make ornaments out of them.

Supplies

Large slow cooker	Ribbon
Small slow cooker	Electric mixer
Artificial seedling tree	8 dessert cups
3 mini-loaf pans (disposable foil pans are okay)	9 x 13-inch glass baking dish

Timeline

1. Set the table. Place the artificial tree in the center of the table. You'll hang cookies on it later.
2. Five hours before serving time, start the Turkey Breast Roast with Cinnamon Sweet Potatoes.
3. Bake the Edible Ornament Cookies. Store in an airtight container with wax paper between the layers.
4. Two and a half to 3 hours before serving time, start the Broccoli Casserole.
5. Make the Christmas-Style Waldorf Salad, cover, and place it in the refrigerator until serving time.
6. Prepare the Strawberry-Banana Christmas Parfaits and place in the refrigerator until serving time.

7. Make and bake the Banana-Nut Bread.
8. Make the Cranberry Chutney.

Last 15 minutes
9. Hang the Edible Ornament Cookies on the artificial tree (in the center of the table).
10. When the Turkey Breast Roast with Cinnamon Sweet Potatoes is finished, remove the foil pouch.
11. Remove the Turkey Breast Roast, place it in a 9 x 13-inch glass baking dish, and cut away the netting.
12. Open the foil pouch and pour the sweet potato and pineapple mixture around the turkey breast roast. Take it to the table.
13. Put the Broccoli Casserole into a serving dish and take it to the table.
14. Take the Waldorf salad, cranberry chutney, banana bread, and parfaits to the table.

Grocery List

Frozen Foods
1 (3-pound) boneless turkey breast roast
1 (16-ounce) bag frozen broccoli pieces
1 (12-ounce) container fat-free dessert whipped topping

Fresh Fruits and Vegetables
6 medium sweet potatoes
1 small red bell pepper (only ½ cup needed)
2 Granny Smith apples
2 Red Delicious apples
1 heart of celery (only 1 stalk of celery needed)
2 very ripe bananas
1 (12-ounce) bag cranberries (only 1 cup needed)
1 large navel orange

Staple Items
1 (8-ounce) can pineapple tidbits
1 (8-ounce) can pineapple chunks
1 (23-ounce) jar cinnamon applesauce (only ½ cup needed)
1 (23-ounce) jar no-sugar-added applesauce (only ½ cup needed)
1 (4-ounce) can mushroom pieces
1 (8-ounce) can water chestnuts

Dairy
1 dozen eggs (7 egg whites needed)
1 (16-ounce) container low-fat ricotta cheese (only 1 cup needed)
1 (2-quart) container fat-free, low-carb milk (only 1¼ cups needed)

Baking Items
¼ cup dark brown sugar
1 (5-pound) bag whole wheat flour (only 3 cups needed)

1 (2-pound) bag all-purpose flour
(only 3½ cups needed)
1 (9.7-ounce) bag Splenda Granular
(4¾ cups needed)
4 teaspoons baking soda
1 (3-ounce) container red sugar
crystals
1 (6-ounce) bag dried cranberries
(only ⅓ cup plus 2 tablespoons
needed)
1 (2.25-ounce) bag walnuts
(5 tablespoons needed)
1 (21-ounce) can strawberry pie filling
2 (1.7-ounce) boxes instant sugar-free
banana cream pudding mix
1 (8-ounce) can nonfat cooking spray

Seasonings/Condiments
1 tablespoon steak seasoning blend (I
use Tone's brand with coarse salt)
1 teaspoon ground allspice
½ teaspoon ground cinnamon
1 teaspoon vanilla extract
2 teaspoons almond extract
1 (8-ounce) fat-free red wine vinaigrette
salad dressing (only ⅓ cup
needed)
1 (2.5-ounce) imitation butter-flavored
sprinkles, such as Butter Buds
(only 1 tablespoon needed)
¼ cup light whipped salad dressing

Other
1 (15.5-ounce) jar sugar-free raspberry
jam (only 2 tablespoons needed)

🍲 Turkey Breast Roast with Cinnamon Sweet Potatoes

The steak seasoning on this turkey is fabulous. Great idea!

1 (3-pound) boneless turkey breast roast	1 (8-ounce) can pineapple chunks, drained
1 tablespoon steak seasoning blend (I use Tone's)	1/4 cup dark brown sugar
6 medium-size sweet potatoes, peeled and quartered (about 4 1/2 cups)	1/2 teaspoon ground cinnamon

- Spray a slow cooker with nonfat cooking spray.
- Place the turkey breast roast in the slow cooker and rub the steak seasoning blend over the top of the turkey.
- Spray a piece of aluminum foil with nonfat cooking spray.
- Place the sweet potatoes and pineapple on the foil and sprinkle the brown sugar and cinnamon over the top of them.
- Fold the foil over and roll the ends together to form a sealed pouch.
- Place the foil pouch on top of the turkey breast roast, cover, and cook on high for 4½ hours or until no longer pink.
- When the turkey is done, remove the foil pouch from the slow cooker, place the turkey breast roast in a 9 x 13-inch glass baking dish, open the foil pouch, and place the potatoes around the turkey. Pour some of the juice in the slow cooker over the turkey and potatoes.
- Serve immediately.

Note: I use a Butterball brand but didn't use the gravy packet that came with it. Cook with the netting on, but cut and remove the netting before serving. For a crispy, golden brown skin, put the poultry in a 9 x 13-inch casserole dish and bake it in the oven at 500 degrees for 5 to 10 minutes. Let it rest for at least 15 to 20 minutes to help it retain more of its juices before cutting.

Yield: 8 servings (4 ounces turkey and ½ cup potato mixture)

Calories: 326 (4% fat); Total Fat: 2g; Cholesterol: 116mg; Carbohydrate: 35g; Dietary Fiber: 3g; Protein: 42g; Sodium: 369mg; Diabetic Exchanges: 4 very lean meat, 2 starch, 1 other carbohydrate

⏱ **Preparation time:** 15 minutes
Cooking time: 4 to 4½ hours
Total time: 4 hours 15 minutes to 4 hours 45 minutes

🥘 🍽 Broccoli Casserole

I love the flavor combination of this vegetable dish.

1 (16-ounce) bag frozen broccoli pieces	¹/₂ cup red bell pepper, chopped
1 (4-ounce) can mushroom pieces, drained and juice discarded	1 (8-ounce) can water chestnuts, drained and chopped
¹/₃ cup fat-free red wine vinaigrette salad dressing	1 tablespoon imitation butter-flavored sprinkles
	Salt

- Spray a slow cooker with nonfat cooking spray.
- Place all the ingredients in the slow cooker, stir, cover, and cook on low for 2½ to 3 hours.
- When finished add salt to taste and serve immediately in a pretty serving bowl.

Yield: 8 (½-cup) servings

Calories: 44 (0% fat); Total Fat: 0g; Cholesterol: 0mg; Carbohydrate: 10g; Dietary Fiber: 3g; Protein: 2g; Sodium: 213mg; Diabetic Exchanges: 2 vegetable

🕐 **Preparation time:** 10 minutes
Cooking time: 2½ to 3 hours

✸ Edible Ornament Cookies

These cookies are wonderful to serve within hours of baking. Fat-free or reduced fat cookies taste great when they are freshly baked, but do not bake them a day or two in advance because they will lose their delicious flavor and texture.

4¹/2 cups Homemade Sweet Baking Mix (page 220)	2 teaspoons almond extract
¹/2 cup no-sugar-added applesauce	¹/2 cup all-purpose flour
3 egg whites	I (3-ounce) container red sugar crystals

- Preheat the oven to 350 degrees.
- Spray four cookie sheets with nonfat cooking spray.
- In a large mixing bowl stir with a spatula the Homemade Sweet Baking Mix, applesauce, egg whites, and almond extract until well mixed.
- Add the flour and knead with your hands until the dough forms a stiff ball. The dough will not be sticky. If it is sticky, add a little more flour 1 teaspoon at a time.
- On a floured surface roll the dough with a rolling pin until it is ⅛ inch thick.
- Dip the cookie cutters into excess flour and then press the cookie cutters firmly into the rolled-out dough, putting the shapes close together. Set aside the scraps of dough to re-roll.
- Using a pancake turner place the cut-out cookie dough on prepared cookie sheets.
- Re-roll any scraps, cut into shapes, and place on the cookie sheets.
- Spray the tops of the cookies with nonfat cooking spray and sprinkle generously with the red sugar.
- Bake for 6 minutes.
- To use these cookies as ornaments for the Christmas tree, with a twisting motion poke a hole with a straw about a ½ inch from the top of each freshly baked cookie.
- Cut forty-five 18 to 20-inch-long pieces of red or white ribbon.*
- Put a piece of ribbon through the hole in each cookie and tie it in a knot, making a 1-inch loop for hanging.
- Curl the extra ribbon by pulling one blade of scissors down the extra length of ribbon.

- Store in an airtight container. Place wax paper between the layers.
- Hang the cookies on the Christmas tree using the loop right before serving dinner.

Note: To save time measuring and cutting curling ribbon, wrap curling ribbon around a 10 to 12-inch basket 45 times, and cut through all of the ribbon with a very sharp pair of scissors. You should have 45 pieces of ribbon.

Yield: 45 (1-cookie) servings

(Nutritional information per cookie)
Calories: 50 (0% fat); Total Fat: 0g; Cholesterol: 0mg; Carbohydrate: 11g; Dietary Fiber: 0g; Protein: 1g; Sodium: 60mg; Diabetic Exchanges: 1/2 starch

Preparation time: 24 minutes
Baking time: 6 minutes
Total time: 30 minutes or less

Keeping the Peace during Family Gatherings

Most of us have our family challenges, some greater than others. Rather than denying that the challenges exist and then getting stressed out about it, acknowledging the challenges and having a plan in order to "keep the peace during the family gathering" can be a good thing.

- Park so you are able to leave early, if needed.
- If you get stressed out, go for a walk to "regroup."
- Try not to spend too much time in the same room with people that drain your energy.
- Preoccupy yourself by playing a game with the children or cleaning up rather than talking with someone who bothers you?

🍲 Christmas-Style Waldorf Salad

Who'd ever guess this was made with so few fats or calories? It's every bit as delicious as the high-fat, high-calorie traditional recipe. The cranberries add an extra little zip that my guests really enjoyed, and using two different types of apples not only added a delicious flavor combination, but beauty as well.

2	Granny Smith apples	1	plus 1 tablespoons finely chopped walnuts
2	Red Delicious apples		
1	celery stalk, chopped	¹/₄	cup light whipped salad dressing
¹/₃	cup finely chopped dried cranberries	¹/₄	cup fat-free dessert whipped topping

- With the peel on, chop the apples into ½-inch pieces. You should have about 6 cups of chopped apples.
- In a large mixing bowl combine the apples, celery, cranberries, 1 tablespoon walnuts, salad dressing, and whipped topping. Stir until well mixed.
- Sprinkle the remaining 1 tablespoon walnuts over the top.

Yield: 12 (½-cup) servings

Calories: 58 (28% fat); Total Fat: 2g; Cholesterol: 1mg; Carbohydrate: 11g; Dietary Fiber: 1g; Protein: 0g; Sodium: 48mg; Diabetic Exchanges: ½ fruit, ½ fat

🕐 **Preparation time:** 15 minutes
Total time: 15 minutes

♥♥ Strawberry-Banana Christmas Parfaits

The color combination of these pretty parfaits is just right for adding Christmas pizzazz to any table.

I cup low-fat ricotta cheese	I (2I-ounce) can strawberry pie filling
I¼ cups fat-free, low-carb milk	
2 (I.7-ounce) boxes instant sugar-free banana cream pudding mix	2 tablespoons finely chopped dried cranberries
I (8-ounce) container fat-free dessert whipped topping	

- Beat the ricotta cheese with an electric mixer, scraping the bowl often.
- Add the milk and pudding mix and beat for 1 to 2 minutes with the mixer.
- With a spatula stir in the whipped topping.
- Stir the dried cranberries into the strawberry pie filling.
- Into each of eight dessert cups place ¼ cup of the cream mixture, then ¼ cup of the strawberry filling, then ¼ cup of the cream mixture, and then ¼ cup of the strawberry filling.
- Cover and keep chilled until ready to serve.

Yield: 8 servings

Calories: 216 (6% fat); Total Fat: 1g; Cholesterol: 8mg; Carbohydrate: 41g; Dietary Fiber: 1g; Protein: 5g; Sodium: 594mg; Diabetic Exchanges: 3 other carbohydrate

⊣ **Preparation time:** 10 minutes

🍲 Banana-Nut Bread

I don't think I'll eat high-fat banana bread made with processed white flour ever again. You'd never know I used so few nuts because the whole wheat adds an extra-nutty flavor and texture. Definitely a healthy recipe you can enjoy completely guilt free.

¹/₂	cup cinnamon applesauce	1	teaspoon vanilla extract
¹/₂	cup liquid egg substitute or 4 egg whites, beaten	2	cups Homemade Whole Wheat Sweet Baking Mix (page 220)
2	very ripe bananas, mashed	3	tablespoons finely chopped walnuts

- Preheat the oven to 350 degrees.
- Spray three mini-loaf pans with nonfat cooking spray.
- In a medium bowl with an electric mixer beat together the applesauce, egg substitute, banana, and vanilla until well blended.
- With a spatula stir in the baking mix until all of the ingredients are blended.
- Pour the batter into the prepared pans. Sprinkle the tops lightly with the nuts.
- Bake for 15 minutes or until a toothpick inserted in the center comes out dry.

Yield: 3 mini-loaves or 12 (2-slice) servings

Calories: 92 (14% fat); Total Fat: 2g; Cholesterol: 0mg; Carbohydrate: 18g; Dietary Fiber: 2g; Protein: 3g; Sodium: 115mg; Diabetic Exchanges: 1 starch

🕐 **Preparation time:** 10 minutes
Baking time: 15 minutes
Total time: 25 minutes

Cranberry Chutney

The natural sweetness of the fruits in this slightly sweet, yet tangy, chutney goes perfectly with ham or turkey. My mouth waters thinking about how good it is on both of these entrées. It would also be good with warm biscuits.

1	cup fresh or frozen cranberries	1	teaspoon ground allspice
1	large navel orange, peeled, seeded, and chopped (also cut the white part off under the peel)	2	tablespoons sugar-free raspberry jam
1	large red apple, cored not peeled	3/4	cup Splenda Granular
1	(8-ounce) can pineapple tidbits, drained		

- In a food processor finely chop the cranberries, orange, and apple.
- Pour the chopped fruit into a medium-size mixing bowl along with the pineapple, allspice, raspberry jam, and Splenda.
- Stir until completely mixed.
- Ready to eat, or cover and keep chilled until ready to serve.

Yield: 10 (¼-cup) servings

Calories: 43 (0% fat); Total Fat: 0g; Cholesterol: 0mg; Carbohydrate: 12g; Dietary Fiber: 2g; Protein: 0g; Sodium: 2mg; Diabetic Exchanges: 1 fruit

Preparation time: 10 minutes

Seafood Dinner Menu

Serves 6

Spicy Seafood Soup (page 131)
Seafood-Topped Tossed Salad (page 127)
Salmon Topped with Creamy Shrimp Sauce (page 130)
Bell Pepper Medley (page 132)
Whole Wheat Buttermilk & Basil Biscuits (page 129)
Minty Angel Dessert Cups (page 128)

Edible Centerpiece

Place a large, clear glass bowl upside down in the middle of the table. Lift the bowl slightly and put several silk poinsettia blooms under the bowl. When the Whole Wheat Buttermilk and Basil Biscuits are done baking, place them on a clear, glass serving plate and place the plate on top of the upside down bowl for an edible centerpiece.

Supplies

Large clear glass bowl
Silk poinsettia blooms
6 dessert glasses

Clear glass serving plate
Baking sheet
Jelly-roll pan

Timeline

1. Set the table before you start cooking so that it will be ready when the guests arrive.
2. About 1½ hours before serving time, prepare the Seafood-Topped Tossed Salad and the dressing. Do not add the dressing to the salad. Cover the salad and the dressing and place in the refrigerator until serving time.
3. Prepare the Minty Angel Dessert Cups, cover, and place in the refrigerator until serving time.
4. Make the Whole Wheat Buttermilk and Basil Biscuits, but do not put them in the oven.
5. Make the Salmon Topped with Creamy Shrimp Sauce. While the salmon is in the oven, start the Spicy Seafood Soup.
6. While the soup is simmering, make the Bell Pepper Medley.

Last 15 minutes

7. Put the biscuits in the oven, prepare the shrimp sauce, and take the salmon out of the oven. Spoon the shrimp sauce down the center of the salmon. Sprinkle with the lemon pepper for color.
8. Add the dressing to the salad and toss. Place on the table.
9. Place the biscuits on a clear glass serving plate and place in the middle of the table.
10. Ladle the soup into bowls and place on the table.
11. Bring everything to the table.

Grocery List

Frozen Foods
1 (12-ounce) container fat-free dessert whipped topping
1 (16-ounce) bag frozen, fat-free, diced hash browns (only ½ bag needed)
1 (16-ounce) bag frozen bell pepper stir-fry mixture

Fresh Fruits and Vegetables
2 (11-ounce) bags spring mix salad greens (only 1½ needed)
1 pint grape tomatoes (only 17 tomatoes needed)
1 (1-ounce) package fresh basil
1 tablespoon minced garlic (from a jar is fine)
1 (8-ounce) package pre-sliced fresh mushrooms (in produce)
1 bunch parsley, optional (only 6 sprigs needed)

Staple Items
1 (14-ounce) can diced tomato
2 (14.5-ounce) cans fat-free chicken broth (3 cups needed)
1 (10¾-ounce) can 98% fat-free tomato soup
1 (8-ounce) can water chestnuts

Meats
1 (2-pound) package salmon fillet, boneless
3 (12-ounce) bags frozen cooked cocktail shrimp (2½ bags needed)
½ pound imitation crabmeat

Dairy
1 (2-quart) container fat-free, low-carb milk (only 1 cup needed)
1 pint low-fat buttermilk (only ½ cup needed)
1 tablespoon Parmesan cheese
1 (4-ounce) container low-fat feta cheese crumbles (only 2 table-spoons needed)
1 tablespoon light real butter

Baking Items
1 (1-ounce) box instant sugar-free vanilla pudding mix
1 (1.75-ounce) box individual packets Splenda (only 1 individual packet needed)
1 (5-pound) bag whole wheat flour (only 3 cups needed)
1 (1.9-ounce) box Splenda Granular (only ½ cup needed)

2 teaspoons baking soda
1 (8-ounce) can nonfat cooking spray
Green sugar crystals, optional

Seasonings/Condiments
1 (12-ounce) jar cocktail sauce (only
    ½ cup needed)
½ cup fat-free mayonnaise
½ cup fat-free whipped salad
    dressing
1 tablespoon light mayonnaise
1 (1-ounce) bottle mint extract (only
    ½ teaspoon needed)
Liquid green food coloring (6 drops
    needed)
1 (2.5-ounce) package imitation
    butter-flavored sprinkles, such as
    Butter Buds (only 1 tablespoon
    needed)
1¼ teaspoons lemon pepper

1 teaspoon Mrs. Dash Table Blend
1 (6-ounce) can Old Bay seasoning,
    found in the spice aisle (only
    3 teaspoons needed)
½ teaspoon garlic salt

Other
1 (15-ounce) jar cocktail onions
    (found in the pickle aisle)
1 (3-ounce) jar reduced-fat crumbled
    bacon bits
1 (12-ounce) angel food cake (only
    ½ needed)
1 (8-ounce) bag spearmint leaf jellied
    candy, optional
1 (12-ounce) bag cinnamon candies,
    such as Red Hots, optional

Seafood-Topped Tossed Salad

Shrimp in our area are so expensive that anytime we put shrimp on a salad the family knows this is a special meal.

1¹/₂ (11-ounce) bags spring mix salad greens (or 11 cups firmly packed)	¹/₃ cup water
¹/₂ cup cocktail sauce	3 tablespoons crumbled reduced-fat bacon bits
¹/₂ cup fat-free whipped salad dressing	³/₄ pound cocktail shrimp, fully cooked* (frozen are fine, just thaw first)
¹/₃ cup cocktail onions, sliced thinly (about 21 onions)	

- Place the lettuce in a large salad bowl.
- In a small bowl with a whisk stir together the cocktail sauce, salad dressing, cocktail onions, water, and bacon bits.
- Remove the tails from the shrimp and cut the shrimp into small pieces.
- Stir the shrimp into the dressing mixture.
- Immediately before serving, pour the shrimp and dressing mixture over the lettuce and toss the salad until the leaves are coated with the dressing.

*Note: Salad shrimp can be substituted; however, sometimes salad shrimp can taste a bit fishy and not have the quality texture or flavor of larger shrimp. This is why I suggested using larger shrimp for this recipe.

Yield: 6 servings

Calories: 121 (14% fat); Total Fat: 2g; Cholesterol: 116mg; Carbohydrate: 10g; Dietary Fiber: 2g; Protein: 15g; Sodium: 587mg; Diabetic Exchanges: 2 very lean meat, ½ other carbohydrate

Preparation time: 15 minutes

☗ Minty Angel Dessert Cups

This lovely dessert tastes and looks too special to be made quickly; yet it is made very quickly.

1/2	(12-ounce) angel food cake, cut into six 1-ounce pieces	1	individual packet Splenda
1	(1-ounce) box instant sugar-free vanilla pudding mix	2	cups fat-free dessert whipped topping
1	cup fat-free, low-carb milk		Green colored sugar crystals (optional)
1/2	teaspoon mint extract		Spearmint leaf-shaped jellied candy
6	drops liquid green food coloring		and cinnamon candies (optional)

- Place one piece of the angel food cake into each of six dessert glasses.
- In a mixing bowl combine the pudding mix, milk, mint extract, food coloring, and Splenda until thoroughly mixed.
- Gently stir the whipped topping in with a spatula.
- Evenly divide the creamy mint mixture among the glasses. This should be about ½ cup per glass.
- If desired, sprinkle the green sugar crystals on top.
- If desired, decorate the dessert cups with holly leaves. Take 1 spearmint leaf candy (a green jellied candy shaped like a leaf with sugar on the outside), and roll the piece of candy between two pieces of wax paper sprinkled with ½ teaspoon of Splenda Granular until the candy is ⅛ inch thick. With a paring knife cut out a holly-leaf shape. Quickly rinse off the extra Splenda with water, and immediately pat the candy dry so that it has a nice green color. For each dessert cut three leaves and press the corners of them together. Then press three red hot candies where the leaves come together. Use one group of leaves to decorate each Minty Angel Dessert Cup. Although this idea is very pretty, it is also very time-consuming; and I'd allow an extra 10 minutes per dessert to decorate with the holly leaves.

Yield: 6 servings

(Nutritional analysis doesn't include holly leaves)
Calories: 140 (0% fat); Total Fat: 0g; Cholesterol: 1mg; Carbohydrate: 29g; Dietary Fiber: 0g; Protein: 4g; Sodium: 434mg; Diabetic Exchanges: 2 other carbohydrate

🕐 **Preparation time:** 10 minutes

Whole Wheat Buttermilk & Basil Biscuits

1/2	cup low-fat buttermilk	17	grape tomatoes
1	tablespoon light mayonnaise	1	tablespoon Parmesan cheese
1/4	cup plus 1/2 teaspoon finely chopped fresh basil	2	tablespoons low-fat feta cheese crumbles
1	cup Homemade Whole Wheat Baking Mix (see page 219)		

- Preheat the oven to 350 degrees.
- Spray a baking sheet with nonfat cooking spray.
- In a medium bowl with a spatula stir together the buttermilk, mayonnaise, and 1/4 cup basil until well mixed.
- Stir in the baking mix and continue stirring until a sticky dough forms. It will look like you don't have enough liquid, but keep stirring.
- Drop the dough onto the prepared baking sheet by rounded tablespoonfuls. This is easiest done by using two measuring tablespoons and scraping the dough off of one measuring spoon with the other.
- Cut the grape tomatoes in half through the middle so that the stem end is on one half and the bottom of the tomato is on the other half.
- Press three tomato halves into the top of each biscuit and place a small piece of the remaining chopped basil on the tomatoes where all three come together.
- Sprinkle 1/4 teaspoon Parmesan cheese on the top of each biscuit.
- Bake for 10 to 12 minutes or until the tops of the biscuits are lightly browned.
- Remove the biscuits from the oven and top each biscuit with 1/2 teaspoon feta cheese crumbles. Return to the top rack and broil for 1 to 1 1/2 minutes. The cheese will be lightly browned and the biscuits will get a crispy crust from broiling.

Note: If you do not have buttermilk you can substitute by putting 1 1/2 teaspoons of lemon juice or vinegar into a measuring cup. Fill to 1/2 cup with fat-free skim milk, and let it sit for 5 minutes before using.

Yield: 11 (1-biscuit) servings

Calories: 50 (19% fat); Total Fat: 1g; Cholesterol: 2mg; Carbohydrate: 8g; Dietary Fiber: 1g; Protein: 2g; Sodium: 121mg; Diabetic Exchanges: 1/2 starch

Preparation time: 15 minutes
Baking time: 10 to 12 minutes
Total time: 27 minutes or less

Salmon Topped with Creamy Shrimp Sauce

This is definitely special.

I	(2-pound) boneless salmon fillet	I	tablespoon minced garlic (from a jar is fine)
I	tablespoon imitation butter-flavored sprinkles	I	(12-ounce) package frozen, fully cooked shrimp, tails removed and cut into ¹/₂-inch pieces
I	plus ¹/₄ teaspoons lemon pepper		
I	tablespoon light real butter (half the fat)	¹/₂	cup fat-free mayonnaise

- Preheat the oven to 350 degrees.
- Put two pieces of aluminum foil about 3 feet long together and fold together a few times to make a seam, creating one large piece of foil.
- Spray the aluminum foil with nonfat cooking spray. Set the foil on a jelly-roll pan with the sprayed side facing up.
- Place the salmon (skin side down) on the foil. Sprinkle the top of the salmon with the imitation butter-flavored sprinkles and 1 teaspoon lemon pepper.
- Fold the foil around the salmon into a loose, but securely closed, tent.
- Cook in the oven for 15 to 20 minutes or until the salmon flakes easily with a fork in the center.
- Do not do this next step until about 3 or 4 minutes before the salmon has finished baking; otherwise the shrimp may overcook and become tough. We want the shrimp to be tender.
- In a 12-inch nonstick skillet melt the butter over medium heat and add the garlic, shrimp, mayonnaise, and the remaining ¹/₄ teaspoon lemon pepper. Cook, stirring often, until the mixture is fully heated. Turn off the heat and cover until the salmon is ready.
- When the salmon is done, very carefully open the foil, folding it back like an unwrapped Christmas present.
- Pour the shrimp sauce down the entire length of the center of the salmon and sprinkle a little lemon pepper on the top for color.
- The entire jelly-roll pan with the opened aluminum foil packet is what we are going to serve the salmon and shrimp on. The presentation of this entrée is another feature that makes this dinner more special.

Yield: 7 (4-ounce) servings

Calories: 222 (7% fat); Total Fat: 6g; Cholesterol: 167mg; Carbohydrate: 4g; Dietary Fiber: 0g; Protein: 36g; Sodium: 452mg; Diabetic Exchanges: 5 lean meat

Preparation time: 10 minutes
Cooking time: 15 to 20 minutes
Total time: 30 minutes or less

Spicy Seafood Soup

This will definitely add zip to your meal.

1	(14-ounce) can diced tomatoes	1	teaspoon Mrs. Dash Table Blend
1/2	(16-ounce) bag frozen fat-free diced hash browns	1/2	(12-ounce) bag frozen cooked cocktail shrimp, tails removed
3	cups fat-free chicken broth	1/2	pound imitation crabmeat, chopped
1	teaspoon Old Bay seasoning		

- In a large soup pan bring the diced tomatoes, hash browns, chicken broth, Old Bay seasoning, and Mrs. Dash to a low boil.
- When at a low boil add the shrimp and crabmeat. Once it comes to a low boil again, turn off heat.
- Serve hot. If desired, place a sprig of fresh parsley on top of each bowl of soup.

Yield: 7 (1-cup) servings

Calories: 101 (7% fat); Total Fat: 1g; Cholesterol: 54mg; Carbohydrate: 12g; Dietary Fiber: 2g; Protein: 11g; Sodium: 663mg; Diabetic Exchanges: 1 very lean meat, 1/2 starch, 1 vegetable

Preparation time: 10 minutes
Cooking time: 15 minutes
Total time: 25 minutes

Bell Pepper Medley

You're gonna love how the colors in this dish enhance and bring out the other colors in your seafood dishes.

1	($10^3/4$-ounce) can 98% fat-free tomato soup (Do not make as directed.)	1	(8-ounce) package presliced fresh mushrooms (in produce)
1	(16-ounce) bag frozen bell pepper stir-fry mixture	1	(8-ounce) can water chestnuts
		2	teaspoons Old Bay seasoning (found in the spice aisle)
		$^1/_2$	teaspoon garlic salt

- Stir the tomato soup, bell pepper mixture, and mushrooms into a large nonstick saucepan until well mixed. Cook over medium heat with the lid on, stirring occasionally, for about 12 minutes.
- While the vegetables are cooking, drain the liquid from the water chestnuts and chop them into tiny pieces.
- Add the water chestnuts, Old Bay seasoning, and garlic salt to the saucepan.
- Continue cooking over medium heat with the lid on and stirring occasionally until vegetables are fully heated and tender, about 2 minutes.
- When the vegetables are finished, drain and discard the excess juice before placing the vegetables in a serving bowl.

Yield: 6 ($^1/_2$-cup) servings

Calories: 80 (0% fat); Total Fat: 0g; Cholesterol: 0mg; Carbohydrate: 16g; Dietary Fiber: 2g; Protein: 3g; Sodium: 598mg; Diabetic Exchanges: 3 vegetable

Preparation time: 5 minutes
Cooking time: 14 minutes
Total time: 19 minutes

Santa's Favorite Steak and Spinach Roll Dinner Menu

Serves 4

Granny's Gourmet Tossed Salad (page 135)
Steak & Spinach Roll (Santa's Favorite) (page 136)
Garlic Smashed Red-Skin Potatoes (page 138)
Holiday Broccoli (page 140)
Christmas Tree Biscuits (page 139)
Candy Cane Ice Cream Cups (page 141)

Edible Centerpiece

Use your finest baking sheet or cover one in aluminum foil and make the Christmas Tree Biscuits as an edible centerpiece. Place several tea-light candles around the biscuits. Do not use too many candles so that guests can easily reach around and get a biscuit.

Supplies

Slow cooker	Cooking string	Blender
Baking sheets	Electric mixer	Tea-light candles

Timeline

1. Set the table. You will be using the Christmas Tree Biscuits as a centerpiece, so leave a space in the middle of the table and use your good baking sheet.
2. About 3½ hours before serving time, start the Steak and Spinach Roll.
3. About 1 hour before serving time, start making the Granny's Gourmet Tossed Salad. Do not put the dressing on until serving time.
4. Forty-five minutes before serving time, make the Garlic Smashed Red-Skin Potatoes.
5. While the potatoes are cooking, make the Christmas Tree Biscuits.
6. Start the Holiday Broccoli.

Last 15 minutes
7. Smash the potatoes and finish the broccoli.
8. Ten minutes before serving, put the Christmas Tree Biscuits in the oven to bake for 8 to 10 minutes.
9. Take the Steak & Spinach Roll out of the slow cooker and place it on a pretty serving platter. Remove the strings from the roll and discard.

10. Take all of the hot food to the table. Light your candles.
11. When everyone has finished eating, clear away the dinner dishes and prepare the Candy Cane Ice Cream Cups. Serve dessert.

Grocery List

Frozen Foods
2 pints low-fat frozen yogurt (only 4 cups needed)

Fresh Fruits and Vegetables
2 pounds red-skin potatoes
1 (1-ounce) bunch fresh basil (only 2 tablespoons needed)
1 pint grape tomatoes (only 5 needed)
1 large head fresh broccoli florets (about 6 cups)
1 medium onion
1 small red bell pepper (only ½ cup needed)
1 Granny Smith apple
1 (10-ounce) bag gourmet lettuces
¼ pound red grapes or pomegranate seeds (only ¼ cup needed)

Staple Items
1 (27-ounce) can spinach
1 (14½-ounce) can stewed tomatoes
1 (8-ounce) can nonfat cooking spray

Meats
1½ pounds eye of round, London Broil, or flank steak

Dairy
1 (4-ounce) container fat-free feta cheese
1 (16-ounce) container fat-free sour cream (only 1½ cups needed)
2 (7.5-ounce) containers refrigerated low-fat buttermilk biscuits (10 in a roll)

1 tablespoon grated Parmesan cheese
1 (2-quart) container fat-free, low-carb milk (only 1 cup needed)

Seasoning/Condiments
1 (8-ounce) bottle fat-free red wine vinaigrette salad dressing (only ½ cup needed)
1 tablespoon of your favorite steak seasoning blend (I use Tone's with coarse salt)
1 (2.5-ounce) jar imitation butter-flavored sprinkles, such as Butter Buds (only 3 tablespoons needed)
¾ teaspoon light salt
¾ teaspoon garlic powder
1 teaspoon dried parsley
½ teaspoon lemon pepper
¼ teaspoon mint extract
Red liquid food coloring (only 4 drops needed)

Other
1 (15-ounce) jar whole cocktail onions (in the condiment aisle)
10 miniature peppermint candy canes

🍲 Granny's Gourmet Tossed Salad

The cute name is from the Granny Smith apples used in this recipe.

1	Granny Smith apple, unpeeled, thinly sliced	1	tablespoon fat-free feta cheese crumbles
1/2	cup fat-free red wine vinaigrette salad dressing	1/4	cup chopped red grapes*
7 1/2	cups gourmet baby lettuces		

- Place the apple in the dressing in a medium bowl. Cover and keep chilled until ready to eat the salad.
- In a large bowl place the lettuces and top with the cheese and grapes.
- Right before serving, toss the salad with the apples and salad dressing mixture. Do not put the salad dressing on too far in advance of serving or the salad will get soggy. Also, make sure the apples are covered with dressing to prevent them from getting dark.

Note: Or substitute ¼ cup fresh pomegranate seeds, which have a terrific cranberry-nutty flavor and texture. I didn't use pomegranate seeds as my first choice because they are not easily available everywhere. If they were easily available, they would be my preference in this recipe.

Yield: 4 servings (or 6 side salads)

(Nutritional information for 4 servings)
Calories: 84 (0% fat); Total Fat: 0g; Cholesterol: 0mg; Carbohydrate: 20g; Dietary Fiber: 3g; Protein: 2g; Sodium: 364mg; Diabetic Exchanges: ½ fruit, 1 other carbohydrate
(Nutritional information for 6 servings)
Calories: 56 (0% fat); Total Fat: 0g; Cholesterol: 0mg; Carbohydrate: 13g; Dietary Fiber: 2g; Protein: 2g; Sodium: 243mg; Diabetic Exchanges: ½ fruit, ½ other carbohydrate

🕐 **Preparation time:** 15 minutes

🍲 Steak & Spinach Roll (Santa's Favorite)

The presentation of this beautiful entrée will make your dinner guests think you are a master chef. No need to tell them differently. How easy this is to prepare will be our little secret. For easier cleanup lay a piece of wax paper over the meat before pounding it.

1 ¹/2 pounds beef round, London broil or flank steak, all visible fat removed from the outside	¹/4 plus ¹/4 cup fat-free feta cheese, crumbled
1 tablespoon your favorite steak seasoning blend (I use Tone's)	1 (14¹/2-ounce) can stewed tomatoes, drained
1 (27-ounce) can spinach, drained	¹/2 cup whole cocktail onions (found in a jar in the condiment aisle)

- Cut ¹/4-inch slices against the grain on both sides of the meat.
- With a rolling pin pound the steak to about ¹/2 inch thickness. This is easiest by turning the steak over periodically and pounding both sides. It takes about 4 to 5 minutes to get the steak to ¹/2 inch thickness. We need the steak to be approximately 6 to 8 inches wide and it does not matter how long it is.
- Sprinkle one side of the steak with steak seasoning.
- Squeeze as much water as possible from the spinach using your hands.
- Wrap six pieces of paper towel around the spinach and squeeze out any remaining liquid. Discard the paper towels.
- In a medium-size bowl stir the spinach and ¹/4-cup feta cheese together until well mixed.
- Place the spinach mixture lengthwise down the center of the steak. Do not spread it over the whole steak; only put it 1¹/2 to 2 inches wide down the center.
- Take 12 to 18-inch pieces of dental floss or cooking string and put it underneath the steak. Fold both sides of the steak up around the spinach mixture and tie the string in a knot. (Some pieces of the steak may overlap and some of the spinach mixture may show. These are both okay.) Tie pieces of string about every two inches all the way down the steak.
- Cut off the excess pieces of string and discard.
- Place the rolled steak in a large slow cooker.
- With your hands place the stewed tomatoes on top of the steak.
- Sprinkle the remaining ¹/4-cup feta cheese on the tomatoes and arrange the onions on top as well.
- Cover and cook on high for 3 hours.

- Remove the cooked roll with tongs and place on a serving platter. Let sit a few minutes before cutting.
- Cut the strings, remove, and discard.
- For a beautiful presentation this is best cut with a very sharp knife at the dining table.

Yield: 5 servings

Calories: 248 (16% Fat); Total Fat: 4g; Cholesterol: 56mg; Carbohydrate: 12g; Dietary Fiber: 4g; Protein: 37g; Sodium: 1479mg; Diabetic Exchanges: 4 very lean meat, 2½ vegetable

Preparation time: 20 minutes
Cooking time: 3 hours
Total time: 3 hours 20 minutes

Blessed with Easy-Free Wrapping

I love the look of a beautifully wrapped gift. To me giving a lovely wrapped present is an extension of myself that affirms the person receiving the gift is extra special to me because of the time and preparation I'd put into wrapping the gift. Sometimes we just don't have the time during the holidays.

This last Christmas I was pressed for time, so I hired my nephew to do the actual wrapping of gifts. I supplied all the wrapping paper, gift-tags, tape, scissors, etc. He wrapped the gifts and I decorated them with ribbons and bows. It cut my time in half and he was worth every penny.

Although a beautifully wrapped present is nice, the attitude of our heart in giving is what is really important. We ought to give because we want to, not because we're trying to impress someone. When dealing with the stress of the holidays it is always important to keep things in perspective.

Garlic Smashed Red-Skin Potatoes

2	pounds red-skin potatoes, about 7 cups when chopped	$^3/_4$	teaspoon light salt
$^1/_2$	cup fat-free sour cream	$^3/_4$	teaspoon garlic powder
2	tablespoons imitation butter-flavored sprinkles	I	teaspoon dried parsley

- Fill a large saucepan with 6 cups water.
- Wash the potatoes and cut them into 1½ to 2-inch chunks, leaving the peel on.
- Put the potatoes in the water. Cover the pan and when the potatoes come to a boil, turn off the heat. Let the potatoes sit in the water for 15 minutes; they will continue to cook.
- Drain the potatoes and put them in a mixing bowl.
- Add the sour cream, butter-flavored sprinkles, light salt, garlic powder, and parsley to the potatoes and mix with an electric mixer or a potato masher.
- Put the potatoes in a serving bowl and sprinkle a little bit of parsley on the top if you wish.

Yield: 6 (1-cup) servings

Calories: 132 (0% fat); Total Fat: 0g; Cholesterol: 3mg; Carbohydrate: 33g; Dietary Fiber: 3g; Protein: 5g; Sodium: 343mg; Diabetic Exchanges: 2 starch

Preparation time: 10 minutes
Cooking time: 15 minutes
Total time: 25 minutes

☐ ♦♦ Christmas Tree Biscuits

Here's an exceptionally easy way to turn ordinary biscuits into something extra-ordinary and special for the holidays.

2	(7.5-ounce) cans low-fat buttermilk biscuits* (10 biscuits per roll; you will need only 19)	5	grape tomatoes, cut in half
		l	tablespoon grated Parmesan cheese
2	tablespoons chopped fresh basil		

- Preheat the oven to 450 degrees.
- Spray a cookie sheet with nonfat cooking spray.
- Place the biscuits right next to each other on the cookie sheet in the shape of a tree. Starting with 1 biscuit on the top, 2 biscuits for the second row, 3 biscuits for the third row, 4 biscuits for the fourth row, and 5 biscuits for the fifth row.
- To make the trunk of the tree, place 2 biscuits under the middle of the bottom row and place 2 biscuits directly underneath those. Make sure all of the biscuits are touching each other.
- Spray the top of the biscuits with nonfat cooking spray.
- Sprinkle the basil evenly over the biscuits, omitting the trunk.
- Place the tomato halves, cut side down, in each spot where 4 biscuits are touching.
- Sprinkle the grated Parmesan cheese evenly over the entire tree.
- Bake for 8 to 10 minutes.
- Let cool a minute or two. Then carefully transfer the tree onto a large plate by using your hands to slide it from the baking sheet.

Note: Look on nutritional label for a brand that only has 1 gram of fat or less per 2-biscuit serving.

Yield: 9½ (2-biscuit) servings

Calories: 113 (17% fat); Total Fat: 2g; Cholesterol: 0mg; Carbohydrate: 20g; Dietary Fiber: 1g; Protein: 3g; Sodium: 540mg; Diabetic Exchanges: 1½ starch

(⌐) **Preparation time:** 8 minutes
Cooking time: 8 to 10 minutes
Total time: 18 minutes or less

Holiday Broccoli

The slightly zesty, lemony flavor is a pleasant surprise guests are sure to enjoy, and the vibrant colors of red and green dress up any holiday table or buffet.

1 head fresh broccoli florets (about 6 cups)*	1/2 teaspoon lemon pepper
1 cup chopped onion (frozen is fine)	1 tablespoon imitation butter-flavored sprinkles
1/2 cup chopped red bell pepper	

- Put 1/2 inch water in the bottom of a large saucepan.
- If you have a steamer basket, put it in the bottom of the saucepan with the water. (If you do not have a steamer basket, don't worry; you can still easily cook this recipe.)
- Place the broccoli in the water or in a steamer basket. Cover with a lid.
- Bring to a boil. Once steam starts lifting the lid, toss in the onions. Do not stir. Cover and cook 2 minutes longer.
- Turn off heat. Toss in the red bell pepper. Do not stir. Cover again and let sit for 8 minutes.
- Remove the vegetables and put them into a serving bowl.
- Gently stir the vegetables with lemon pepper and butter-flavored sprinkles to evenly coat them with seasoning.
- Serve immediately while the vegetables are hot.

Note: To save time purchase precut broccoli florets in the produce section.

Yield: 6 (1/2-cup) servings

Calories: 40 (0% fat); Total Fat: 0g; Cholesterol: 0mg; Carbohydrate: 9g; Dietary Fiber: 2g; Protein: 2g; Sodium: 111mg; Diabetic Exchanges: 2 vegetable

Preparation time: 10 minutes or less
Cooking time: 15 minutes or less
Total time: 25 minutes or less

Candy Cane Ice Cream Cups

Here's an elegant ending to a beautiful meal.

4	plus 5 plus I miniature peppermint candy canes (10 total)	¹/₄	teaspoon mint extract
		4	drops red liquid food coloring
I	cup ice		
4	cups low-fat frozen yogurt		
I	cup fat-free, low-carb milk		

- In a blender put 4 miniature peppermint candy canes. Cover and process until the candy canes are crushed.
- Add the ice, frozen yogurt, milk, mint extract, and food coloring.
- Cover and process on high speed until all the ingredients are well blended, smooth, and creamy. You may need to stop periodically to stir with a spatula to help bring ingredients from the bottom up and vice-versa.
- Put the mix into individual serving cups. This is exceptionally pretty in tall, stemmed glasses.
- Garnish by putting 1 miniature candy cane inside each serving with the loop of the candy cane hanging onto the edge of the glass.
- Crumble the last candy cane in a sealed, zip-top plastic bag with either a rolling pin or a can.
- Sprinkle the candy cane crumbs evenly on top of each dessert.

Yield: 5 (1-cup) servings

Calories: 202 (9% fat); Total Fat: 2g; Cholesterol: 9mg; Carbohydrate: 36g; Dietary Fiber: 0g; Protein: 9g; Sodium: 137mg; Diabetic Exchanges: 2¹/₂ other carbohydrate

Total preparation time: 5 minutes or less

Fancy Shmancy
Sit-Down Dinner

Serves 6

Snow-Capped Icebergs (page 144)
Filet Mignon Topped with Lobster (page 147)
Dilled Smashed Potatoes (page 146)
Asparagus with Crab & Blue Cheese (page 148)
Cheese Filled Breadsticks (page 145)
Virgin Cranberry Mimosas (page 148)
Cranberry Sorbet (page 149)

Centerpiece

Fill a large glass or crystal bowl with red Christmas ornaments and place it in the center of the table for a simple but elegant centerpiece.

Supplies

Large glass or crystal bowl	6 champagne flutes
Red Christmas ornaments	Electric mixer
Baking sheets	Blender

Timeline

1. One and a half hours before serving, set the table. Make your centerpiece.
2. One hour before serving time, prepare the Snow-Capped Icebergs and the dressing, but do not put the dressing on the salads until serving time. Cover each salad and the dressing and refrigerate until ready to serve.
3. Get the Cheese Filled Breadsticks ready, but do not bake them yet. Start the Dilled Smashed Potatoes.
4. While the potatoes are cooking, start making the filet mignon.
5. While the filet mignon is cooking, start making the asparagus.

Last 15 minutes

6. Make the Cranberry Mimosas and take them to the table.
7. Put the breadsticks in the oven to bake. Set the timer for 7 minutes so that they do not burn.
8. Finish the filet mignon.
9. Smash the potatoes. You can wrap a towel around the bowl to help keep the potatoes warm if you wish.
10. Put the dressings and bacon on the salads and place them on the table.

11. Take all of the hot food to the table, including the breadsticks from the oven.
12. After everyone has finished eating, clear away the dinner dishes, and make and serve the Cranberry Sorbet.

Grocery List

Frozen Foods
1 (8-ounce) container fat-free dessert whipped topping (only ¼ cup needed)

Fresh Fruits and Vegetables
1 large head iceberg lettuce
1 (5-pound) bag Russet potatoes (8 cups needed)
1 bunch fresh parsley
2 pounds fresh asparagus spears
1 (12-ounce) bag whole cranberries (only 1 cup needed)

Staple Items
1 (15-ounce) container Italian breadcrumbs (only ¼ cup needed)

Meats
2 pounds beef tenderloin
1 pound imitation or real lobster meat
1 pound imitation crabmeat

Dairy
1 (16-ounce) container fat-free sour cream (only 1¼ cups needed)
1 (4-ounce) container blue cheese crumbles (only 6 tablespoons needed)
1 (12-ounce) roll home-style biscuits (10 in a roll)
1 (8-ounce) package string cheese (only 2½ pieces needed)
1 pound light real butter or margarine (only 2 tablespoons needed)

Baking Items
1 (1.9-ounce) box Splenda Granular (only 1 tablespoon needed)
1 (8-ounce) can nonfat cooking spray

Seasonings/Condiments
⅓ cup fat-free mayonnaise
1 (10-ounce) bottle Worcestershire sauce (only 1 teaspoon needed)
1 (8-ounce) bottle fat-free French salad dressing (only 2 tablespoons needed)
1 (2.5-ounce) bottle imitation butter-flavored sprinkles, such as Butter Buds (2 tablespoons needed)
1 teaspoon dill weed
2½ teaspoons garlic salt
2 tablespoons steak seasoning blend (I use Tone's)
½ teaspoon lemon pepper

Other
1 (3-ounce) jar reduced-fat bacon crumbles (only 1 tablespoon needed)
1 (64-ounce) bottle light cranberry juice cocktail (only 3 cups needed)
1 (25.4-ounce) bottle sparkling red grape juice (only 12 tablespoons needed)
1 (1.2-ounce) container sugar-free raspberry drink mix (only 1 teaspoon needed)

Snow-Capped Icebergs

This includes salad wedges with blue cheese crumbles, French dressing, and bacon. It's a simple salad with a holiday twist. I think this salad dressing tastes best made a few days in advance. The longer the dressing can absorb the flavors of the blue cheese, the better I think it tastes. However, you don't have to make it in advance, and it will taste good as soon as it is made.

$^1/_3$ cup fat-free mayonnaise	2 tablespoons fat-free French dressing
$^1/_2$ cup fat-free sour cream	
1 teaspoon Worcestershire sauce	1 tablespoon reduced-fat bacon crumbles
3 tablespoons blue cheese crumbles	
1 large head iceberg lettuce, cut into 6 wedges	

- In a medium bowl stir together the mayonnaise, sour cream, Worcestershire sauce, and blue cheese crumbles. Cover and keep chilled until ready to eat.
- Divide the wedges of iceberg lettuce among six salad plates.
- Place 2 tablespoons blue cheese dressing on the top of each wedge of iceberg lettuce.
- Drizzle 1 teaspoon French dressing on top, and then sprinkle $^1/_2$ teaspoon bacon bits over the top.
- Best served right away.

Yield: 6 servings

Calories: 78 (23% fat); Total Fat: 2g; Cholesterol: 10mg; Carbohydrate: 12g; Dietary Fiber: 2g; Protein: 4g; Sodium: 284mg; Diabetic Exchanges: 1 vegetable, $^1/_2$ other carbohydrate, $^1/_2$ fat

Preparation time: 15 minutes or less

Cheese Filled Breadsticks

It's hard to believe cheese filled breadsticks that taste this yummy can be low fat.

2½ (1-ounce) individual string cheese sticks
1 (12-ounce) roll home-style biscuits, 10 in a roll
¼ cup Italian breadcrumbs
Garlic salt

- Preheat the oven to 400 degrees.
- Spray a baking sheet with nonfat cooking spray.
- Cut each string cheese stick in half lengthwise, and cut it in half again.
- Stretch the biscuit and place the quartered piece of string cheese in the biscuit.
- Pinch the biscuit closed around the string cheese.
- Spray the stuffed biscuit with nonfat cooking spray and roll it in the breadcrumbs.
- Place on the prepared baking sheet and sprinkle lightly with garlic salt.
- Bake for 7 to 8 minutes.

Yield: 10 stuffed breadsticks

Calories: 118 (24% fat); Total Fat: 3g; Cholesterol: 5mg; Carbohydrate: 18g; Dietary Fiber: 1g; Protein: 4g; Sodium: 527mg; Diabetic Exchanges: 1 starch, ½ fat

Preparation time: 10 minutes
Cooking time: 7 to 8 minutes
Total time: 18 minutes or less

Dilled Smashed Potatoes

We know this makes twelve servings and the menu serves only six, but they're so good, we think you'll want extras—just in case.

8	cups russet potatoes (not peeled)	I	teaspoon dill weed
2	tablespoons imitation butter-flavored sprinkles	$^3/_4$	cup fat-free sour cream
		I	teaspoon garlic salt

- In a large saucepan or Dutch oven bring to a boil enough water to cover the potatoes.
- Chop the potatoes into 1-inch pieces and put them into the boiling water.
- Bring the water to a boil again, cover the pan, and turn off the heat.
- Let the potatoes sit and continue to cook for 15 to 20 minutes.
- When the potatoes are tender, drain the water and put the potatoes into a large mixing bowl.
- Add the butter-flavored sprinkles, dill weed, sour cream, and garlic salt.
- Mix with an electric mixer or a potato masher until the potatoes are creamy. You will still have lumps in the potatoes.
- Place in a pretty serving bowl. Serve immediately.

Yield: 12 (½-cup) servings

Calories: 97 (0% fat); Total Fat: 0g; Cholesterol: 3mg; Carbohydrate: 22g; Dietary Fiber: 2g; Protein: 3g; Sodium: 159mg; Diabetic Exchanges: 1½ starch

Preparation time: 10 minutes
Cooking time: 15 to 20 minutes
Total time: 30 minutes or less

Filet Mignon Topped with Lobster

This exquisite meal is super pricey to make and tremendously delicious. Because I no longer serve prime rib for the holidays (too fat for me) I substitute this for special occasions.

2	pounds beef tenderloin	$^1/_2$	teaspoon garlic salt
2	tablespoons steak seasoning blend (I used Tone's)	1	pound imitation or real lobster meat
2	tablespoons light butter or margarine	1	teaspoon finely chopped fresh parsley

- Preheat a large cast-iron skillet over high heat.
- Spray the tenderloin with nonfat cooking spray. Do not spray the pan.
- Rub the outside of the beef with the steak seasoning.
- Cook the beef on high heat for about 15 minutes, turning the tenderloin a quarter turn every 3 to 4 minutes so the entire outside is seared. Remove from the skillet and place on a platter to rest for 3 to 4 minutes. (As the meat rests, it will continue to cook.) I recommend medium rare to medium. It should still be juicy and reddish-pink in the middle.
- While the meat is resting, in a nonstick skillet over medium heat melt the butter with the garlic salt and cook the lobster until heated, about 2 to 3 minutes, stirring occasionally.
- Spoon the lobster meat over the beef and sprinkle with the parsley.
- You can lay several sprigs of fresh parsley along the tenderloin for an extra garnish if desired.

Note: You may want to cut your tenderloin in half so it can fit in the pan easier. However, serving one long piece of tenderloin is impressive.

Yield: 8 servings (3 ounces beef and 2 ounces lobster meat)

Calories: 232 (33% fat); Total Fat: 8g; Cholesterol: 84mg; Carbohydrate: 6g; Dietary Fiber: 0g; Protein: 32g; Sodium: 1088mg; Diabetic Exchanges: 4 lean meat, $^1/_2$ other carbohydrate

Preparation time: 5 minutes or less
Cooking time: 20 minutes or less
Total time: 25 minutes or less

Asparagus with Crab & Blue Cheese

Asparagus just doesn't get any more delicious than this.

2	pounds fresh asparagus spears, about 7 cups	1/2	teaspoon lemon pepper
1	cup water	3	tablespoons blue cheese crumbles, firmly packed
1	pound imitation crabmeat	1	teaspoon parsley
1/2	teaspoon garlic salt		

- In a large skillet place the asparagus spears and water.
- Cover and cook on medium-high heat for 5 minutes.
- Place the crabmeat over the top of the asparagus.
- Sprinkle the garlic salt, lemon pepper, and blue cheese over the crab.
- Cover and cook 3 to 4 minutes.
- Before serving, sprinkle the parsley down the center.

Yield: 6 (¾-cup) servings

Calories: 133 (15% fat); Total Fat: 2g; Cholesterol: 18mg; Carbohydrate: 14g; Dietary Fiber: 3g; Protein: 13g; Sodium: 801mg; Diabetic Exchanges: 1½ very lean meat, 1½ vegetable, ½ other carbohydrate

Preparation time: 5 minutes
Cooking time: 8 to 9 minutes
Total time: 14 minutes or less

ii Virgin Cranberry Mimosas

This is normally an alcoholic beverage made with champagne and fruit juice combined; however, I wanted an alcohol-free version so the entire family could enjoy it.

3	cups light cranberry juice cocktail	12	tablespoons alcohol-free sparkling red grape juice

- Fill each champagne glass with ½ cup light cranberry juice cocktail

- Add 2 tablespoons sparkling red grape juice. (There are approximately 5 ounces in a champagne glass.)

Note: Chill your juices ahead of time so they are cold when served.

Yield: 6 servings

Calories: 39 (0% fat); Total Fat: 0g; Cholesterol: 0mg; Carbohydrate: 10g; Dietary Fiber: 0g; Protein: 0g; Sodium: 38mg; Diabetic Exchanges: ½ fruit

🕐 **Preparation time:** 5 minutes or less

Cranberry Sorbet

Just the right blend of tartness and sweetness that makes this very refreshing after a heavy holiday meal.

1 cup whole cranberries, frozen	1¼ cups water
2½ cups ice cubes	1 tablespoon Splenda Granular
1 teaspoon sugar-free raspberry drink mix	¼ cup fat-free dessert whipped topping

- Place the cranberries, ice cubes, raspberry drink mix, water, Splenda, and whipped topping in a blender.
- Cover and process on high for 2 to 3 minutes. Turn the blender off occasionally and push the ice cubes down with a long handled spatula. Keep mixing until the sorbet has a smooth and creamy consistency.
- Immediately spoon into seven individual dessert cups. If you do not have dessert cups, tall, stemmed glasses filled with sorbet would make the end of any holiday meal extraordinary.

Yield: 7 (½-cup) servings

Calories: 11 (0% fat); Total Fat: 0g; Cholesterol: 0mg; Carbohydrate: 3g; Dietary Fiber: 1g; Protein: 0g; Sodium: 2mg ; Diabetic Exchanges: Free

🕐 **Preparation time:** 5 minutes or less

Yuletide Pork Roast Dinner

Serves 6

Cream of Spinach Soup (page 153)
Yuletide Pork Roast with Lemon Pepper & Rosemary (page 152)
Savory Rice Stuffing (page 155)
Breakaway Broccoli (page 157)
Pumpkin Custard (page 154)
Cut-Out Glazed Sugar Cookies (page 156)

Edible Centerpiece

Place a plain artificial green wreath in the center of the table. Place the Cut-Out Glazed Sugar Cookies on top as decorations for the wreath. If desired, place pretty, colored, thin ribbon on the greenery too. Place a candle in the middle.

Supplies

2 slow cookers	A plain artificial green wreath
7 (5-ounce) ceramic ramekins	A wide candle
Roasting pan	Electric mixer
Baking sheets	Dutch oven

Timeline

1. The morning of your party set your table using red and green napkins.
2. Start the Yuletide Pork Roast 3 hours before serving time if you are cooking it on high and 6 hours before serving if you are cooking it on low.
3. Three hours before serving time make the Cream of Spinach Soup.
4. Prepare the custard and refrigerate until ready to serve.
5. Two and a half hours before serving time, bake the sugar cookies.
6. While the cookies are baking, make the glaze, brush or spread the glaze over the cookies, and let it dry slightly.
7. Make your centerpiece.
8. About 30 minutes before serving time, start the Breakaway Broccoli.
9. While the broccoli is cooking, start the Savory Rice Stuffing.

Last 15 minutes

10. Drain the water from the broccoli, add the feta cheese and dressing to the Breakaway Broccoli, cover, and keep warm.

11. Place the pork roast on a serving platter. Bring all of the food to the table while it is hot.
12. You can put the soup in a soup tureen, if you have one, or ladle it into rye bread bowls or soup bowls and serve immediately. Don't forget to light your candle in the centerpiece.
13. When everyone has finished eating, clear away the dinner dishes and serve the Pumpkin Custard.

Grocery List

Frozen Foods
2 (5.2-ounce) boxes low-fat, fully cooked breakfast sausage links
1 (10-ounce) bag frozen chopped onion (only 1 cup needed)

Fresh Fruits and Vegetables
1 large head fresh broccoli (7 cups florets needed)
1 small white onion

Staple Items
1 (27-ounce) can spinach
1 (10¾-ounce) can 98% fat-free cream of celery soup
1 (6.2-ounce) box instant brown rice (only 2 cups needed)
1 (6-ounce) box chicken-flavored stuffing mix

Meats
2 pounds pork tenderloin

Dairy
1 pint fat-free liquid nondairy creamer (only 1 cup needed)
1 pint fat-free half-and-half (only 1 cup needed)
1 (8-ounce) liquid egg substitute (only ¾ cup needed)
1 pound reduced-fat margarine (only ½ cup needed)
2 eggs

1 (4-ounce) container fat-free feta cheese crumbles (only ¼ cup needed)

Baking Items
1 (30-ounce) can pumpkin pie mix (only 1½ cups needed)
1 (1.9-ounce) box Splenda Granular (only 1 cup needed)
1 (1-pound) box confectioners' sugar (only 1¼ cups needed)
1 teaspoon baking powder
1 (2-pound) bag all-purpose flour (only 2 cups plus 2 tablespoons needed)
1 (8-ounce) can nonfat cooking spray

Seasonings/Condiments
1 (8-ounce) bottle reduced-fat red wine vinaigrette salad dressing (only ¼ cup needed)
2½ teaspoons lemon pepper seasoning
¼ teaspoon celery salt
1½ teaspoons dried rosemary
1 teaspoon garlic salt
¼ teaspoon dried sage
½ teaspoon paprika
½ teaspoon ground allspice
Dash of cinnamon, optional
1 (2.5-ounce) jar imitation butter-flavored sprinkles (only 7½ tablespoons needed)

1 (1-ounce) jar vanilla extract (only
    1 teaspoon needed)
1 (1-ounce) jar almond or vanilla
    extract (only 1¼ teaspoons
    needed)
6 drops liquid food coloring, optional

Other
6 large rye Kaiser rolls, optional

Yuletide Pork Roast with Lemon Pepper & Rosemary

The savory blend of spices will leave everyone asking for more.

2	teaspoons lemon pepper seasoning	1	teaspoon dried rosemary
½	teaspoon ground allspice	2	pounds pork tenderloin, all visible fat removed
2	tablespoons imitation butter-flavored sprinkles	½	teaspoon paprika
¼	teaspoon celery salt		

- Spray the inside of a slow cooker with nonfat cooking spray.
- In a small mixing bowl combine the lemon pepper, allspice, butter-flavored sprinkles, celery salt, and rosemary.
- Place the pork tenderloin in the slow cooker and rub the spice mixture all over the pork.
- Sprinkle the paprika over the top.
- Cover and cook on high for 3 hours or on low for 6 hours.
- When the pork roast has finished cooking, remove it with tongs and slice into eight equal servings. Pour some of the juice over each serving.

Yield: 8 servings

Calories: 141 (26%fat); Total Fat: 4g; Cholesterol: 74mg; Carbohydrate: 2g; Dietary Fiber: 0g; Protein: 24g; Sodium: 258mg; Diabetic Exchanges: 3 lean meat

Preparation time: 5 minutes
Cooking time: 3 hours on high or 6 hours on low
Total time: 3 hours 5 minutes or 6 hours 5 minutes

🍲 Cream of Spinach Soup

This smooth, creamy, and rich soup is liked even by people in our family who don't like spinach. I made this the night we were decorating with Christmas lights outside, and it felt so soothing warming up at dinner with a hot bowl of this. There wasn't a single drop left over.

2	(5.2-ounce) boxes low-fat, fully cooked breakfast sausage links, cut into very thin slices vertically	I	cup frozen chopped onion (fresh is fine too)
I	(27-ounce) can spinach, not drained	2¹/₂	tablespoons imitation butter-flavored sprinkles (found in spice aisle)
I	(10³/₄-ounce) can 98% fat-free cream of celery soup (Do not make as directed.)	¹/₂	teaspoon lemon pepper
I	cup fat-free, liquid nondairy creamer	6	large rye Kaiser rolls (optional)

- Spray a slow cooker with nonfat cooking spray.
- Gently stir together the sausage, spinach, soup, creamer, onion, butter-flavored sprinkles, and lemon pepper until all of the ingredients are well mixed.
- Cover and cook for 3 hours on high.
- If desired, hollow out 6 large rye Kaiser rolls and ladle the soup into the bread bowls.

Yield: 7 (1-cup) servings

(Nutritional information does not include roll)
Calories: 168 (14% fat); Total Fat: 2g; Cholesterol: 23mg; Carbohydrate: 22g; Dietary Fiber: 2g; Protein: 10g; Sodium: 1054mg; Diabetic Exchanges: 1 lean meat, 1¹/₂ vegetable, 1 other carbohydrate

🕐 **Preparation time:** 5 minutes or less
Cooking time: 3 hours
Total time: 3 hours 5 minutes or less

Pumpkin Custard

Here's a delicious union of two Christmas favorites: custard and pumpkin pie.

1¹/2 cups pumpkin pie mix, includes spices	1 teaspoon vanilla extract
¹/2 cup Splenda Granular	³/4 cup liquid egg substitute
1 cup fat-free half-and-half	Ground cinnamon

- Preheat the oven to 325 degrees.
- Fill a roasting pan with ¹/2 inch very hot water and place it in the oven.
- In a mixing bowl whisk together the pumpkin pie mix, Splenda, half-and-half, vanilla, and egg substitute until well blended.
- Pour the mixture evenly into seven ramekins (small, 5-ounce porcelain cups).
- Place the ramekins in the water in the roasting pan.
- Sprinkle the top of each with a dash of cinnamon.
- Bake for 25 minutes or until the centers are almost set but not fully. You want the center to be a tad bit wobbly.
- Remove from the oven, let rest a few minutes, and then place in the refrigerator. As it cools the custard will set more.
- Serve chilled.

Note: Custards are thickened with eggs, whereas puddings are thickened with flour or cornstarch.

Yield: 7 (5-ounce porcelain cup) servings

Calories: 103 (0% fat); Total Fat: 0g; Cholesterol: 0mg; Carbohydrate: 20g; Dietary Fiber: 1g; Protein: 6g; Sodium: 163mg; Diabetic Exchanges: 1¹/2 other carbohydrate

Preparation time: 5 minutes
Baking time: 25 minutes
Total time: 30 minutes or less

Savory Rice Stuffing

The savory blend of rosemary and sage enhances this brown rice stuffing.

3¹/4 cups water	¹/4 teaspoon dried sage
2 tablespoons imitation butter-flavored sprinkles	2 cups instant brown rice
¹/2 teaspoon dried rosemary	1 (6-ounce) box chicken-flavored stuffing mix

- In a medium-size saucepan place the water, butter-flavored sprinkles, and the seasonings and bring to a boil over high heat.
- Add the rice and let the rice come to a boil.
- Reduce the heat to low, cover, and simmer 5 minutes.
- Remove from the heat and stir in the stuffing mix.
- Let the mix sit for 5 minutes and then fluff with a fork.

Yield: 9 (½-cup) servings

Calories: 151 (9% fat); Total Fat: 1g; Cholesterol: 1mg; Carbohydrate: 30g; Dietary Fiber: 1g; Protein: 4g; Sodium: 376mg; Diabetic Exchanges: 2 starch

Preparation time: 5 minutes
Cooking time: 10 minutes
Total time: 15 minutes

♥♥ Cut-Out Glazed Sugar Cookies

These cookies are wonderful to serve within hours of baking. Fat-free or reduced-fat cookies taste great when they are freshly baked. Do not bake them a day or two in advance because they will lose their delicious flavor and texture.

Cookie Recipe	2	cups plus 2 tablespoons all-purpose flour
$^1/_2$ cup reduced-fat margarine (I stick)		
$^1/_2$ teaspoon almond or vanilla extract	Cookie Glaze Recipe	
$^1/_2$ cup confectioners' sugar	$^3/_4$	cup confectioners' sugar
$^1/_2$ cup Splenda Granular	$^3/_4$	teaspoon almond or vanilla extract
2 egg whites	2	tablespoons warm water
I teaspoon baking powder	6	drops food coloring (optional)

- For the cookie recipe, preheat the oven to 350 degrees.
- With an electric mixer beat together the margarine, almond or vanilla extract, confectioners' sugar, Splenda, and egg whites until well blended.
- With a spatula stir in the baking powder and flour until well mixed.
- Transfer the dough to a lightly floured surface and knead a few times until there are no more lumps.
- Roll the dough on the lightly floured surface with a rolling pin until it is $^1/_8$ inch thick.
- Dip a cookie cutter into excess flour and then press the cookie cutter firmly into the rolled-out dough, putting the shapes close together. Transfer the cut-out shapes of cookie dough to the cookie sheets. Knead the scraps of dough and re-roll with a rolling pin. Cut out more cookies and place them on a cookie sheet as above. Discard any remaining scraps.
- Bake for 6 minutes.
- While the cookies are baking, make the cookie glaze recipe. In a small bowl stir together with a fork the confectioners' sugar, extract, water, and food coloring.
- With a pancake turner remove the baked cookies from the cookie sheet and place them on aluminum foil.
- With a clean, small pastry brush, paint brush, or butter knife, spread the glaze over the warm cookies fresh from the oven.

Note: If your cookies are stored in a sealed container or covered with plastic wrap, this glaze becomes runny and can make your cookies soggy.

Yield: 24 (1-cookie) servings

Preparation time: 24 minutes
Baking time: 6 minutes
Total time: 30 minutes

Breakaway Broccoli

Just as children with great anticipation break away bows and wrappings from Christmas packages to get to their gift, dinner guests often break into this dish and start nibbling away before dinner is ready to begin.

1 teaspoon garlic salt	1/4 cup fat-free feta cheese crumbles
7 cups fresh broccoli florets	1/4 cup reduced-fat red wine vinaigrette
1 small white onion, sliced and rings separated	

- Put 1 inch of water into a large saucepan or Dutch oven along with the garlic salt. (If you have one, use a vegetable steamer basket in the bottom of the pan.)
- Add the broccoli to the water. Bring the water to a full boil over high heat. Once at a full boil cover and cook for 5 minutes.
- Add the onion rings and cover. Turn off the heat. Let the onions and broccoli steam for 7 minutes or until the onion rings are tender.
- Drain the water and put the vegetables in a serving bowl.
- Gently toss the cooked vegetables with the feta cheese and salad dressing.

Yield: 6 (½-cup) servings

Preparation time: 10 minutes or less
Cooking time: 12 minutes
Total time: 22 minutes or less

Homey Ham Dinner

Serves 6

Tossed Salad with Smooth Cranberry Salad Dressing (page 161)
Christmas Skillet Ham Steaks (page 164)
Sweet Potatoes with Caramelized Onions (page 163)
Onion Muffin Tops (page 162)
Gingerbread & Eggnog Dessert Cups (page 160)

Centerpiece

Fill a Christmas tin, loaf pan, or Bundt cake pan with florist foam. Press tall tapered candles that match the color theme of your table into the foam. Cut fresh pieces from your Christmas tree or use artificial greenery along with Christmas tree ornaments to decorate and cover the florist foam. Light the candles before dinner.

Supplies

Eight dessert cups	Christmas tin, loaf pan, or Bundt pan
Florist foam	Electric mixer
Tall tapered candles	Christmas tree ornaments

Timeline

1. Make your centerpiece.
2. Set your table. (Better yet, have your spouse or children help do it.)
3. One and a half hours before serving time, make the Gingerbread and Eggnog Dessert Cups and put them in the refrigerator until you are ready to serve dessert.
4. One and a quarter hours before serving time, make the Tossed Salad with Smooth Cranberry Salad Dressing. Do not add the salad dressing until serving time. Cover the salad and the dressing and place in the refrigerator until serving time.
5. One hour before serving time, make the Onion Muffin Tops.
6. Fifty minutes before serving time, put the Onion Tops in the oven.
7. While the muffins are baking, start the Sweet Potatoes with Caramelized Onions.
8. When the muffins are finished, place them in a basket lined with a pretty napkin. Place the basket of muffins on your table.

9. Twenty-five minutes before serving time, start the ham steaks.
10. Cover the ham steaks and keep them warm while you finish the sweet potatoes.

Last 15 minutes:
11. Put the dressing and almonds on the salads and place the salads on the table.
12. Bring the ham steaks and sweet potatoes to the table. Make sure your candles are lit.
13. When everyone has finished, clear away the dinner plates and serve the Gingerbread and Eggnog Dessert Cups.

Grocery List

Frozen Foods
1 (2-quart) container sugar-free, low-fat frozen vanilla yogurt (only 4 cups needed)
1 (10-ounce) bag frozen chopped onion; fresh is okay too (1 cup needed)

Fresh Fruits and Vegetables
2 (11-ounce) bags spring mix salad greens
2 small onions (in addition to the 1 cup frozen)
3 medium sweet potatoes (3 cups needed)
1 green apple

Staple Items
1 (1-pound) box gingersnap cookies (only 21 cookies needed)
1 (8-ounce) can jellied cranberry sauce (only 2/3 cup needed)
1 (23-ounce) jar no-sugar-added applesauce (only 1/4 cup needed)
1 (8-ounce) can crushed pineapple

Meats
6 (3-ounce) extra-lean, smoked, boneless ham steaks, fully cooked

Dairy
1 (2-quart) container fat-free, low-carb milk (only 2 1/2 cups needed)
1 (16-ounce) container fat-free sour cream (only 2/3 cup needed)
2 eggs (or 1/4 cup liquid egg substitute)
1 pound light butter (only 1 tablespoon needed)

Baking Items
1 (1.5-ounce) package fat-free, sugar-free vanilla instant pudding mix
1 (1.9-ounce) box Splenda Granular (only 2 tablespoons needed)
1 (2.25-ounce) bag sliced almonds, toasted (only 2 tablespoons needed)
1 (40-ounce) box reduced-fat, all-purpose baking mix (only 2 cups needed)
1 pound dark brown sugar (only 3/4 cup plus 1 tablespoon needed)
1 (20-ounce) can light cherry pie filling
1 (8-ounce) can nonfat cooking spray
1 (6-ounce) bag dried cranberries, optional (only 1/4 cup needed)

Seasonings/Condiments
1 (8-ounce) jar prepared horseradish
  (only 2 teaspoons needed)
1 tablespoon minced dried onion
  (or Mrs. Dash Minced Onion
  Medley)
1 (2.5-ounce) jar imitation butter-
  flavored sprinkles, such as Butter
  Buds (only 2 tablespoons
  needed)

½ teaspoon ground allspice

Other
1 tablespoon lemon juice

👫 Gingerbread & Eggnog Custard Dessert Cups

Okay, so I cheated a bit by using store-bought gingersnap cookies. This dessert is super rich and thick. Here's an interesting tidbit: Eggnog came from England, and the word nog *is an English term for ale.*

4	cups sugar-free, low-fat vanilla frozen yogurt	I	(1.5 ounce package) fat-free, sugar-free vanilla instant pudding mix
³/4	cup fat-free, low-carb milk	21	gingersnaps, crushed (set aside ¹/4 cup)

- In a large mixing bowl with an electric mixer combine the frozen yogurt, milk, and pudding mix until creamy.
- Stir in the gingersnap crumbs.
- Spoon into eight dessert cups, and sprinkle with the remaining gingersnap crumbs, evenly dividing the crumbs among each serving.

Yield: 8 (½-cup) servings

Calories: 160 (11% fat); Total Fat: 2g; Cholesterol: 3mg; Carbohydrate: 29g; Dietary Fiber: 0g; Protein: 6g; Sodium: 424mg; Diabetic Exchanges: 1 skim milk, 1 other carbohydrate

🕐 **Preparation time:** 10 minutes or less
  Total time: 10 minutes or less

Tossed Salad with Smooth Cranberry Salad Dressing

The unique ingredient combination of this flavorsome salad dressing is very smooth. Most people don't realize I use canned cranberry sauce.

2 (11-ounce) bags spring mix salad greens, about 7 cups firmly packed	2 teaspoons prepared horseradish
2/3 cup jellied cranberry sauce	2 tablespoons Splenda Granular
2/3 cup fat-free, low-carb milk	2 tablespoons toasted sliced almonds
2/3 cup fat-free sour cream	1/4 cup dried cranberries (optional)

- Divide the lettuce evenly among six salad plates.
- Put the jellied cranberry sauce in a small microwave-safe dish and microwave for 30 seconds.
- To the cranberry sauce add the milk, sour cream, horseradish, and Splenda. Stir until well mixed.
- Pour the salad dressing evenly over each plate of lettuce only immediately before you are ready to eat. Otherwise the salad will get soggy and wilted.
- Sprinkle with the toasted almonds and, if desired, top with cranberries.

Yield: 6 servings

(Nutritional information does not include cranberries)
Calories: 115 (10% fat); Total Fat: 1g; Cholesterol: 5mg; Carbohydrate: 21g; Dietary Fiber: 3g; Protein: 5g; Sodium: 84mg; Diabetic Exchanges: 1 vegetable, 1 other carbohydrate

Preparation time: 5 minutes or less
Cooking time: 1 minute
Total time: 6 minutes or less

⊟ Onion Muffin Tops

The enticing aroma of these fragrant muffins lures everyone into the kitchen even before the muffins are done baking. They appear as if they came from a professional bakery with the pretty browned onions baked on top.

1	small onion, thinly sliced, not frozen (about $3/4$ cup)	1	tablespoon lemon juice
2	egg whites (or $1/4$ cup liquid egg substitute)	2	cups reduced-fat, all-purpose baking mix*
1	cup minus 1 tablespoon fat-free, low-carb milk	$1/4$	cup no-sugar-added applesauce
		1	tablespoon minced dried onion (or Mrs. Dash Minced Onion Medley)

- Preheat the oven to 400 degrees.
- Spray twenty cups of two muffin pans with nonfat cooking spray.
- Separate the onion rings and place in small nonstick skillet that has been sprayed with nonfat cooking spray. Cook on high heat for about a minute or two, just enough time to sear the onions until lightly browned, stirring occasionally. Remove from the heat.
- In a medium-size mixing bowl combine the egg whites, milk, lemon juice, baking mix, applesauce, and dried onion. Use a spatula and stir the ingredients until blended. The batter will be lumpy.
- Put $1/8$ cup (or 2 tablespoons) batter in each prepared muffin tin cup.
- Place several cooked onion rings on top of each muffin.
- Bake for 12 minutes.

*Note: I used reduced-fat Bisquick.

Yield: 10 (2-muffin top) servings

Calories: 110 (13% fat); Total Fat: 2g; Cholesterol: 1mg; Carbohydrate: 20g; Dietary Fiber: 1g; Protein: 4g; Sodium: 310mg; Diabetic Exchanges: $1\frac{1}{2}$ starch

⊥ **Preparation time:** 10 minutes
Baking time: 12 minutes
Total time: 22 minutes or less

Sweet Potatoes with Caramelized Onions

I love the crunchiness of the onion with the sweetness of the potatoes.

1 pound sweet potatoes, peeled, sliced 1/4 inch thick and quartered	1/4 cup dark brown sugar, firmly packed
1 tablespoon light butter	2 tablespoons imitation butter-flavored sprinkles
1 onion, thinly sliced and separated into rings	

- Fill a large saucepan or Dutch oven with about 5 cups of water and bring to a boil.
- Add the potatoes to the water and let it come to a boil again. Cover the pan and turn off the heat. Let the potatoes continue to cook for 7 to 10 minutes.
- Place the butter into a large skillet over medium-high heat. When the butter is melted, add the onion rings. Cook, stirring frequently, until the onions are lightly browned.
- When the potatoes are tender, drain and place them in a serving bowl. Add the brown sugar, butter-flavored sprinkles, and onions and stir gently.
- Immediately soak the skillet in hot water to make it easier to clean.

Yield: 6 (1/2-cup) servings

Calories: 115 (8% fat); Total Fat: 1g; Cholesterol: 3mg; Carbohydrate: 27g; Dietary Fiber: 3g; Protein: 2g; Sodium: 173mg; Diabetic Exchanges: 1 starch, 1 other carbohydrate

Preparation time: 10 minutes
Cooking time: 7 to 10 minutes
Total time: 20 minutes or less

Christmas Skillet Ham Steaks

This is a wonderful idea to use if you are having a dinner party and you are short on time. This recipe is very fast. It could not make a prettier presentation.

6	(3-ounce) extra-lean, smoked, boneless ham steaks, fully cooked	I	(8-ounce) can crushed pineapple, drained
I	(20-ounce) can light cherry pie filling	1/2	teaspoon allspice
I	cup frozen chopped onion (Fresh is okay too.)	I	green apple cored, peeled, and cut into 1/4-inch slices
		I	tablespoon firmly packed dark brown sugar

- Spray a 12-inch nonstick skillet with nonfat cooking spray.
- Place the ham steaks in the skillet and place on medium-high heat.
- Cook for 2 to 3 minutes and then turn the steaks.
- Spread the pie filling over the ham steaks and then add the onion and pineapple.
- Sprinkle the allspice evenly over all and lay the apple slices on top in a pretty pattern. Sprinkle the brown sugar over all.
- Cover and let cook for 5 minutes or until completely heated.

Yield: 6 servings

Calories: 186 (18% fat); Total Fat: 4g; Cholesterol: 38mg; Carbohydrate: 20g; Dietary Fiber: 2g; Protein: 17g; Sodium: 1096mg; Diabetic Exchanges: 3 lean meat, 1 fruit, 1/2 other carbohydrate

Preparation time: 5 minutes
Cooking time: 7 to 8 minutes
Total time: 13 minutes or less

Southern Country Ham Dinner

Serves 8

Mini Ham with Sweet Sauce (page 167)
Holiday Turnip Greens with Potatoes (page 171)
Cranberry-Apple Warm, Sweet & Spicy Chutney (page 170)
Sweet Potato Mini Muffins (page 169)
Peachy Pumpkin Dish (page 172)
Old-Fashioned Bread Pudding (page 168)

Edible Centerpiece

For an edible centerpiece place the Sweet Potato Mini Muffins in a pretty basket lined with a cloth napkin that matches the colors of the table settings. Place a color-coordinating bow on the handle of the basket. For extra dimension and appeal, place another cloth napkin on a cake plate. Place the pretty basket filled with warm muffins on top of the cloth-covered cake plate.

Supplies

2 slow cookers   Electric mixer
2 mini muffin pans   A bread basket

Timeline

1. Set the table.
2. Three hours and 15 minutes before serving time, start the Mini Ham.
3. As soon as the ham is cooking, start the Old-Fashioned Bread Pudding.
4. Make the cream sauce that goes on the bread pudding, cover, and refrigerate.
5. About 45 minutes before serving time, make the Sweet Potato Mini Muffins.
6. While the muffins are baking, make the Cranberry-Apple Warm, Sweet & Spicy Chutney and keep warm until serving time by letting it stay in the pan. Simply remove the pan from the heat and cover. If desired, wrap the entire pan with a large towel to help it retain heat.
7. Take the muffins out of the oven and make your centerpiece.
8. Twenty-five minutes before mealtime, prepare the turnip greens and keep warm.

Last 15 minutes:
9. While the turnip greens are cooking, make the Peachy Pumpkin Dish.

10. Remove the ham from the slow cooker, slice it, and pour the sauce over the ham slices.
11. Take all the hot food to the table.
12. When everyone has finished eating, clear away the dishes and serve the Old-Fashioned Bread Pudding with cream sauce over the top.

Grocery List

Fresh Fruits and Vegetables
3 Granny Smith apples
3 Red Delicious apples

Staple Items
1 (16-ounce) loaf light whole-grain sliced bread
1 (8-ounce) can pineapple slices (only 5 slices needed)
1 (23-ounce) jar cinnamon applesauce (2¼ cups needed)
2 (15-ounce) cans sweet potatoes (1½ cups needed)
2 (14-ounce) cans chopped turnip greens
1 (14.5-ounce) can diced tomatoes
1 (15-ounce) can sliced potatoes
2 (29-ounce) cans yellow-cling peaches in light syrup

Meats
1 (2-pound) 96% fat-free mini ham
1 pound extra-lean honey ham lunch meat

Dairy
3 (8-ounce) cartons liquid egg substitute
4 (1-pint) containers, fat-free half-and-half (6½ cups needed)

Baking Items
1 pound dark brown sugar (only ½ cup needed)
3 (1.9-ounce) boxes Splenda Granular (only 4¾ cups needed)

1 (5-pound) bag whole wheat flour (only 3 cups needed)
2 teaspoons baking soda
1 (6-ounce) bag dried cranberries (only ¼ cup needed)
1 (12-ounce) package raisins (only 1 cup needed)
1 (1-ounce) box fat-free, sugar-free instant vanilla pudding mix
1 (15-ounce) can pure pumpkin (not with spices already in it)
1 (8-ounce) can nonfat cooking spray

Seasonings/Condiments
1 teaspoon ground allspice
1 (0.6-ounce) container ground cinnamon (4¾ teaspoons needed)
1½ teaspoons vanilla extract
½ teaspoon light salt
1 (2.5-ounce) bottle imitation butter-flavored sprinkles, such as Butter Buds (only 4½ tablespoons needed)
1 teaspoon lemon pepper
½ teaspoon pumpkin pie spice
¼ teaspoon ground cloves

Other
1 (6-ounce) jar maraschino cherries (only 4 needed)
1 (12-ounce) bottle diet cola (only 1 cup needed)
Toothpicks

🍲 Mini Ham with Sweet Sauce

Everyone loved this ham.

1	(2-pound) 96% fat-free mini ham	1/2	cup dark brown sugar
1	(8-ounce) can pineapple slices	1/4	teaspoon ground cloves
4	red maraschino cherries	1/4	teaspoon ground cinnamon
1	cup diet cola		

- Spray a slow cooker with nonfat cooking spray.
- Secure the pineapple slices to the top and sides of the ham using toothpicks. Secure 1 cherry in the center of each pineapple slice with a toothpick.
- Place the ham in the slow cooker and pour the diet cola over the ham.
- Cover and cook on high for 2 hours.
- After 2 hours, in a small saucepan add the brown sugar, cloves, cinnamon, and juices from the slow cooker.
- Cook and stir until boiling and pour the sauce back into the slow cooker over the ham.
- Cover and cook for 1 more hour.
- Remove the ham from the slow cooker and place on a pretty serving plate. Place the glaze in a small bowl.
- Remove the toothpicks right before you are ready to slice the ham. Pour some of the glaze over each slice of ham.

Yield: 8 (4-ounce) servings

Calories: 184 (20% fat); Total Fat: 4g; Cholesterol: 54mg; Carbohydrate: 19g; Dietary Fiber: 0g; Protein: 19g; Sodium: 1415mg; Diabetic Exchanges: 4 very lean meat, 1 1/2 other carbohydrate

🕐 **Preparation time:** 15 minutes
Cooking time: 3 hours
Total time: 3 hours 15 minutes

🍲 Old-Fashioned Bread Pudding

Not just any run of the mill bread pudding here, folks. It's good to the last bite. I found a few children licking the plate when they were all done because it was so good.

2	(8-ounce) cartons liquid egg substitute	1	(16-ounce) loaf light whole-grain sliced bread, cut into ¹/₂-inch pieces, dry*
2	plus 1 teaspoons ground cinnamon		
4	plus 2¹/₂ cups fat-free half-and-half	1	(1-ounce) box fat-free, sugar-free instant vanilla pudding mix, dry (do not make as directed)
1	cup Splenda Granular		
1	cup raisins		

- Spray a small 3½-quart slow cooker with nonfat cooking spray.
- In a large bowl stir together the egg substitute, 2 teaspoons cinnamon, 4 cups half-and-half, and Splenda together until well mixed.
- Stir in the raisins and bread until the bread is saturated with the mixture.
- Pour into the prepared slow cooker and cover.
- Cook on high for 1 hour.
- Reduce the heat to low and cook another 2 hours or until a thermometer reaches 160 degrees when placed in the center of the bread pudding.
- Beat together the remaining 2½ cups half-and-half and the pudding mix in a medium bowl with a whisk to make a cream sauce; cover and refrigerate. Once the cream sauce is well blended, stir in the remaining 1 teaspoon cinnamon.
- When the bread pudding is fully cooked, serve hot and spoon ¼ cup cream sauce on each serving.
- If desired, heat the cream sauce for 30 to 45 seconds before putting it on top of the pudding.

Note: Leave the bread out overnight to dry, or you can put it in a 200-degree oven for 10 to 15 minutes.

Yield: 12 (½-cup) servings

Calories: 232 (2% fat); Total Fat: 1g; Cholesterol: 0mg; Carbohydrate: 48g; Dietary Fiber: 7g; Protein: 16g; Sodium: 506mg; Diabetic Exchanges: 2 very lean meat, 1 starch, 1 fruit, 1 other carbohydrate

🕐 **Preparation time:** 15 minutes
Cooking time: 3 hours
Total time: 3 hours 15 minutes

☺ Sweet Potato Mini Muffins

Oh, man! These are so good.

1/4 cup cinnamon applesauce	1 teaspoon vanilla extract
1/2 cup liquid egg substitute or 4 egg whites, beaten	1/2 teaspoon light salt
	1 teaspoon ground cinnamon
1 1/2 cups canned sweet potatoes, mashed*	2 cups Homemade Whole Wheat Sweet Baking Mix (page 220)

- Preheat the oven to 350 degrees.
- Spray 1 large or 2 small mini-muffin tins with nonfat cooking spray.
- In a medium bowl with an electric mixer beat together the applesauce, egg substitute, sweet potatoes, vanilla, salt, and cinnamon together until well blended.
- With a spatula stir in the baking mix until all of the ingredients are well mixed.
- Spoon 1 1/2 tablespoons batter into each prepared muffin tin.
- Bake for 15 minutes or until a toothpick inserted in the center of the muffins comes out dry.

Note: You will use most of a 29-ounce can. Simply drain the canned sweet potatoes (also known as yams). Discard the juice. Mash the sweet potatoes with a potato masher or fork and then measure 1 1/2 cups for the recipe.

Yield: 12 (2-mini-muffin) servings

Calories: 90 (3% fat); Total Fat: 0g; Cholesterol: 0mg; Carbohydrate: 19g; Dietary Fiber: 2g; Protein: 3g; Sodium: 201mg; Diabetic Exchanges: 1 1/2 starch

⏱ **Preparation time:** 15 minutes
Baking time: 15 minutes
Total time: 30 minutes

Cranberry-Apple Warm, Sweet & Spicy Chutney

It's sweet; it's tart; it's fantastic.

3	Granny Smith apples, finely chopped, peel on	6	tablespoons Splenda Granular
3	Red Delicious apples, finely chopped, peel on	1	teaspoon allspice
2	cups cinnamon applesauce	$^1/_4$	cup finely chopped dried cranberries

- In a nonstick saucepan cook the apples, applesauce, Splenda, allspice, and dried cranberries over medium-high heat for about 8 minutes.
- Serve warm.

Yield: 12 (½-cup) servings

Calories: 65 (0% fat); Total Fat: 0g; Cholesterol: 0mg; Carbohydrate: 17g; Dietary Fiber: 2g; Protein: 0g; Sodium: 2mg; Diabetic Exchanges: 1 fruit

Preparation time: 10 minutes
Cooking time: 8 minutes
Total time: 18 minutes

☺ Holiday Turnip Greens with Potatoes

This dish is as satisfying as any southern comfort dish can get.

2	(14-ounce) cans chopped turnip greens, drained	I	pound honey ham lunch meat, extra-lean, cut into $^{1}/_{2}$-inch pieces
I	(14.5-ounce) can diced tomatoes, drained	$2^{1}/_{2}$	tablespoons imitation butter-flavored sprinkles
I	(15-ounce) can sliced potatoes, drained	2	teaspoons Splenda Granular
		I	teaspoon lemon pepper

- Over medium heat in a large saucepan cook the turnip greens, tomatoes, potatoes, and ham together until fully heated; this takes about 5 minutes.
- Stir in the imitation butter-flavored sprinkles, Splenda, and lemon pepper.

Yield: 14 ($^{1}/_{2}$-cup) servings

Calories: 70 (18% fat); Total Fat: 1g; Cholesterol: 22mg; Carbohydrate: 8g; Dietary Fiber: 2g; Protein: 8g; Sodium: 671mg; Diabetic Exchanges: 1 very lean meat, $^{1}/_{2}$ starch

Preparation time: 10 minutes or less
Cooking time: 5 minutes
Total time: 15 minutes or less

⛫ Peachy Pumpkin Dish

This is one of those dishes that tastes even better than I'd hoped it would when I began creating it. The pumpkin base is smooth and creamy with full slices of sweet peaches throughout.

2 tablespoons imitation butter-flavored sprinkles	$^1/_2$ teaspoon ground cinnamon
	$^1/_2$ teaspoon pumpkin pie spice
$^1/_2$ teaspoon vanilla extract	2 (29-ounce) cans yellow-cling
$1^1/_4$ cups Splenda Granular	peaches in light syrup, drain and
1 (15-ounce) can pure pumpkin (not with spices already in it)	discard juice

■ In a medium-size nonstick saucepan over medium heat stir together the butter-flavored sprinkles, vanilla, Splenda, pumpkin, cinnamon, pie spice, and peaches until well mixed. Cook until fully heated, 4 to 5 minutes.

■ Put into a serving bowl and serve while nice and hot.

Note: It's also great to serve fat-free dessert whipped topping and crushed reduced-fat vanilla wafers on the side.

Yield: 12 (½-cup) servings

Calories: 93 (0% fat); Total Fat: 0g; Cholesterol: 0mg; Carbohydrate: 23g; Dietary Fiber: 2g; Protein: 1g; Sodium: 70mg; Diabetic Exchanges: 1 fruit, ½ other carbohydrate

⏱ **Preparation time:** 5 minutes
Cooking time: 5 minutes
Total time: 10 minutes

Stuffed Cornish Hens

Serves 6

Stuffed Cornish Hens with Acorn Squash & Apples (page 176)
Cucumber & Beet Salad (page 180)
Cranberry-Nut Bread (page 179)
Cranberry-Cinnamon Tapioca Pudding (page 178)
Guiding Star Cookies (page 175)

Edible Centerpiece

Place the Guiding Star Cookies on any plain, colored wreath, set it on the table, and place a large candle in the center for an edible centerpiece.

Supplies

A plain, colored wreath   Star-shaped 2-inch cookie cutter
Large oblong slow cooker   3 mini loaf pans (disposable foil ones are okay)
Large candle   6 dessert cups
Electric mixer

Timeline

1. Set the table.
2. Five and a half hours before serving time, start the Stuffed Cornish Hens with Acorn Squash and Apples.
3. Make the Guiding Star Cookies. (Cover baked cookies with plastic wrap on plates to prevent them from drying out.)
4. Make your centerpiece, but *do not put cookies on it yet.*
5. One hour before serving time, make the Cranberry-Cinnamon Tapioca Pudding.
6. While the pudding is cooling, make the Cranberry-Nut Bread.
7. Make the Cucumber and Beet Salad. Keep chilled until ready to eat.

Last 15 minutes:

8. Place the Cornish hens on a platter, and place the acorn squash and apples around them. Place the platter on the table.
9. Slice the Cranberry-Nut Bread.
10. Bring all of the food to the table including the Cucumber and Beet Salad and the Cranberry-Cinnamon Tapioca Pudding. Place the Guiding Star Cookies on the wreath.

Grocery List

Fresh Fruits and Vegetables
4 Granny Smith apples
2 large or 3 small acorn squash
1 seedless cucumber
1 bunch of seedless green grapes for garnish, optional

Staple Items
1 (6-ounce) box cornbread stuffing
1 (14.5-ounce) can chicken broth
1 (15-ounce) can sliced beets

Meats
3 Cornish hens (1½ pounds each)

Dairy
1 pint low-carb, fat-free French vanilla liquid creamer (only ½ cup needed)
1 (2-quart) container fat-free, low-carb milk (only 2¾ cups needed)
2 eggs
1 (8-ounce) package liquid egg substitute (or 2 more eggs)

Baking Items
1 (6-ounce) package dried cherries (only ⅓ cup needed)
1 (6-ounce) bag sweetened dried cranberries (only 1¼ cups needed)
1 (2.25-ounce) bag chopped walnuts (only 3 tablespoons needed)
1 (14-ounce) bag shredded coconut (only 2 tablespoons needed)
1 (1.9-ounce) box Splenda Granular (4½ cups needed)
1 (2-pound) bag all-purpose flour (only 3 cups needed)
1 (5-pound) bag whole wheat flour (3 cups needed)
4 teaspoons baking soda

1 pound dark brown sugar (only ½ cup needed)
1 (12-ounce) can red raspberry filling, in the baking aisle (only ¼ cup needed)
1 (8-ounce) box minute tapioca (only 3 tablespoons needed)
1 (8-ounce) can nonfat cooking spray

Seasonings/Condiments
1 teaspoon almond extract
1 (0.6-ounce) container ground cinnamon
¼ cup fat-free mayonnaise
1 (8-ounce) bottle fat-free Italian salad dressing (only ½ cup needed)
Lawry's Seasoned Salt, optional
Paprika, optional

Other
1 (1.8-ounce) box sugar-free, orange-flavored drink mix (only ¾ cup drink needed)

☐ ✦ Guiding Star Cookies

You can be sure the aroma of these cookies baking will guide many wise men (and children) into your kitchen.

2 cups Homemade Sweet Baking Mix (page 220)	$1/4$ cup red raspberry filling (Found in baking aisle in a 12-ounce can)
$1/2$ cup fat-free, low-carb French vanilla liquid creamer	2 tablespoons shredded coconut

- Preheat the oven to 350 degrees.
- Spray two cookie sheets with nonfat cooking spray.
- In a large mixing bowl stir with a spatula the baking mix and creamer until a stiff dough forms. Put the dough on a lightly floured surface and knead a few times until there are no more lumps.
- Roll the dough with a rolling pin until it is $1/8$ inch thick. Dip a 2-inch star-shaped cookie cutter into the excess flour. Then press the cookie cutter firmly into the rolled-out dough, putting the shapes close together. Knead the scraps of leftover cookie dough together briefly and repeat the step.
- Using a pancake turner, place the cut-out stars on the prepared cookie sheets.
- Bake for 5 minutes.
- Remove the baked cookies from the cookie sheet and place on aluminum foil.
- While the cookies are still warm, spread a thin layer of raspberry filling on the tops of all of the cookies.
- Lightly sprinkle the center of each star with shredded coconut.

Note: Do not bake them a day or two in advance because they will lose their delicious flavor and texture.

Yield: 20 cookies

Calories: 46 (0% fat); Total Fat: 0g; Cholesterol: 0mg; Carbohydrate: 10g; Dietary Fiber: 0g; Protein: 1g; Sodium: 65mg; Diabetic Exchanges: $1/2$ starch

Preparation time: 25 minutes or less
Baking time: 5 minutes
Total time: 30 minutes or less

⟨🍲⟩ Stuffed Cornish Hens with Acorn Squash & Apples

I really like the tartness of the Granny Smith apples along with the touch of sweetness in the cherries for the stuffing. The bird is so tender it falls off the bone, and the squash and apples topped lightly with seasoning salt make a wonderful orchard medley.

3 Cornish hens (1½ pounds each)	7 cups acorn squash, peeled, chopped into 1½ to 2-inch pieces (2 large or 3 small squash)
1 (6-ounce) box cornbread stuffing	
⅓ cup dried cherries, finely chopped	
3½ plus 1 cups Granny Smith apples, cored, chopped, not peeled	½ cup dark brown sugar
	Seasoned salt and/or paprika (optional)
1 cup chicken broth	1 bunch green seedless grapes for garnish (optional)

- Spray a large oblong slow cooker with nonfat cooking spray.
- Rinse the Cornish hens in cold water.
- In a large mixing bowl combine the stuffing mix, dried cherries, and 1 cup chopped apple.
- Heat the chicken broth in the microwave for 2 minutes or until hot and pour it over the stuffing mix, stirring until thoroughly mixed.
- Place the stuffing in each rinsed Cornish hen, dividing the stuffing evenly among the hens.
- Put the stuffed hens into the prepared slow cooker.
- Peel and chop the squash and place it in a large mixing bowl. Put the remaining 3½ cups of the chopped apples into the bowl with the squash. Add the brown sugar and stir until well mixed.
- Take two large pieces of foil, fold the long sides together to form one large piece of foil, and spray with nonfat cooking spray.
- Transfer the squash and apples to the foil. Fold the foil over the pile of squash and apples and roll the edges to seal the packet.
- Place the packet of squash and apples into the slow cooker on top of the hens.
- Cover the slow cooker and cook on high for 4½ to 5 hours.
- When the hens are completely cooked through, remove the foil. Using tongs, remove the hens from the slow cooker and place in a 9 x 13-inch glass baking dish or on a platter. Cut each Cornish hen in half using a sharp knife or kitchen scissors. Surround the hens with the squash and apple

mixture. Sprinkle the paprika over the Cornish hens for a great presentation.

■ Sprinkle seasoned salt over the tops of the Cornish hens and the squash and apple mixture and garnish with the grapes, if desired.

Note: For a crispy, golden brown skin, put the hens in a 9 x 13-inch casserole dish and bake them in the oven at 500 degrees for 5 to 10 minutes.

Yield: 6 servings (½ stuffed Cornish hen, 1 cup squash and apple mixture)

(Nutrition information without skin)
Calories: 505 (11% fat); Total Fat: 6g; Cholesterol: 133mg; Carbohydrate: 78g; Dietary Fiber: 10g; Protein: 35g; Sodium: 693mg; Diabetic Exchanges: 4 lean meat, 3 starch, 1 fruit, 1 other carbohydrate

Preparation time: 25 minutes
Cooking Time: 4½ to 5 hours
Total time: 5 to 5½ hours

Cranberry-Cinnamon Tapioca Pudding

Here's an old-fashioned, home-style favorite with a snappy holiday twist, made quickly and easily the way today's busy cooks need and want. Here's an interesting tidbit: Cinnamon is the bark from a tree in the cinnamon family.

1/3 cup Splenda Granular	2/3 cup plus 1 tablespoon finely chopped sweetened dried cranberries
3 tablespoons minute tapioca	
2 3/4 cups fat-free, low-carb milk	1 teaspoon almond extract
2 egg whites, beaten	Ground cinnamon

- In a medium-size nonstick saucepan stir together the Splenda, tapioca, milk, and egg whites until well mixed. Let the mixture sit for 5 minutes.
- Place on medium heat and, stirring constantly, cook until the mixture comes to a full rolling boil.
- Remove from the heat and stir in 2/3 cup cranberries and the almond extract.
- Let cool 10 minutes.
- Put 1/2 cup pudding into individual dessert cups or tall, stemmed glasses.
- Lightly sprinkle the tops with a dash of the cinnamon and the remaining 1 tablespoon cranberries.
- Serve warm or chilled. I like it best chilled because it's thicker; however, my assistants like it warm.

Yield: 6 (1/2-cup) servings

Calories: 112 (0% fat); Total Fat: 0g; Cholesterol: 2mg; Carbohydrate: 20g; Dietary Fiber: 1g; Protein: 7g; Sodium: 115mg; Diabetic Exchanges: 1 very lean meat, 1 1/2 other carbohydrate

Preparation time: 5 minutes
Cooking and cooling time: 20 minutes
Total time: 25 minutes

🍲 Cranberry-Nut Bread

I like how the whole wheat in this recipe makes this fruit bread taste a lot nuttier and the texture heavier than if I were to use white flour.

1/4	cup fat-free mayonnaise	1/2	cup finely chopped sweetened dried cranberries
1/4	cup liquid egg substitute or 2 egg whites, beaten	2	cups Homemade Whole Wheat Sweet Baking Mix (page 220)
3/4	cup sugar-free, orange-flavored drink	3	tablespoons finely chopped walnuts

- Preheat the oven to 350 degrees.
- Spray three mini loaf pans with nonfat cooking spray.
- In a medium bowl with an electric mixer beat together the mayonnaise, egg, orange drink, and cranberries until well blended.
- With a spatula stir in the baking mix until all of the ingredients are mixed.
- Pour the batter into the prepared pans. Sprinkle the top of each loaf with 1 tablespoon finely chopped walnuts.
- Bake for 15 to 20 minutes or until a toothpick inserted in the center comes out clean.

Yield: 3 mini loaves or 12 (2-slice) servings

Calories: 90 (15%); Total Fat: 2g; Cholesterol: 1mg; Carbohydrate: 18g; Dietary Fiber: 2g; Protein: 3g; Sodium: 145mg; Diabetic Exchanges: 1 starch

🕐 **Preparation time:** 10 minutes
Baking time: 15 to 20 minutes
Total time: 30 minutes or less

⌂ Cucumber & Beet Salad

These colors are gorgeous together for Christmas.

I (15-ounce) can beets, sliced, drained and ½ cup liquid reserved	I teaspoon Splenda Granular
½ cup fat-free Italian salad dressing	I seedless cucumber, sliced (about 3 cups)*

- In a pretty serving bowl stir together the reserved beet juice, salad dressing, and Splenda.
- Gently toss the cucumber slices and beets with the dressing.
- Cover and keep chilled until ready to eat.

Note: To make these prettier, do not peel the cucumbers. Instead, run the tines of a fork down the sides of the cucumber skin to give it a lovely frilled edge before cutting it into slices.

Yield: 8 (½-cup) servings

Calories: 31 (0% fat); Total Fat: 0g; Cholesterol: 0mg; Carbohydrate: 7g; Dietary Fiber: 1g; Protein: 1g; Sodium: 305mg; Diabetic Exchanges: 1½ vegetable

(⌐) **Total preparation time:** 15 minutes

Turkey Buffet

Serves 14

Turkey Breast with Cloves & Warm Fruit Chutney **(page 184)**
Green Beans & Potato Casserole **(page 186)**
Sausage Stuffing **(page 190)**
Punch Bowl Christmas Salad **(page 188)**
Cran-Nutty Mini Biscuits **(page 189)**
Pumpkin Trifle **(page 187)**

Edible Centerpiece

Place an eight-inch red candle in the center of the Pumpkin Trifle. Place silk poinsettia blossoms around the base of the trifle bowl and around the candle as well. Light the candle for dinner; however, remove the candle and poinsettia blossoms before serving the trifle. (See photo on page 187.)

Supplies

2 punch bowls	A candle
Trifle bowl	Silk poinsettia blossoms
2 large slow cookers	
Christmas tree cake mold (if you want to shape the stuffing)	

Timeline

1. Six hours before serving time, start the Turkey Breast with Cloves and Warm Fruit Chutney.
2. Put the plates, silverware, and napkins on the buffet table. You will be using the Pumpkin Trifle as a centerpiece so leave a space in the middle of the table for it.
3. Four and a half hours before serving time, start the Green Beans and Potato Casserole.
4. One and a quarter hours before serving time, prepare the Pumpkin Trifle, cover, and place it in the refrigerator until serving time.
5. Prepare two of the Punch Bowl Christmas Salads. Do not put any dressing on them. Cover the salads and place them in the refrigerator until serving time.
6. Thirty-five minutes before serving time, make the Cran-Nutty Mini Biscuits. Bake later.

Last 15 minutes:
7. Preheat the oven.
8. Prepare the Sausage Stuffing.

Last 8 minutes:
9. Put the biscuits in the oven to bake.
10. Put the trifle in the middle of the buffet table, add a candle and poinsettia blossoms, and light the candle.
11. Remove the turkey from the slow cooker and place it on a serving tray.
12. Put the Green Beans and Potato Casserole into a serving bowl.
13. Take all of the food to the table. Don't forget to get a salad and the dressing out of the refrigerator. You can put both of the salads out, or you can put one out and get the other one out when the first one is empty.
14. When ready for dessert remove the candle and poinsettia blossoms before serving the Pumpkin Trifle.

Grocery List

Frozen Foods
2 (1-pound) bags frozen green beans
1 (8-ounce) container fat-free dessert whipped topping (only half of an 8-ounce container needed)
1 (10-ounce) bag frozen, or fresh, chopped onion (only 1 cup needed)

Fresh Fruits and Vegetables
1 pound red grapes
4 (11-ounce) bags spring mix salad greens
15 cherry tomatoes for garnishing Christmas tree-shaped stuffing, optional
Fresh parsley for garnishing Christmas tree-shaped stuffing, optional

Staple Items
1 (16-ounce) can whole cranberry sauce
1 (30-ounce) can pineapple tidbits
2 (7-ounce) cans mushroom pieces
2 (12-ounce) jars fat-free chicken gravy
2 (14-ounce) cans wax beans
3 (15-ounce) cans white potatoes, sliced
2 (6-ounce) boxes cornbread stuffing mix

Meats
4½ pounds fully cooked deli-style turkey breast, mesquite flavored
1 pound low-fat turkey sausage

Dairy
1 (8-ounce) package fat-free cream cheese

1 (2-quart) container fat-free, low-carb milk (only 2 cups needed)

1 (4-ounce) container fat-free feta cheese crumbles (only ½ cup needed)

4 eggs or 4 ounces liquid egg substitute

1 slice cheese for the star if making Christmas tree-shaped stuffing, optional

Baking Items

1 (30-ounce) can pumpkin pie mix, includes spices (only 2 cups needed)

1 (2.25-ounce) chopped walnuts (only 3 tablespoons needed)

2 (1.7-ounce) packages sugar-free, fat-free instant vanilla pudding mix

3 (14.5-ounce) cans tart red cherries in water

1 (6-ounce) bag dried cranberries (only ¾ cup needed)

1 (2.25-ounce) bag toasted sliced almonds

1 (1-ounce) bottle almond extract (only 1 teaspoon needed)

1 (5-pound) bag whole wheat flour (only 3 cups needed)

1 (1.9-ounce) box Splenda Granular

2 teaspoons baking soda

1 (8-ounce) can nonfat cooking spray

Seasonings/Condiments

1 (1.5-ounce) container whole cloves

1½ teaspoons ground allspice

1 (2.5-ounce) bottle imitation butter-flavored sprinkles, such as Butter Buds

¼ cup fat-free mayonnaise

1 (16-ounce) bottle of your favorite salad dressing

Other

1 (10-ounce) angel food cake

3 (3-ounce) jars 30% less-fat real bacon pieces

🐹 🍲 Turkey Breast with Cloves & Warm Fruit Chutney

If you like spiced ham, you will love this turkey. This has a very Christmasy flavor.

1 (4½-pound) fully cooked deli-style turkey breast, mesquite flavored*	1 (14.5-ounce) can red tart cherries in water, drained
⅓ (1½-ounce) container whole cloves	1 (30-ounce) can pineapple tidbits, drained
1 (16-ounce) can whole berry cranberry sauce	1½ teaspoons ground allspice

- Spray a large oblong slow cooker with nonfat cooking spray.
- Press cloves about 1 inch apart covering the entire turkey breast, except the bottom, or if using half of a larger breast, don't put cloves on the cut side.
- Place clove-studded turkey breast in the slow cooker.
- In a large bowl stir together cranberry sauce, cherries, pineapple, and allspice with a spatula until well mixed.
- With your hands press the fruit mixture onto the turkey so that it is completely covered. Some fruit will fall off and that's okay.
- Cover and cook on low for 5½ hours.
- Remove the turkey with tongs and place in either a 9 x 13-inch glass casserole dish or a platter.
- Spoon the fruit chutney out with a slotted spoon and place around the turkey.
- Pour the juice into a gravy boat or bowl with a ladle.
- Let the turkey breast sit for a few minutes before serving. For a dramatic and pretty serving presentation, serve with the cloves still in the turkey. However, please inform guests to remove the cloves before eating.
- If desired, decorate the serving platter with a sprig of fresh rosemary on each of the corners of the platter or a green silk Christmas decoration.

Note: I use a 9-pound breast from Sam's Club. I cut it in half, placing the cut side in the slow cooker, and save the remaining half for later.

Yield: 14 (approximately 4-ounce cooked) servings

Calories: 236 (5% fat); Total Fat: 1g; Cholesterol: 52mg; Carbohydrate: 24g; Dietary Fiber: 1g; Protein: 31g; Sodium: 1472mg; Diabetic Exchanges: 4 very lean meat, 1 fruit, ½ other carbohydrate

Preparation time: 15 minutes
Cooking time: 5½ hours
Total time: 5 hours 45 minutes

❄ ❄ ❄

Missing Christmas Cookies

Mom was an excellent planner. She would begin her Christmas baking in November. She would bake and decorate dozens of frosted sugar cookies, put them on plates (six to a plate) in plastic bags, and store them in the freezer in our garage until Christmastime. The week before Christmas my mom had me regularly fetch things from the freezer, and each time I went out there the cookies called to me. Rather than just take one cookie off one plate, I thought it would be better to take one from each plate. *Mom won't remember if she put five or six cookies on each plate,* I thought. They were so good with their sweet frosting. Every time Mom would send me to the freezer I was tempted. *Mom will think she only put four cookies on each plate,* I thought the second time. Before I knew it the plates were down to only two cookies each. Christmas Eve arrived and Mom started getting things ready for the evening. "Dawn", my Mother said with her sweet, loving voice. "Honey, do me a favor and go out to the freezer and get those frosted sugar cookies we made together earlier this fall."

"What Christmas cookies, Mom?" I asked, looking up at her with my big, brown, pitiful eyes and my knees trembling.

"The Christmas cookies we made before Thanksgiving. You know the ones."

My lower lip started quivering and big pools of tears flooded my eyes, running down my cheeks. And with that gush of words came a purging of detailed, step-by-step plays of how I unintentionally ate every cookie.

Continued on next page

Continued from previous page

All of my siblings stood there, staring at me, dumbfound and in total disbelief with their mouths wide open and eyes bulging from their heads. I can't remember the punishment I received from my parents. Whatever the punishment, it was nothing compared to the guilt and shame I felt. What I ate the most of wasn't frosted sugar cookies; it was humble pie. Believe me, I never did it again.

 Green Beans & Potato Casserole

This is a southern-inspired dish that's delicious at Christmas.

2 (7-ounce) cans mushroom pieces, drained	3 (15-ounce) cans white potatoes, sliced and drained
2 (12-ounce) jars fat-free chicken gravy	1/2 cup reduced-fat bacon bits
2 (14-ounce) cans wax beans	2 tablespoons imitation butter-flavored sprinkles
2 (1-pound) bags frozen green beans	

- Spray a large slow cooker with nonfat cooking spray.
- Put the mushroom pieces, chicken gravy, wax beans, green beans, potatoes, bacon pieces, and butter-flavored sprinkles into the slow cooker.
- Stir gently, cover, and cook for 4½ hours on low.

Yield: 14 (1-cup) servings

Calories: 107 (9% fat); Total Fat: 1g; Cholesterol: 10mg; Carbohydrate: 20g; Dietary Fiber: 4g; Protein: 6g; Sodium: 864mg; Diabetic Exchanges: 1 starch, 1 vegetable

Preparation time: 5 minutes
Cooking time: 4½ hours
Total time: 4 hours 35 minutes

⏲ Pumpkin Trifle

Pretty layers of pumpkin and cream filling make my mouth water.

1	(10-ounce) angel food cake, cut into bite-size pieces	2	(1.7-ounce) packages sugar-free, fat-free instant vanilla pudding mix
2	cups pumpkin pie mix, includes seasoning	1	(8-ounce) package fat-free cream cheese
4	plus 2 teaspoons finely chopped walnuts	2	cups fat-free, low-carb milk
		4	ounces fat-free dessert whipped topping (half an 8-ounce container)

- Mix the angel food cake, pumpkin pie mix, and 4 teaspoons walnuts in a large bowl.
- In a large mixing bowl stir together the vanilla pudding mix, cream cheese, milk, and dessert whipped topping.
- In a large trifle bowl or large glass bowl put 1⅓ cups of the pudding mixture on the bottom. Then place 1½ cups of pumpkin mixture on top of the cream mixture. Repeat the layers.
- Top with 1⅓ cups of the cream mixture.
- Sprinkle with the remaining 2 teaspoons chopped walnuts.

Yield: 15 (½-cup) servings

Calories: 149 (5% fat); Total Fat: 1g; Cholesterol: 3mg; Carbohydrate: 28g; Dietary Fiber: 1g; Protein: 6g; Sodium: 546mg; Diabetic Exchanges: ½ very lean meat, 2 other carbohydrate

🕐 **Preparation time:** 20 minutes or less

⬡ Punch Bowl Christmas Salad

Because this takes up so much space, I keep my salads cold by storing them covered in our garage to free up room in our refrigerator. Another idea is to store in a large cooler with ice. You will make two of these.

1 cup red grape halves	$^1/_4$ cup fat-free feta cheese crumbles
2 (11-ounce) bags spring mix salad greens or 15 cups firmly packed	$^1/_4$ cup finely chopped dried cranberries
1 (14.5-ounce) can tart red cherries in water, chilled* and drained (found in the baking aisle)	$^1/_4$ cup 30%-less-fat real bacon pieces
	2 tablespoons toasted sliced almonds

- Layer in a large punch bowl starting from the bottom: the red grapes, 8 cups spring mix, cherries, 7 cups spring mix, feta cheese, cranberries, bacon pieces, and almonds.
- Cover and keep chilled until ready to eat. Serve with your favorite salad dressings on the side.

Note: To save time store in the refrigerator when unpacking from the grocery store.

Yield: 8 servings

Calories: 84 (18% fat); Total Fat: 2g; Cholesterol: 5mg; Carbohydrate: 14g; Dietary Fiber: 3g; Protein: 5g; Sodium: 189mg; Diabetic Exchanges: $^1/_2$ lean meat, 1 fruit

 **Preparation time:** 10 minutes

☗ Cran-Nutty Mini Biscuits

The tops of these biscuits look like they are covered in cranberry-colored confetti. The whole wheat helps enhance the nutty flavor and texture.

4 egg whites or ¹/₂ cup liquid egg substitute	¹/₄ cup fat-free mayonnaise
2 cups Homemade Whole Wheat Sweet Baking Mix (page 220)	2 plus 2 tablespoons finely chopped dried cranberries
1 teaspoon almond extract	1 tablespoon finely chopped walnuts

- Preheat the oven to 350 degrees.
- Spray two baking sheets with nonfat cooking spray.
- In a medium mixing bowl stir together the egg whites, sweet baking mix, almond extract, mayonnaise, and 2 tablespoons cranberries.
- Drop by the rounded teaspoonful onto the prepared baking sheets. You can put 15 on each baking sheet. These mini biscuits are small and do not rise much.
- In a small bowl stir together the remaining 2 tablespoons dried cranberries and the walnuts until well mixed.
- With your fingers sprinkle the cranberry/walnut mixture on tops of the biscuits.
- Gently press the cranberries and walnuts into the biscuits to help them adhere.
- Bake for 6 to 7 minutes.

Yield: 15 (2-mini-biscuits) servings

Calories: 60 (9% fat); Total Fat: 1g; Cholesterol: 0mg; Carbohydrate: 12g; Dietary Fiber: 2g; Protein: 3g; Sodium: 122mg; Diabetic Exchanges: 1 starch

⊣ **Preparation time:** 18 minutes or less
Baking time: 6 to 7 minutes
Total time: 25 minutes or less

Sausage Stuffing

1	pound low-fat turkey sausage	4 tablespoons imitation butter-flavored sprinkles
1	cup frozen chopped onion (fresh is fine)	
3	cups water	2 (6-ounce) boxes cornbread stuffing mix

- In a large nonstick skillet cook the sausage over high heat until fully cooked, and then crumble it. Remove the meat from the skillet.
- Do not rinse out the skillet. Cook the onions in the sausage drippings over high heat for about 2 to 3 minutes or until tender. (They will brown a little from the meat juices.)
- Add the water and butter-flavored sprinkles. Bring to a boil.
- Add the stuffing mix and the crumbled, cooked sausage and stir until well mixed. Cover with a lid. Turn heat off. Let rest for 5 minutes before serving.

Note: For a unique serving presentation, press the cooked stuffing into a Christmas tree cake mold that has been sprayed with nonfat cooking spray. Turn the mold onto a serving plate and top with fresh parsley, a piece of sliced cheese cut into a star shape, and five groupings of three small cherry tomatoes.

Yield: 16 (½-cup) servings

Calories: 125 (12% fat); Total Fat: 2g; Cholesterol: 14mg; Carbohydrate: 18g; Dietary Fiber: 1g; Protein: 7g; Sodium: 643mg Diabetic Exchanges: ½ lean meat, 1 starch

Preparation time: 7 minutes
Cooking time: 8 minutes
Total time: 15 minutes

Chapter Four

Kids' Birthday Party for Jesus
Ages 3 to 10

A n easy rule of thumb when it comes to figuring out how many children one parent can comfortably handle at a party without being too overwhelmed is to have one guest for however old your child is in years. Example: If your child is five years old, having five children at the party is a good number.

Decorate the room using red and green balloons and happy birthday streamers. Use birthday paper or foam plates, napkins, and cups for easy cleanup. Make a "Happy Birthday, Jesus" banner.

Games, Craft Ideas, and Party Activity Ideas

- You can make your own game of Pin the Star on the Top of the Tree using construction paper and tape.
- Using construction paper and crayons, have the children create Christmas cards to be given to nursing home residents who do not have any family.
- Take the children Christmas caroling at a nursing home. (That way the children won't complain about being cold.) Call a nursing home ahead of time to ask what time would be good. In the invitation explain what you will be doing and request permission from the parents.
- Bake some Cut-Out Glazed Sugar Cookies (page 156) and let the children frost and decorate them. Have extra paper plates and large zip-top bags for the children to take home a few cookies to share with their families. Have on hand old blouses or shirts that the children can wear backwards as smocks to protect their clothing. For easier cleanup you can line the floor and the table with newspaper before frosting the cookies.
- Read the Christmas story about Jesus's birth to the children found in the Bible or go to the library and get an illustrated children's version of the story.
- Have each child practice the principle of giving by having each one bring a gift for a needy children's program such as Toys for Tots. Call your local church or Red Cross for worthy charities in your area. Other ideas include: blankets, hats, scarves, mittens, etc. for the homeless or good, clean, used winter clothing for the less fortunate.
- Have the kids sing "Happy Birthday" to Jesus. After singing, have the kids blow out their own candles on their cupcakes.

Kids' Birthday Party Menu

Grilled Cheese Christmas Puzzle Sandwich (page 197)
Snow-Covered Holiday Fruit Cups (page 196)
Dill Dip with Assorted Vegetables (page 196)
Snow-Topped Birthday Cupcakes (page 194)
Snow Frosting (page 195)
Kiddy Christmas Cocktail (page 198)

Edible Centerpiece

Using eighteen cupcakes, write one letter in red or green decorating gel to spell out *Happy Birthday, Jesus*. If desired, place a birthday candle in each cupcake, put the cupcakes on a tray, and place it in the middle of the table. Place a bouquet of helium balloons in the center of the table with the cupcakes.

Supplies

Christmas-tree shaped (1-inch)
   cookie cutter
Star-shaped (1-inch) cookie cutter

Clear plastic cups
Electric mixer

Timeline

1. Decorate the party room. For easier cleanup, use a plastic "Happy Birthday" tablecloth to cover the table. Make any banners (or have paper and crayons ready and have the kids make a banner) and plan games that you will need.

2. Make the Snow-Topped Cupcakes. Cover until serving time. You can place a toothpick or birthday candles in the cupcakes before you cover them so that the frosting will not stick to the plastic wrap or use a large plastic container with a lid. You will have more cupcakes than you need.

3. Prepare the Dill Dip. This makes eight servings of dip, so if you are having more than eight guests you will want to double this recipe. Cover and refrigerate until serving time.

4. Wash and cut fresh vegetables into Christmas-theme shapes with a small cookie cutter. You should have about ½ cup vegetables per guest. Cover and refrigerate.

5. Make the Snow-Covered Holiday Fruit Cups. Multiply this recipe by the number of guests you are serving. Cover and keep chilled.

Last 15 minutes:

6. Set out the number of plates you'll need on the counter next to where you will be making the sandwiches. Make the Grilled Cheese Christmas Puzzle Sandwiches. Place the pieces next to each other on the plate after you have cut them with the cookie cutter. Multiply this recipe by the number of guests you are serving.

7. Place ½ cup fresh vegetables on each plate with the sandwich and place 2 tablespoons dip in a Christmas-decorated Dixie cup for each guest or spoon the dip directly onto the plate.

8. Because we know the children are going to be overly excited once their unique, Christmas-shaped sandwiches and vegetables are placed in front of them, I encourage you to say a prayer immediately before serving food.

9. Have a "helper" take the plates to the table along with the fruit cups while you make the Kiddy Christmas Cocktails. Serve the Kiddy Christmas Cocktails. Multiply this recipe by the number of guests you are serving.

10. When everyone has finished eating, have the children help clean up by throwing their plates in the garbage.

11. Give each child one cupcake. Light the candles and sing "Happy Birthday" to Jesus. Let the children eat their cupcakes.

12. If desired, do any of the activities, games, or crafts that are given here.

Grocery List (for six servings)

Frozen Foods
1 (8-ounce) container fat-free dessert whipped topping

Fresh Fruits and Vegetables
¼ watermelon (2 cups needed)
2 red bell peppers
2 green bell peppers
1 honeydew melon

Staple Items
1 (23-ounce) jar no-sugar-added applesauce (only ⅓ cup needed)
1 loaf fat-free light bread

Dairy
6 eggs
1 (16-ounce) container fat-free sour cream (only ½ cup needed)
1 pound light margarine or butter
1 (8-ounce) package fat-free Cheddar cheese slices

Baking Items
1 (18.25-ounce) box white cake mix
1 pound sugar (only 1 cup needed)
1 (.68-ounce) tube red or green decorating gel
6 teaspoons Splenda Granular
1 (14-ounce) bag finely shredded coconut

24 birthday candles
1 (8-ounce) can nonfat cooking spray
24 cupcake papers, optional

Seasonings/Condiments
¼ teaspoon cream of tartar
1 teaspoon vanilla extract
½ cup fat-free mayonnaise
1 tablespoon dill weed
½ teaspoon minced onion
½ teaspoon seasoned salt

Other
1 (12-ounce) bag bite-size candy bars
(only 12 mini candy bars needed)

1 (10-ounce) bottle maraschino cherry
juice
1 (2-liter) bottle sugar-free, lemon-
lime soda
1 (6-ounce) jar red maraschino cherries
1 (6-ounce) jar green maraschino
cherries
1 container pretty toothpicks, ideally
frilled at one end (only 6 needed)
1 box Christmas decorated Dixie cups
12 clear plastic cups

Snow-Topped Birthday Cupcakes

The kids will love the candy surprise in the center of these moist and delicious cupcakes.

1 (18.25-ounce) box white cake mix	12 mini candy bars, halved
4 egg whites	Snow Frosting (see next page)
⅓ cup no-sugar-added applesauce	1 (.68-ounce) tube red or green
1 cup water	decorating gel (in the baking aisle)

- Preheat the oven to 375 degrees.
- Line 24 muffin cups with cupcake papers or spray muffin tins with nonfat cooking spray.
- In a large mixing bowl combine the cake mix, egg whites, applesauce, and water. Stir with an electric mixer until well blended.
- Into each prepared muffin tin, place 2 tablespoons cupcake batter, then half a candy bar (cut side down), and top with 1 tablespoon plus 1 teaspoon of the cupcake batter.
- Bake for 10 minutes.
- While the cupcakes are baking, make the Snow Frosting (see next page).
- Remove the cupcakes from the oven and let cool slightly.
- Turn one cupcake at a time upside down into the Snow Frosting and twist as you pull it out.

- Place the cupcakes on a tray and with the writing gel, make one letter on each of the eighteen cupcakes to spell out *Happy Birthday, Jesus.*
- Put the tray of cupcakes in the middle of the table as a centerpiece.

Note: You can freeze these cupcakes.

Yield: 24 frosted cupcakes

Calories: 179 (18% fat); Total Fat: 4g; Cholesterol: 1mg; Carbohydrate: 35g; Dietary Fiber: 1g; Protein: 2g; Sodium: 186mg; Diabetic Exchanges: 2½ other carbohydrate, ½ fat

Preparation time: 20 minutes
Baking time: 10 minutes
Total time: 30 minutes

Snow Frosting

This frosting is perfect to quickly frost cupcakes.

1	cup sugar	2	egg whites
¼	teaspoon cream of tartar	1	teaspoon vanilla extract
⅓	cup water		

- In a small saucepan heat the sugar, cream of tartar, and water over medium.
- Stir and cook until bubbly and sugar is dissolved.
- Combine the egg whites and vanilla in a medium glass mixing bowl.
- Slowly pour the sugar syrup into the egg whites beating with an electric mixer on high speed until soft peaks form or about 7 minutes.

Yield: 3 cups

(nutrition analysis per entire recipe)
Calories: 823 (0% fat); Total Fat: 0g; Cholesterol: 0mg; Carbohydrate: 201g; Dietary Fiber: 0g; Protein: 7g; Sodium: 113mg; Diabetic Exchanges: NA

Preparation time: 10 minutes
Cooking time: 3 minutes
Total time: 13 minutes

🍲 👫 Dill Dip

Using a small 1-inch cookie cutter, cut red bell pepper into star shapes and green bell pepper into Christmas tree shapes and serve these along with assorted raw vegetables with this dip.

¹/₂ cup fat-free sour cream	¹/₂ teaspoon minced onion
¹/₂ cup fat-free mayonnaise	¹/₂ teaspoon seasoned salt
I tablespoon dill weed	

- In a small mixing bowl stir together the sour cream, mayonnaise, dill weed, minced onion, and seasoned salt.
- Cover and refrigerate until serving time.

Yield: 8 (2-tablespoon) servings

Calories: 30 (0% fat); Total Fat: 0g; Cholesterol: 4mg; Carbohydrate: 5g; Dietary Fiber: 0g; Protein: 1g; Sodium: 228mg; Diabetic Exchanges: ¹/₂ other carbohydrate

🕐 **Preparation time:** 5 minutes or less

👫 Snow-Covered Holiday Fruit Cups

What a lovely way to serve fruit with a holiday flair. Multiply this recipe by the number of guests you are serving.

¹/₃ cup bite-size pieces watermelon	2 tablespoons fat-free dessert whipped topping
¹/₂ plus ¹/₂ teaspoon Splenda Granular	
¹/₄ cup bite-size pieces honeydew melon	¹/₂ teaspoon finely shredded coconut

- Put the watermelon pieces in a small mixing bowl. Sprinkle with ½ teaspoon Splenda and stir gently.
- Put the honeydew melon pieces in a small mixing bowl. Sprinkle with ½ teaspoon Splenda and stir gently.
- In a holiday-theme plastic cup place the watermelon, then the honeydew melon.
- Top each cup with 2 tablespoons dessert whipped topping and then with ½ teaspoon of coconut.
- Serve immediately or cover and chill until ready to serve.

Yield: 1 serving

Calories: 52 (0% fat); Total Fat: 0g; Cholesterol: 0mg; Carbohydrate: 12g; Dietary Fiber: 1g; Protein: 1g; Sodium: 16mg; Diabetic Exchanges: 1 fruit

🕐 **Preparation time:** 10 minutes

Grilled Cheese Christmas Puzzle Sandwich

This is a creative and fun way to get finicky eaters to eat nutritiously.

2 teaspoons light margarine or butter	1 (^{3}/4-ounce) slice fat-free Cheddar cheese
2 slices fat-free light bread	

- Spread a teaspoon of margarine on one side of each slice of bread.
- Place the cheese slice between the bread slices so the unbuttered sides are next to the cheese and the buttered sides are showing.
- Cook the sandwich in a nonstick skillet or on a griddle on medium-high heat for about 1 or 2 minutes on each side or until golden brown.
- Remove from the heat.
- Let cool a minute or two.
- Using a Christmas cookie cutter, cut out a holiday shape from the sandwich.
- Place the cut out shape on a plate next to the remaining part of the sandwich.
- Make sure the sandwich puzzle is cool enough before serving so children don't burn their mouths.

Note: Simply multiply this recipe by the number of children you are serving. Usually most 12-inch skillets can comfortably fit four sandwiches at a time.

Yield: 1 sandwich puzzle

Calories: 145 (24% fat); Total Fat: 4g; Cholesterol: 4mg; Carbohydrate: 19g; Dietary Fiber: 7g; Protein: 11g; Sodium: 493mg; Diabetic Exchanges: 1 lean meat, 1½ starch

🕐 **Preparation time:** 1 minute
Cooking time: 4 minutes or less
Total time: 5 minutes or less

♀♂ Kiddy Christmas Cocktail

When I was a little girl, for my sixth birthday my mother took me out for a special birthday meal, just her and me. I vividly remember as if it were just yesterday how very special I felt when she ordered me a kiddy cocktail. I am confident the children at this party will feel special, too, with such a drink made just for them.

2	tablespoons maraschino cherry juice	2	red maraschino cherries
3	ice cubes	1	green maraschino cherry
²⁄₃	cup sugar-free lemon-lime soda	1	pretty toothpick, ideally frilled at one end

- In a clear plastic Christmas cup place 2 tablespoons cherry juice in the bottom of the cup.
- Place 3 ice cubes in the cup.
- Very gently and slowly pour ²⁄₃ cup lemon-lime soda into the cup. You want the cherry juice to stay at the bottom to see a pretty red layer of color on the bottom of the cup.
- Garnish by placing in the cup a colored toothpick holding one green cherry between two red cherries.

Note: Multiply this recipe by the number of guests you have.

Yield: 1 kiddy cocktail

Calories: 40 (0% fat); Total Fat: 0g; Cholesterol: 0mg; Carbohydrate: 8g; Dietary Fiber: 0g; Protein: 0g; Sodium: 23mg; Diabetic Exchanges: ½ other carbohydrate

⊙ **Preparation time:** 5 minutes or less

Chapter Five

Cookie and Candy Exchange

A cookie and candy exchange is a fun way to have a large variety of cookies and candy for the holidays without spending many hours baking or having to purchase a gazillion ingredients.

Every person who comes to the cookie and candy exchange is called a member. Each member brings only one kind of homemade cookie or candy. However, each member needs to bring *one dozen* of that certain cookie *for each member participating.* So if there are five members participating in the exchange, then the members will bring five dozen each of whatever treat they are bringing. If there are seven members, each member will bring seven dozen, and so on.

It is super easy to organize. Simply follow these easy steps, and you are on your way to a fun-filled cookie and candy exchange that very well may become a yearly tradition in your home once you see how easy it is to do.

Easy Step-by-Step Directions for Organizing a Cookie and Candy Exchange

1. Select a day, time, and location where invited guests can exchange cookies and candy.
2. Contact the guests by either telephone or e-mail, and invite them to participate in a cookie and candy exchange. Give them a date to RSVP so you know who is coming and what type of cookie or candy they plan to bring. Each guest that chooses to participate in the exchange becomes a member for that year's cookie and candy exchange.
3. Write a list of everyone you invited; check off who is able to come and what cookie or candy each person is bringing. Not having this list can mean lots of doubles or triples of the same kind of cookie.
4. Count the number of members participating and that is the number of dozens each member will need to bring. If you have too many of one type of cookie, you can ask those members if they have another favorite cookie or candy that they would like to bring.

199

5. Inform the members of the total number of dozens they will need to bring. *Remind each member that it is very important to put only one dozen cookies or candies (regardless of how many total dozens each member brings) in a sealed, closed container along with enough copies of the recipe for all members.* This way each member can have one dozen of whatever it is she (or he) is bringing, along with a dozen cookies or candies from each of the other members and a copy of all the recipes.

   I have seen containers as extravagant as beautiful little baskets and tins and as simple as paper plates covered in plastic wrap or small plastic zip-top bags.

6. A few days prior to the event call or e-mail to remind the members of the time, date, and step number five of these instructions.

7. The day of the event make sure you have an empty table or countertop large enough for everyone to put the cookies or candy. (Ping-pong tables and pool tables work great.)

8. On separate 8½ x 11-inch sheets of paper write the names of each member attending. Place the paper with the member's name on it in the designated area on the table or counter where you would like her (or him) to place her goodies to exchange.

9. Give each member a bag in which to carry her cookies and candy home. Have each member take one plate (bag or container) of a dozen cookies (or candies) that each member brought to the exchange.

10. If desired, look in the back of this book in the index for an assortment of delicious holiday beverages you can serve during the exchange.

Great Places to Organize Cookie and Candy Exchanges

Work

Church

Small Groups

Sunday School Classes

Weight-Loss Groups

Neighbors

Friends

Exercise Groups

Great Recipes to Make for a Cookie and Candy Exchange

Look in index for more cookie and candy recipes.

☝ Butterscotch-Oatmeal Bar Cookies

This is one of my favorites.

³/₄ cup dark brown sugar	1¹/₂ cups Homemade Sweet Baking Mix
4 egg whites	(page 220)
1 cup cinnamon-flavored applesauce	3 cups quick cooking oats
1 teaspoon vanilla extract	1 cup butterscotch morsels

- Preheat the oven to 375 degrees.
- Spray a 10 x 15-inch jelly-roll pan with nonfat cooking spray.
- In a large bowl with an electric mixer beat the brown sugar, egg whites, applesauce, and vanilla together until well mixed.
- Slowly add the baking mix and oats until well blended.
- Spread the dough evenly in the prepared jelly-roll pan.
- Sprinkle the butterscotch morsels over the dough and press them into the dough.
- Bake for 15 minutes.
- Let the cookies cool in the pan for 2 minutes before cutting.
- Cut into 48 squares.

Yield: 48 (1-cookie) servings

Calories: 73 (22% fat); Total Fat: 2g; Cholesterol: 0mg; Carbohydrate: 13g; Dietary Fiber: 1g; Protein: 1g; Sodium: 29mg; Diabetic Exchanges: 1 other carbohydrate

🕐 **Preparation time:** 10 minutes
Baking time: 15 minutes
Total time: 25 minutes

⏺ Cherry Cream Cookies

These cheerful cookies are so cute with their red sugar sprinkles on top and cherry-red cream filling center. Children especially like their burst of cherry flavor.

4	egg whites or ¹/₂ cup liquid egg substitute	l	tablespoon red colored sugar (found in the baking aisle)
2	cups plus 2 tablespoons Homemade Sweet Baking Mix (page 220)		Filling:
l	teaspoon almond extract	8	tablespoons fat-free cream cheese
¹/₄	cup fat-free mayonnaise	³/₄	teaspoon sugar-free cherry drink mix (do not make as directed)

- Preheat the oven to 350 degrees.
- Spray two cookie sheets with nonfat cooking spray.
- In a medium-size mixing bowl with a spatula stir the egg whites, baking mix, almond extract, and mayonnaise until well mixed.
- Drop by rounded teaspoonfuls onto the prepared cookie sheets. You can put fifteen cookies per sheet. These cookies are small and do not rise much.
- Sprinkle the tops with the red sugar.
- Bake for 6 to 7 minutes.
- While the cookies are baking, put the cream cheese and the cherry drink mix in a small bowl and stir with a spatula until blended.
- Remove the cookies from the pans and let cool slightly.
- Cut each cookie in half horizontally and spread the center with a small amount (about ³/₄ teaspoon) of the cream cheese mixture.

Yield: 30 (1-cookie) servings

Calories: 34 (0% fat); Total Fat: 0g; Cholesterol: 1mg; Carbohydrate: 6g; Dietary Fiber: 0g; Protein: 2g; Sodium: 85mg; Diabetic Exchanges: ¹/₂ starch

⏱ **Preparation time:** 18 minutes or less
Baking time: 6 to 7 minutes
Total time: 25 minutes or less

⊡ ∗∗ Christmas Wreath Cookies

This is an old-fashioned recipe we made as children with my mom, but it is made here lower in fat and calories. Every time I make these, the kids eat them so fast and are always asking, "Mom, where did all of the cookies go?"

2	tablespoons reduced-fat margarine	1	teaspoon green food coloring
3	cups miniature marshmallows	4	cups cornflakes
1/2	teaspoon almond extract	56	cinnamon candies

- In a medium-size nonstick saucepan melt the margarine over low heat.
- When the margarine is melted, add the marshmallows, stirring constantly.
- When the marshmallows are melted and the mixture is smooth, remove from the heat and stir in the almond extract and green food coloring.
- Stir in the cereal.
- Onto a piece of wax paper that has been sprayed with nonfat cooking spray, place 1/4-cup mounds of the cereal mixture. Spray your hands with nonfat cooking spray, if needed, and shape the mounds into wreaths.
- Decorate each wreath with four cinnamon candies.
- Let cool to harden.

Yield: 14 (1-cookie) servings

Calories: 76 (6% fat); Total Fat: 1g; Cholesterol: 0mg; Carbohydrate: 18g; Dietary Fiber: 0g; Protein: 1g; Sodium: 75mg; Diabetic Exchanges: 1 other carbohydrate

Preparation time: 10 minutes
Cooking time: 10 minutes
Total time: 20 minutes

🍯 Cranberry Spice Cookies

These are so nutritious that I'll enjoy three or four for a quick breakfast.

3 cups Homemade Whole Wheat Sweet Baking Mix (page 220)	1 teaspoon ground cinnamon
4 egg whites	1 teaspoon almond extract
1/2 cup cinnamon-flavored applesauce	1 cup chopped sweetened dried cranberries
1/2 teaspoon ground cloves	

- Preheat the oven to 350 degrees.
- Spray two cookie sheets with nonfat cooking spray.
- In a large mixing bowl stir together the baking mix, egg whites, applesauce, cloves, cinnamon, almond extract, and cranberries until well mixed.
- Drop by rounded teaspoonfuls onto the prepared cookie sheets.
- Bake for 6 to 7 minutes or until the bottoms are lightly browned.

Yield: 40 (1-cookie) servings

Calories: 37 (0% fat); Total Fat: 0g; Cholesterol: 0mg; Carbohydrate: 8g; Dietary Fiber: 1g; Protein: 1g; Sodium: 48mg; Diabetic Exchanges: 1/2 other carbohydrate

Preparation time: 10 minutes or less
Baking time: 7 minutes (per 2 dozen)
Total time: 24 minutes or less

☐ Date Squares

Everyone gave these two thumbs up.

¹/₂	cup light butter, softened	I	cup rolled oats, regular or quick
I	teaspoon ground cinnamon		cooking
¹/₂	cup brown sugar	¹/₂	cup date filling* (found in baking
I	cup Homemade Whole Wheat		aisle)
	Sweet Baking Mix (page 220)	3	tablespoons Grape-Nuts cereal

■ Preheat the oven to 350 degrees.

■ Spray a jelly-roll pan with nonstick cooking spray.

■ In a medium bowl with an electric mixer on the lowest speed beat together the butter, cinnamon, sugar, baking mix, and oats until well mixed and crumbly.

■ Take two-thirds of the crumbly mixture with your hands and very firmly squeeze it into a log about 2 inches wide down the center of the jelly-roll pan. Flatten the top of the log so it is only about ½ inch thick.

■ Spread the date filling down the center of the log.

■ Stir the cereal into the remaining crumb mixture until well mixed. Then sprinkle the remaining crumb mixture on top of the date filling, and with your hands gently press the crumb mixture into the bar to help the crumb topping adhere.

■ With a sharp knife cut the log into 2-inch pieces. You'll have twelve pieces total.

■ Arrange the pieces on the jelly-roll pan so they are not touching each other.

■ Bake for 10 to 12 minutes or until lightly browned on the bottom.

■ Let cool on the pan for 2 minutes before removing.

■ With a very sharp knife, cut each piece in half.

*Note: Other flavors of filling can be used instead of date filling. We tested with apricot and raspberry fillings. Each tasted fantastic.

Yield: 24 (1-piece) servings

Calories: 80 (25% fat); Total Fat: 2g; Cholesterol: 7mg; Carbohydrate: 14g; Dietary Fiber: 1g; Protein: 1g; Sodium: 61mg; Diabetic Exchanges: 1 other carbohydrate

🕐 **Preparation time:** 5 minutes
Baking time: 15 minutes
Total time: 20 minutes

🍲 ⚕️ Dirty Snowball Candy

This is actually nothing more than very lightly chocolate-covered mini marshmallows that have a wonderful sweet and salty thing going on. My children and their friends, along with my husband, gobbled this up about as quickly as I made it. I have to admit it is addictive.

1 (2-ounce) cube of a (24-ounce) package chocolate-flavored almond bark* (In the baking aisle.)	1/4 teaspoon popcorn salt (Popcorn grains of salt are finer than regular salt and it goes farther.)
1 (10.5-ounce) bag mini marshmallows	

- In a large microwave-safe bowl, melt the chocolate for 2 to 3 minutes in a carousel microwave, stirring every 30 seconds. Once the chocolate is completely melted, stir the marshmallows in with the chocolate with a spatula that has been sprayed with nonfat cooking spray. Stir until well coated. There will be some spots that are not completely covered with chocolate. That is okay.
- Sprinkle lightly with the popcorn salt and stir again.
- Put the mix in a bowl.
- Cover with plastic wrap and store in a cool, dry location.

Note: There are 12 (2-ounce) cubes in a package. You need only one for this recipe.

Yield: 12 (½-cup) servings

Calories: 102 (12% fat); Total Fat: 1g; Cholesterol: 1mg; Carbohydrate: 23g; Dietary Fiber: 0g; Protein: 1g; Sodium: 68mg; Diabetic Exchanges: 1½ other carbohydrate

🕐 **Preparation time:** 2 minutes
Cooking time: 2 to 3 minutes
Total time: 5 minutes

☐ Divinity Candy

2 egg whites	1 teaspoon vanilla extract
1/2 cup Splenda Granular	Pinch of light salt
1 1/2 cups sugar	1/4 cup very finely chopped pecans
1/4 cup water	(optional)
1/4 cup white corn syrup	1/2 teaspoon light salt (optional)

- Beat the egg whites in a large glass bowl until stiff peaks form.
- In a medium nonstick saucepan bring the Splenda, sugar, water, and corn syrup to a full boil while stirring constantly.
- Continue boiling until the mixture reaches 245 degrees on a candy thermometer or when the mix forms a soft ball when a teaspoon is dropped into cold water.
- Slowly pour the mixture into the beaten egg whites, beating constantly with an electric mixer on medium-high speed.
- Add the vanilla and salt, beating the candy mixture until it is almost hard.
- Drop by teaspoonfuls onto wax paper by pushing the candy off of one spoon with another spoon.
- After completely mixing the candy until it is almost hard, stir or knead in the pecans and salt if desired. Roll by teaspoonfuls into balls and place on wax paper.

Note: To test a candy thermometer, place it in boiling water. It should read 212 degrees.

Yield: 40 (1-piece) servings

Calories: 37 (0% fat); Total Fat: 0g; Cholesterol: 0mg; Carbohydrate: 10g; Dietary Fiber: 0g; Protein: 0g; Sodium: 7mg; Diabetic Exchanges: 1/2 other carbohydrate

Preparation time: 10 minutes
Cooking time: 13 minutes
Total time: 23 minutes

⏱ 👫 Easiest Sugar Drop Cookies

Sugar cookies don't get any easier or tastier than this, folks. These are super moist and soft. Do not frost these yummy cookies; the confectioners' sugar is enough sweetness. These freeze and store well.

1	(8-ounce) container fat-free dessert whipped topping	1	(18.25-ounce) box white cake mix, dry (do not make as directed)
2	egg whites	1/4	cup confectioners' sugar

- Preheat the oven to 350 degrees.
- Spray three cookie sheets with nonfat cooking spray.
- In a large bowl mix the whipped topping and egg whites with a spatula until combined.
- Add the cake mix and stir until well blended.
- Scoop the dough by tablespoonfuls and dip it into the confectioners' sugar. Using another spoon, scrape the dough onto the prepared cookie sheets.
- Bake for 10 to 12 minutes or until the cookies are set in the middle.

Yield: 39 (1-cookie) servings

Calories: 70 (17% fat); Total Fat: 1g; Cholesterol: 0mg; Carbohydrate: 13g; Dietary Fiber: 0g; Protein: 1g; Sodium: 90mg; Diabetic Exchanges: 1 other carbohydrate

Preparation time: 10 minutes
Baking time: 10 to 12 minutes
Total time: 22 minutes or less

☐ Homemade Caramels

I love homemade caramels. There's just nothing like smooth, sweet, creamy caramel melting in your mouth. As with almost all of my recipes, I have once again created a lower-calorie version of an old-time family favorite.

³/4 cup white corn syrup	¹/2 cup fat-free, reduced-calorie French vanilla coffee creamer
1 cup dark brown sugar	
¹/2 cup light butter	¹/4 teaspoon light salt
	¹/2 teaspoon vanilla extract

- Spray a small jelly-roll pan with nonfat cooking spray.
- Remove items from one shelf in the freezer to make room for the jelly-roll pan.
- Place a kitchen towel on the freezer shelf.
- In a medium-size nonstick saucepan over medium-high heat, cook the corn syrup, brown sugar, butter, creamer, and salt together for about 15 minutes or until the mixture reaches 245 degrees on a candy thermometer. (It is important that you make sure it reaches 245 degrees. If it is any lower, the candy will be runny.)
- Remove the pan from the heat and stir in the vanilla until well blended.
- Pour the caramel into the prepared pan. Be careful—the caramel is very hot!
- Put the pan in the freezer for 10 minutes on top of the kitchen towel to help speed up the cooling process.
- Once it is cooled, cut the caramel into 64 pieces.
- If desired, roll up each flat square into a small log, and wrap each piece in wax paper that has been cut into 3 x 3-inch squares by rolling the wax paper around the candy and twisting the ends. (Or have the kids do it.)

Note: To test a candy thermometer, place it in boiling water. It should read 212 degrees.

Yield: 64 (1-piece) servings

Calories: 34 (19% fat); Total Fat: 1g; Cholesterol: 3mg; Carbohydrate: 7g; Dietary Fiber: 0g; Protein: 0g; Sodium: 21mg; Diabetic Exchanges: ¹/2 other carbohydrate

Preparation time: 5 minutes
Cooking time: 25 minutes
Total time: 30 minutes

⭘ Light Baklava

This is a much lighter version that is every bit as tasty as the traditional high-fat recipe. It is not sickeningly sweet like the original, and you can eat this guilt free.

$1/2$ teaspoon ground cinnamon	Nonfat cooking spray
6 tablespoons finely chopped walnuts	$1/2$ cup honey
	$1/2$ cup water
I cup Grape-Nuts cereal	36 cupcake papers (optional)
$1/2$ (16-ounce) package phyllo (fillo) dough, 20 half-sheets	

- Preheat the oven to 350 degrees.
- Spray a 10 x 15-inch jelly-roll pan with nonfat cooking spray.
- In a small mixing bowl stir together the cinnamon, walnuts, and cereal.
- Place 3 layers of phyllo dough in the middle of the jelly-roll pan, spraying nonfat cooking spray between each layer.
- Sprinkle 3 tablespoons of the nut mixture over the dough.
- Repeat layering the phyllo dough and the nut mixture three times and place 5 sheets of phyllo over the top of the last nut mixture, making sure that each layer is sprayed with nonfat cooking spray.
- Cut the baklava with a sharp knife into eighteen squares, and cut each square diagonally to form a triangle.
- Bake for 17 minutes or until golden brown.
- While the baklava is baking, bring the honey and water just to a boil, stirring occasionally. Reduce the heat and simmer for 10 minutes.
- When the baklava is done, spoon the hot honey mixture over the hot baklava. Let it cool slightly before handling.
- You can place the baklava on a serving tray or, for a professional appearance, place each piece of baklava into a cupcake paper.

Yield: 36 (1-piece) servings

Calories: 54 (17% fat); Total Fat: 1g; Cholesterol: 0mg; Carbohydrate: 11g; Dietary Fiber: 1g; Protein: 1g; Sodium: 45mg; Diabetic Exchanges: $1/2$ other carbohydrate

Preparation time: 13 minutes or less
Baking time: 17 minutes
Total time: 30 minutes or less

⏲ Maraschino Chocolate Cookies

These are great for curbing your craving for chocolate without blowing a bunch of calories unnecessarily, and they are oh-so-pretty with their bright red cherry on top.

36 maraschino cherries	4 egg whites or $^1/_2$ cup liquid egg substitute
I (10.25-ounce) chocolate fudge brownie mix, dry (do not make as directed)	$^3/_4$ cup whole wheat flour

- Preheat the oven to 350 degrees.
- Spray two cookie sheets with nonfat cooking spray.
- Set the maraschino cherries out on paper towels and lightly pat dry with another paper towel.
- In a medium-size mixing bowl stir with a spatula the brownie mix, egg whites, and flour, adding the flour a little at a time.
- Once the ingredients are well mixed and the dough is thick and sticky, drop by rounded teaspoonfuls onto the prepared cookie sheets. This is easiest to do by pushing the dough off of one measuring teaspoon with a second measuring teaspoon.
- Gently press 1 maraschino cherry into each cookie just enough so the cherry is resting in the middle of the cookie. You want to see at least half of the cherry.
- Bake for 7 to 8 minutes. Let the cookies cool a few minutes before eating.

Yield: 36 (1-cookie) servings

Calories: 56 (16% fat); Total Fat: 1g; Cholesterol: 0mg; Carbohydrate: 10g; Dietary Fiber: 1g; Protein: 1g; Sodium: 37mg; Diabetic Exchanges: $^1/_2$ other carbohydrate

⏲ **Preparation time:** 10 minutes or less
Baking time: 8 minutes or less
Total time: 18 minutes or less

⛴ Mocha Mini Cookies

I love the flavor of these tender, soft cookies that are melt-in-your mouth delicious.
Plus, to think we can eat them guilt free during the holidays is an added bonus.

3	tablespoons instant coffee granules	1	(18.25-ounce) box chocolate cake mix, dry (do not make as directed)
1	(8-ounce) container fat-free dessert whipped topping	1	(2.5 ounce) container chocolate candy sprinkles (found in baking aisle)
2	egg whites		

- Preheat the oven to 350 degrees.
- Spray two cookie sheets with nonfat cooking spray.
- In a medium mixing bowl with a spatula stir the coffee granules, whipped topping, egg whites, and cake mix until well mixed.
- Drop by rounded teaspoonfuls onto the prepared cookie sheets.
- Sprinkle the tops of the cookies lightly with the chocolate candy sprinkles.
- Bake for 5 minutes, or until set but not brown.
- Remove from the oven and let the cookies cool on a baking sheet for 2 minutes before removing.

Note: This recipe makes six dozen cookies. If desired bake a couple dozen at a time and keep the remaining cookie dough covered in the refrigerator until ready to bake.

Yield: 72 (1-cookie) servings

Calories: 41 (19% fat); Total Fat: 1g; Cholesterol: 0mg; Carbohydrate: 8g; Dietary Fiber: 0g; Protein: 1g; Sodium: 49mg; Diabetic Exchanges: ½ other carbohydrate

Preparation time: 15 minutes
Baking time: 7 minutes per 2 dozen
Total time: 36 minutes total for 6 dozen

Pastry Roll-Ups

These could not be any quicker to make.

| 10 | half-sheets phyllo (fillo) dough* | ¹/₂ cup confectioners' sugar |
| 10 | tablespoons ready-to-use apricot or date filling | |

- Preheat the oven to 400 degrees.
- Spray one cookie sheet with nonfat cooking spray.
- Place one sheet of phyllo dough on a cutting board or on the counter and spread 1 level tablespoon filling on the 9-inch end of the phyllo dough. Spread the filling very thinly about 2 inches up. (If the filling has separated when you open the can, just stir it.)
- Spray the rest of the sheet with nonfat cooking spray and roll up the dough, starting at the end with the filling. If the dough cracks when you are rolling it, it will still turn out okay.
- Spray the outside of the roll with nonfat cooking spray and cut the roll into four pieces with scissors.
- Place the four rolls on the prepared pan with the seam side down. Repeat until you have used all of the phyllo dough.
- Bake for 5 minutes.
- Roll in the confectioners' sugar and place on a serving tray. (These need to cool for 4 or 5 minutes before you eat them. Even though you can touch the outside, the inside is still very hot and can burn your mouth.)

Note: These are the 9 x 13-inch-size sheets or cut five 9 x 26-inch-size sheets in half.

Yield: 40 (1-pastry roll-up) servings

Calories: 24 (0% fat); Total Fat: 0g; Cholesterol: 0mg; Carbohydrate: 5g; Dietary Fiber: 0g; Protein: 0g; Sodium: 14mg; Diabetic Exchanges: ¹/₂ other carbohydrate

Preparation time: 10 minutes
Cooking time: 5 minutes
Total time: 15 minutes

🍲 Peanut Butter Cookies

These are about as traditional at our Christmas Cookie Exchanges as the turkey is for Christmas dinner.

1/4	cup imitation butter-flavored sprinkles (found in spice aisle)	1	cup reduced-fat peanut butter (25% less fat than regular)
1	cup applesauce	1	cup dark brown sugar
1	teaspoon vanilla extract	4	cups Homemade Whole Wheat
4	egg whites		Sweet Baking Mix (page 220)

- Preheat the oven to 375 degrees.
- Spray cookie sheets with nonfat cooking spray.
- In a large mixing bowl with an electric mixer beat together the butter-flavored sprinkles, applesauce, vanilla, egg whites, and peanut butter until well blended.
- Add the brown sugar and continue beating until well mixed.
- Using a spatula stir in the sweet baking mix until ingredients are well mixed.
- Drop rounded teaspoonfuls of the dough on the prepared cookie sheets.
- Using a fork that has been sprayed with nonfat cooking spray, press the fork down lightly on the top of the cookie. Turn the fork and press again to make a crisscross pattern on the top of each cookie.
- Bake for 5 minutes or until soft-set. (If desired, bake a few at a time and keep the cookie dough covered in the refrigerator for freshly baked cookies at the drop of a hat when unexpected company drops by.)
- Remove from the oven and let the cookies cool on the baking sheet for 2 minutes before removing.

Variations: For different variations add 3 peanut butter chips or chocolate chips or chopped nuts on top of each cookie before baking. However, remember that adding these ingredients will increase your fats and calories.

Yield: 96 (1-cookie) servings

Calories: 40 (23% fat); Total Fat: 1g; Cholesterol: 0mg; Carbohydrate: 7g; Dietary Fiber: 1g; Protein: 1g; Sodium: 63mg; Diabetic Exchanges: 1/2 other carbohydrate

Preparation time: 5 minutes
Baking time: 7 minutes per 2 dozen
Total time: 33 minutes for 8 dozen

🍴 Sticky Toffee Squares

This is a cross between a candy and a cookie. It's anything but low calorie, but I have reduced the fats and calories dramatically, so at least it isn't as fattening as it used to be. The key here is trying to eat only a piece or two, not a whole bunch—which for me is difficult to do because it tastes so fine.

40 fat-free saltine crackers	¹/₃ cup mini semisweet chocolate chips
1 cup light butter	
1 cup dark brown sugar	

- Preheat the oven to 400 degrees.
- Empty a shelf in the freezer to make room for a jelly-roll pan. Place a kitchen towel on the shelf of the freezer so that you can place the jelly-roll pan on it later.
- Line an 11½ x 17-inch jelly-roll pan with aluminum foil. Curl up the foil around the edge to keep the ingredients on the foil. Spray the foil with non-fat cooking spray.
- Place the saltines on the prepared jelly-roll pan so the sides of the crackers touch each other but do not overlap.
- Melt the butter in a medium-size nonstick saucepan over medium-high heat, stirring constantly.
- Once the butter is completely melted, add the brown sugar and bring it to a boil. Once it begins boiling, boil for exactly 3 minutes, stirring constantly.
- Carefully and slowly pour the boiling mixture over all the crackers.
- With a fork press any crackers that float to the top under the brown sugar mixture, making sure all the crackers are evenly coated and covered with the brown sugar mixture.
- Bake in the oven for 5 minutes.
- When done, any crackers that are not covered in syrup can be flipped over using two forks to ensure that each cracker is completely covered. Sprinkle the chocolate chips lightly over the top.
- Place in the freezer for 10 minutes to quicken the cooling time and then finish cooling in the refrigerator.
- Cut into 40 pieces with a very sharp knife. This is easily done by cutting in between the crackers. Place the Sticky Toffee Squares in a single layer on serving plates.

Note: These are very sticky, so if you want to stack these in more than one layer, place wax paper in between the layers.

Yield: 40 (1-cookie) servings

Calories: 58 (41% fat); Total Fat: 3g; Cholesterol: 8mg; Carbohydrate: 9g; Dietary Fiber: 0g; Protein: 1g; Sodium: 60mg; Diabetic Exchanges: ½ other carbohydrate

Preparation time: 10 minutes
Cooking time: 20 minutes
Total time: 30 minutes

☐ Snickerdoodles

These cookies taste just like Grandma used to make, except they don't have all of the fat.

1¹/₂	teaspoons ground cinnamon	2	egg whites
3	tablespoons sugar	1	(18.25-ounce) box white cake mix,
4	ounces fat-free dessert whipped topping (half of an 8-ounce container)		dry (do not make as directed)
		1	teaspoon cream of tartar
		2	tablespoons all-purpose flour

- Preheat the oven to 350 degrees.
- Spray three cookie sheets with nonfat cooking spray.
- In a small bowl mix together the cinnamon and the sugar.
- In a large mixing bowl combine the whipped topping, egg whites, cake mix, cream of tartar, and flour. The dough will be stiff, but still sticky to the touch.
- Spray your hands with nonfat cooking spray and roll 1 rounded teaspoon of dough at a time in your hands to form a ball.
- Roll the ball in the cinnamon-sugar mixture and place on the prepared pan.
- Bake for 7 minutes.

Yield: 60 (1-cookie) servings

Calories: 44 (18% fat); Total Fat: 1g; Cholesterol: 0mg; Carbohydrate: 8g; Dietary Fiber: 0g; Protein: 1g; Sodium: 58mg; Diabetic Exchanges: ¹/₂ other carbohydrate

Preparation time: 20 minutes
Cooking time: 7 minutes
Total time: 27 minutes

Homemade Baking Mix

Use these mixes only as directed in my recipes. I do not know how well they will work in your own recipes, since I have not tested them. Also, do not interchange *the whole wheat for the all-purpose mix or vice versa, because these mixes have been tested only as directed in each recipe. I cannot guarantee a quality product when baking mixes are substituted for each other and not used as directed.*

3 cups all-purpose flour	2 teaspoons baking soda
¹/₂ cup Splenda Granular	

- Combine the flour, Splenda, and baking soda in a large mixing bowl. Stir until well mixed.
- Store in a plastic zip-top bag or sealed container until ready to use. Fluff with a whisk or fork before measuring.

Variation: **Homemade Whole Wheat Baking Mix:** Simply substitute whole wheat flour for the all-purpose flour in this recipe. This mix should be stored in the freezer or refrigerator, because whole wheat flour has a small amount of fat and it could spoil.

Yield: 3½-cups

(Nutrition information per entire recipe)
Homemade Baking Mix
Calories: 1413 (2% fat); Total Fat: 4g; Cholesterol: 0mg; Carbohydrate: 298g; Dietary Fiber: 10g; Protein: 39g; Sodium: 2525mg; Diabetic Exchanges: NA
Homemade Whole Wheat Baking Mix
Calories: 1268 (5% fat); Total Fat: 7g; Cholesterol: 0mg; Carbohydrate: 273g; Dietary Fiber: 44g; Protein: 49g; Sodium: 2535mg; Diabetic Exchanges: NA

⊣ **Preparation time:** 5 minutes

Homemade Sweet Baking Mix

3	cups all-purpose flour	2	teaspoons baking soda
2	cups Splenda Granular		

- Mix the flour, Splenda, and baking soda in large bowl. Stir until well mixed.
- Store in a zip-top bag or sealed container in a cool place. Fluff with a whisk or fork before measuring.

Variation: **Homemade Whole Wheat Sweet Baking Mix:** Simply substitute whole wheat flour for the all-purpose flour. This mix settles during storage. Fluff with a whisk or fork before measuring. This mix should be stored in the freezer or refrigerator because whole wheat flour has a small amount of fat and it could spoil.

Yield: 4½ cups

(Nutrition information per entire recipe)
Homemade Sweet Baking Mix
Calories: 1557 (2% fat); Total Fat: 4g; Cholesterol: 0mg; Carbohydrate: 334g; Dietary Fiber: 10g; Protein: 39g; Sodium: 2525mg; Diabetic Exchanges: NA
Homemade Whole Wheat Sweet Baking Mix
Calories: 1412 (4% fat); Total Fat: 7g; Cholesterol: 0mg; Carbohydrate: 309g; Dietary Fiber: 44g; Protein: 49g; Sodium: 2535mg; Diabetic Exchanges: NA

Preparation time: 5 minutes

Chapter Six

Edible Gifts

T he way to a man's heart is through his stomach.

Maybe it's because I love to eat; I don't really know why, but I absolutely love getting gifts that I can eat. There are two very special Christmas gifts that I (to this day) still treasure the thought of, and those gifts were: In 1994 my husband's cousin made and gave our family a vast array of assorted homemade cookies. In 2002 my neighbors, Donna and Todd Frendt, gave me a plate of homemade cookies.

I was going through a difficult time in my life during both of those times, and these gifts made their loving kindness that much more appreciated. And even now edible gifts are still tops on my list. No matter how great of a cook or baker you are, who doesn't appreciate a gift of something you can eat?

There are numerous recipes throughout this book that would make wonderful gifts. These are just some of my favorites.

Yuletide Roll Cake

The Yule log was a log of freshly cut wood that would be carried to the house on Christmas Eve in celebration of a good year and in hopes of a good year to come in a lot of European countries. With the passing of big fireplaces, the Yule log was replaced by a cake decorated to look like a log and eaten with the Christmas Eve meal.

1 (18.25-ounce) box chocolate cake mix	1 cup raspberry no-sugar-added fruit preserves
6 egg whites	1/2 (8-ounce) container fat-free dessert whipped topping
1/2 cup water	
Chocolate frosting (next page)	15 red maraschino cherries with stems (optional)
1/4 cup confectioners' sugar	

- Preheat the oven to 350 degrees.
- Line a 10 x 15-inch jelly-roll pan with wax paper and spray with nonfat cooking spray.
- Combine the cake mix, egg whites, and water in a large mixing bowl.
- Beat the batter on low speed for 30 seconds. Increase the speed to medium and beat for 2 minutes.
- Pour the cake batter into the prepared pan and spread evenly.
- Bake for 13 to 15 minutes or until the cake springs back when touched.
- While the cake is baking, lay a clean kitchen towel on the counter and sprinkle the confectioners' sugar over one side of the towel. Make the Low-Fat Chocolate Frosting and cover it.
- When the cake is done, turn the pan over, placing the cake on the sugar-dusted towel. Remove the wax paper. Starting at either of the short sides, roll up the cake and the towel together.
- Place the cake roll into the freezer to cool for 7 minutes.
- Unroll the cake and spread the raspberry preserves evenly over the cake. Spread the whipped topping over the raspberry preserves and roll the cake (without the towel) to enclose the filling. Place the cake seam side down on a cake plate.
- Frost the outside of the cake, but not the ends of the cake (so you can see the roll), with the Low-Fat Chocolate Frosting recipe that follows.
- Use the tines of the fork and run down the sides of the cake to make the frosting look like bark on the side of a tree.

- If desired, garnish with 3 maraschino cherries at each corner and on top in the middle of the cake.
- If desired, you can place two tea light candles on top of the log, one at each end. Cut a small hole where each candle will be placed so the candles can sit in the hole.

Yield: 10 (1-inch) slices

Calories: 313 (14% fat); Total Fat: 5g; Cholesterol: 0mg; Carbohydrate: 62g; Dietary Fiber: 3g; Protein: 5g; Sodium: 369mg; Diabetic Exchanges: 4 other carbohydrate, 1 fat

Preparation time: 15 minutes
Baking time: 15 minutes
Total time: 30 minutes or less

Low-Fat Chocolate Frosting

$1/4$ cup light margarine	$1/2$ teaspoon vanilla extract
$1/4$ cup cocoa	$1^1/4$ cups confectioners' sugar
1 tablespoon Splenda Granular (or 3 tablespoons confectioners' sugar)	

- Mix the margarine, cocoa, Splenda, and vanilla with an electric mixer in a mixing bowl on low speed until well blended.
- Slowly add the confectioners' sugar.
- Beat the mixture with an electric mixer until creamy and smooth.
- Spread over cake roll.

Yield: 12 (1-tablespoon) servings

Calories: 73 (24% fat); Total Fat: 2g; Cholesterol: 0mg; Carbohydrate: 14g; Dietary Fiber: 0g; Protein: 0g; Sodium: 25mg; Diabetic Exchanges: 1 other carbohydrate, $1/2$ fat

Preparation time: 5 minutes or less

Chocolate-Covered Raisin Cookies in a Jar

Even Mrs. Claus would be happy to receive this gift. Once you make the jar, photocopy the directions for making the cookies and tape them to the jar.

¹/₄ cup powdered cocoa	¹/₂ cup dark brown sugar
1¹/₂ cups Homemade Sweet Baking Mix (page 220)	1 cup raisins, packed
	¹/₄ cup real semisweet mini chocolate chips

- In a 1-quart wide-mouth canning jar layer the cocoa, baking mix, brown sugar, and raisins. Press everything down firmly into the jar with a spatula.
- Wrap the chocolate chips in a piece of clear plastic wrap and put them in the jar. It may be a snug fit.
- Tighten the lid of the canning jar securely in place.
- Make a copy of the lower part of this page and cut it out. Glue these directions to a pretty card, cut a hole in the middle of the card and tie the card to the top of the jar.

Note: To enhance the sweetness of the cookies add ¹/₂ teaspoon of light salt to the baking mix.

Yield: Makes 1 (1-quart) jar

Calories: 43 (0% Fat); Total Fat: 0g; Cholesterol: 0mg; Carbohydrate: 9g; Dietary Fiber: 0g; Protein: 1g; Sodium: 23mg; Diabetic Exchanges: ¹/₂ other carbohydrate

 Preparation time to make jar: 15 minutes or less

Chocolate Covered Raisin Cookies in a Jar

2 cups fat-free dessert whipped topping   2 egg whites

- Preheat oven to 350 degrees. Spray cookie sheets with nonfat cooking spray.
- Remove chocolate chips from jar and set aside.
- Stir together jar of cookie mix, dessert whipped topping, and egg whites until well mixed.
- Using two spoons drop cookie dough by rounded teaspoonful onto prepared baking sheets. Sprinkle top of the cookies with the chocolate chips.
- Bake for 5 to 6 minutes or until soft set, but do not overbake.
- Let the cookies cool on the baking sheet for 2 minutes before removing.

Yield: 48 (1-cookie) servings

Soft Fudge

This is the best fudge.

5 plus 2 tablespoons light butter, softened	3 tablespoons fat-free sweetened condensed milk (not evaporated)
2³/4 cups confectioners' sugar	1 teaspoon vanilla extract
¹/2 cup powdered cocoa	¹/2 cup real semisweet mini-morsels
¹/4 teaspoon light salt	chocolate chips (in baking aisle)

- Line an 8 or 9-inch square pan with wax paper.
- In a medium-size bowl with an electric mixer on low speed beat together the 5 tablespoons butter, confectioners' sugar, cocoa, salt, milk, and vanilla until well blended. The mixture will be super stiff.
- *Do not do this next step until the first step is completely finished.* In another medium bowl melt the remaining 2 tablespoons butter with the chocolate chips in a carousel microwave. Stir the chocolate and butter together after 1 minute. Cook for 1 more minute and stir. If needed, continue cooking for 30 seconds and then stir until the chocolate is completely melted. *Do not boil.* Simply cook enough to completely melt the chocolate.
- With a spatula put all of the melted chocolate chips into the first bowl. Stir with the spatula until ingredients are well mixed and then knead the fudge with your hands for about a minute longer.
- With your hands press the fudge into the prepared pan.
- Cut into 64 (1-inch) pieces.

Variation: For **Fudgy Balls,** follow the fudge recipe exactly and then roll each piece of fudge into a ball with your hands.

Yield: 64 (1-inch) pieces

Calories: 40 (26% fat); Total Fat: 1g; Cholesterol: 2mg; Carbohydrate: 7g; Dietary Fiber: 0g; Protein: 0g; Sodium: 15mg; Diabetic Exchanges: ¹/2 other carbohydrate

Preparation time: 15 minutes or less
Cooking time: 2 minutes
Total time: 17 minutes or less

Caramel Popcorn

I'm the oldest of seven children and my siblings ask every year, "Are you going to make homemade caramel corn again?" That tells you how good it is.

³/₄ cup dark brown sugar, firmly packed	1 (3-ounce) bag 94% fat-free microwave buttered popcorn, not popped
6 tablespoons light butter	
3 tablespoons light corn syrup	¹/₄ teaspoon baking soda
¹/₄ teaspoon light salt	¹/₄ teaspoon vanilla extract

- Preheat the oven to 275 degrees.
- Cover two large jelly-roll pans with aluminum foil and then spray the foil with nonfat cooking spray.
- In a large nonstick Dutch oven over medium-high heat cook the sugar, butter, corn syrup, and salt until it comes to a full boil, stirring constantly.
- Reduce the heat to medium and continue boiling for 5 minutes without stirring.
- While the caramel is boiling, cook the popcorn in the microwave as directed on the bag. Keep freshly cooked, popped popcorn in the bag and lay a dish towel over the bag to help keep it warm.
- Remove the caramel from the heat and stir in the baking soda and vanilla until well blended.
- Spray a very large glass mixing bowl with nonfat cooking spray (for easier cleanup).
- Pour the popcorn into the bowl.
- Drizzle the caramel over the popcorn and stir with a very large spoon that has been sprayed with nonfat cooking spray until all the popcorn is well coated. *Be very careful. The caramel is extremely hot.*
- Pour the caramel-coated popcorn onto the prepared jelly-roll pans.
- Bake for 8 minutes, stirring after 5 minutes.
- Stir one last time after baking to help evenly coat the popcorn with the caramel.
- Let cool several minutes before serving so nobody burns their mouth. Or cool completely before storing in airtight containers.

Note: The process of making this caramel corn happens quickly, so you should have all of your cooking utensils and supplies out and ready to use before you begin. Also, to save on cleanup time, spray all of your cooking utensils with nonfat cooking spray right before you use each utensil, bowl, or pan. For easier cleanup keep a kitchen sink full of hot, sudsy water to put the caramel-covered cooking utensils and pan into as soon as you have finished using them.

Yield: 12 (1-cup) servings

Calories: 108 (26% fat); Total Fat: 3g; Cholesterol: 10mg; Carbohydrate: 20g; Dietary Fiber: 1g; Protein: 1g; Sodium: 136mg; Diabetic Exchanges: 1½ other carbohydrate, ½ fat

Preparation time: 5 minutes or less
Cooking time: 15 minutes or less
Total time: 20 minutes or less

✲✲ Snowballs (Coconut Cookies)

These tiny cookies remind me of expensive gourmet cookies found at specialty shops, where they are usually extremely expensive. Put these into a cute snow-theme tin or cookie jar for an edible gift that will be delicious to the last bite.

1	(18.25 ounce) box French vanilla cake mix, dry (do not make as directed)	1	teaspoon coconut extract
		2	tablespoons water
2	egg whites	1/2	cup very finely chopped coconut

- Preheat the oven to 350 degrees.
- Spray two cookie sheets with nonfat cooking spray.
- With your hands mix the cake mix, egg whites, coconut extract, and water until all the ingredients are mixed.
- Roll 1 teaspoon of the dough at a time in your hands to form a ball. Roll the ball in the chopped coconut. If the coconut is not sticking to the dough, spray it with a little nonfat cooking spray before rolling it in the coconut. You can fit 45 cookies on the cookie sheet at one time.
- Bake for 7 to 8 minutes.

Note: To save time with this recipe, have the kids help roll the balls of dough. These freeze and store well.

Yield: 90 (1-cookie) servings

Calories: 27 (24% fat); Total Fat: 1g; Cholesterol: 0mg; Carbohydrate: 5g; Dietary Fiber: 0g; Protein: 0g; Sodium: 39mg; Diabetic Exchanges: 1/2 other carbohydrate

⏲ **Preparation time:** 22 minutes
Cooking time: 7 to 8 minutes
Total time: 30 minutes

Hard Candy

For an inexpensive gift that will look like a million bucks, purchase a pretty candy dish and fill it with this holiday favorite hard candy made with only a fraction of the sugar.

1 cup sugar	$^1/_4$ teaspoon liquid food coloring
1 cup Splenda Granular	1 to 2 teaspoons candy flavoring
$^2/_3$ cup light corn syrup	1 tablespoon confectioners' sugar
$^3/_4$ cup water	

- Spray a jelly-roll pan with nonfat cooking spray.
- In a large saucepan mix together the sugar, Splenda, corn syrup, and water.
- Cook and stir over medium-high heat until the sugar dissolves.
- Bring the mixture to a boil without stirring and let it continue cooking for about 15 minutes, or until drops of the syrup form brittle threads when placed in a cup of cold water.
- Remove from the heat and stir in the food coloring.
- When the boiling stops, add the flavoring and stir.
- Pour onto the prepared jelly-roll pan.
- Let cool in the refrigerator for 5 minutes.
- Sprinkle the confectioners' sugar lightly over the candy and break it into small pieces.

Note: Candy flavoring can usually be bought at drug stores, candy-making stores, or specialty baking and candy-making supply stores. Match your candy flavoring with the food coloring. If you use cinnamon candy flavoring, use red food coloring. If you use mint candy flavoring, use green food coloring. If you use lemon candy flavoring, use yellow food coloring.

Yield: $1^1/_2$ cups hard candy pieces or 12 (2-tablespoon) servings

Calories: 129 (0% fat); Total Fat: 0g; Cholesterol: 0mg; Carbohydrate: 34g; Dietary Fiber: 0g; Protein: 0g; Sodium: 22mg; Diabetic Exchanges: 2 other carbohydrate

Preparation time: 10 minutes
Cooking time: 20 minutes
Total time: 30 minutes

Four-Day Gingerbread House

This gingerbread house can be completed in four days, thirty minutes each day. The first day you will make the dough. The second day you will roll the dough and bake it. The third day you will assemble the house, and the fourth day you get to decorate it.

3½ cups Homemade Whole Wheat Sweet Baking Mix (page 220)	2 plus 2 egg whites
2 teaspoons ground ginger	⅓ cup light molasses
½ teaspoon ground cloves	2 tablespoons light margarine
	3 cups confectioners' sugar

Day One

- Place the baking mix, ginger, cloves, 2 egg whites, molasses, and margarine in a large mixing bowl.
- Stir until crumbly and then knead the dough with your hands. Keep mixing until the dough forms a ball. It will seem like there is not enough liquid; but be patient, the dough will come together.
- Wrap the dough in plastic wrap and place it in the refrigerator.

Preparation time: 10 minutes

Day Two

- Preheat the oven to 350 degrees.
- Lightly spray two cookie sheets with nonfat cooking spray.
- Take the gingerbread dough out of the refrigerator, unwrap it, and place it on a floured surface.
- Sprinkle flour on the dough and roll the dough to about ¼ inch thickness.
- Cut out four 6 x 4-inch rectangular pieces and two house-shaped pieces. (See pattern on page 232)
- Using a spatula, carefully place them on the prepared baking sheets.
- Bake for 6 minutes or until lightly browned on the bottom.
- Place the baked pieces on aluminum foil on a flat surface until the next day.

Preparation time: 10 minutes
Baking time: 6 minutes
Total time: 16 minutes

Day Three

- To prepare the decorator icing, place the confectioners' sugar and the remaining 2 egg whites in a mixing bowl.
- Stir together with an electric mixer until combined, and then turn the mixer on high and whip for 7 to 8 minutes or until the icing forms stiff peaks.
- Put the icing in a quart-size zip-top bag and cut off a small piece of the corner with scissors. The hole should be a little smaller than a dime.
- Cover a cake plate or a piece of cardboard with aluminum foil.
- Take two of the rectangle pieces and turn them over on the counter so that the side that was on the baking sheet is facing up.
- Gently squeeze the zip-top bag and put icing on the 4-inch sides of the gingerbread.
- While you are building, you can put frosting on the bottom edge of each piece so that when you place it on the foil-covered cake plate, the house will stick to it. To build the house take one of the rectangles and one of the house-shaped pieces and push them together so they are perpendicular to each other.
- Take the other house-shaped piece and push it into the icing on the other side of the rectangle.
- Put the second rectangle against the ends of the house-shaped pieces. You might need to hold the pieces together for a minute until they stick. The icing will dry out and become very hard after a few hours.
- Put frosting along the entire top edge of the house and set one of the rectangles on the top to form half the roof. Place the frosting along the edge to form the peak of the roof and put the last rectangle on top.
- Set the house aside so that the frosting will dry. Place the cut zip-top bag into another zip-top bag and refrigerate the frosting so that you can use it to decorate the house the next day.

(⌐) **Preparation time:** 30 minutes or less

Day Four

- Attach gumdrops, starlight mints, Red Hots, candy canes, jelly beans, cookies, pretzels, graham crackers, etc., to your house using the frosting that was left over from day three.

- We tiled our roof with vanilla wafers and made windows with graham crackers. Our door was a piece of a Dr. Phil's Shape-Up Bar that had a chocolate chip handle.
- Be creative and have fun decorating your gingerbread house.

🕐 **Preparation time:** 30 minutes or less

Gingerbread House Pattern

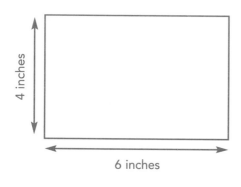

4 inches

6 inches

**2 for the roof
2 for the walls**

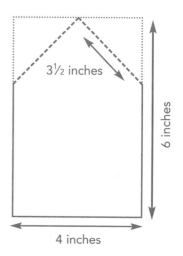

3½ inches

6 inches

4 inches

2 for the side walls

Chapter Seven

Using Leftovers

Leftovers are a bittersweet part of Christmas. As a homemaker, I appreciate leftovers because it helps cut back on my cooking time. Yes, even I (a homemaker who makes only fast and easy recipes) appreciate the ease of using leftovers. Is there anything faster or easier to make for a meal than to pop something into the microwave to reheat?

Unfortunately, like many people, my family doesn't like to eat leftovers of the same thing for more than one day. As a result, this is the reason why I created this using leftovers chapter. My goal is to have delicious, fast, and easy-to-prepare recipes using holiday leftovers that in their final forms will taste and appear as if they were made not using any leftovers at all.

In regard to these leftover recipes, what your family does not know about these foods will not hurt them. Hopefully your family will be like my family and appreciate and enjoy every last bite of our leftover recipes without even realizing they are indeed eating leftovers.

If your family complains about eating leftovers, these recipes are your answer. When your family is savoring every mouthfull (and wanting second servings) of these leftover recipes, be smart and do not tell them the food was made using leftovers from Christmas or that it is low fat, fast, and easy to make. Why burst their bubble? Just let them enjoy. It'll be our little secret.

Chef Dinner Salads

Chef salads are a great way to use leftover holiday meat and still eat light at the same time.

2	(16-ounce) bags iceberg salad mix	2	cups diced cooked ham
1/2	cup fat-free shredded Cheddar cheese	2	cups diced cooked turkey breast
		1	cup fat-free salad dressing
4	hard-cooked egg whites, chopped*		

- Divide the lettuce evenly among four dinner plates.
- Top each salad with the cheese, egg whites, ham, and turkey.
- Cover and keep chilled until ready to serve.
- Do not put dressing on the salads until you are ready to eat, because it will make them soggy.

Note: The yolks are the fattening part of the egg and also where the cholesterol is. However, cats and dogs love the egg yolks and it helps give them a shiny coat.

Yield: 4 (entrée-size) salads

Calories: 315 (17% fat); Total Fat: 6g; Cholesterol: 102mg; Carbohydrate: 16g; Dietary Fiber: 5g; Protein: 48g; Sodium: 1989mg; Diabetic Exchanges: 1½ vegetable, ½ other carbohydrate, 6 very lean meat

 **Preparation time:** 10 minutes or less

Menu Idea: A cup of soup along with some fat-free crackers would round off this chef salad perfectly. For lots of terrific soup recipes look in *Busy People's Slow Cooker Cookbook*. It was selected by *Southern Living* magazine as one of the top ten slow cooker cookbooks.

Creamy Turkey Spread

If you freeze your leftover turkey on Christmas, you can thaw it and use it in this recipe for a spread for a New Year's Eve party.

2 cups chopped cooked turkey breast	1 (0.9 ounce) envelope vegetable soup mix, dry (do not make as directed)
2 (8-ounce) packages fat-free cream cheese, softened	
2/3 cup fat-free sour cream	1/4 cup red bell pepper, chopped

- In a medium-size bowl with a spatula combine the turkey, cream cheese, sour cream, soup mix, and bell pepper together until well mixed.
- Cover and keep chilled until ready to serve.
- Serve with fat-free crackers or celery sticks.

Yield: 30 (2-tablespoon) servings

Calories: 39 (0% fat); Total Fat: 0g; Cholesterol: 12mg; Carbohydrate: 3g; Dietary Fiber: 0g; Protein: 5g; Sodium: 128mg; Diabetic Exchanges: 1 very lean meat

Preparation time: 10 minutes or less

Menu Ideas: Great with fat-free or reduced-fat crackers or as a sandwich spread on light wheat bread. For a complete, well-rounded, and satisfying meal, serve with one of my many super easy-to-make-soups such as these found in *Busy People's Slow Cooker Cookbook*: World's Easiest Vegetable Soup on page 63, Taco Vegetable Soup on page 62, Green Bean Soup on page 55, or Tomato Bisque on page 65.

Gobble-Me-Up Soup

Hey, you laugh at the title now, but once you cook this soup, see if you don't have a hard time not gobbling it up. This is another great way to eat leftover turkey without it tasting like leftover turkey.

2	cups diced cooked turkey breast	1	(16-ounce) jar salsa (Remember, the spicier the salsa, the hotter it'll be.)
2	(16-ounce) packages frozen stir-fry vegetables	$^3/_4$	cup fat-free sour cream
1	(1.5-ounce package) taco seasoning mix	1	cup crushed fat-free light tortilla chips
1	(49.5-ounce) can fat-free chicken broth		

- In a large saucepan mix the turkey breast, vegetables, taco seasoning, chicken broth, and salsa.
- Bring to a boil and reduce the heat to low. Cover and simmer for 10 minutes.
- Put a 1-cup serving in each bowl and top with 1 tablespoon sour cream.
- Sprinkle 1 heaping tablespoon crushed tortilla chips on top of each serving of soup around the sour cream.
- Serve immediately.

Note: If you like a spicier soup, add a few drops of Tabasco sauce.

Yield: 12 (1-cup) servings

Calories: 142 (9% fat); Total Fat: 1g; Cholesterol: 23mg; Carbohydrate: 17g; Dietary Fiber: 3g; Protein: 11g; Sodium: 670mg; Diabetic Exchanges: $^1/_2$ starch, $1^1/_2$ vegetable, 1 very lean meat

Preparation time: 5 minutes or less
Cooking time: 10 minutes or less
Total time: 15 minutes or less

Menu Ideas: This is a complete meal in itself. Usually two servings will make a light meal by itself. Instead of crackers, serve with any one of the delicious fast-and-easy-to-make biscuit or roll recipes found in *Busy People's Low-Fat Cookbook*: Cheese Biscuits on page 63, Pinwheel Dinner Rolls on page 64, Tomato Biscuits on page 59, or Sweet Cornbread on page 60.

Turkey Caesar Salad

Most people will think this recipe is chicken Caesar salad because that is what most people perceive poultry in Caesar salad to be. However, substituting our leftover turkey is a smart way to make it appear as if it is something it is not. You won't hear complaints about eating leftover turkey because people probably won't even realize they are eating leftovers.

2 cups diced cooked skinless turkey breast	$^1/_2$ cup finely grated Parmesan cheese
1 cup fat-free Caesar salad dressing	20 fat-free croutons (optional)
2 medium heads Romaine lettuce, torn into bite-size pieces	Freshly ground black pepper (optional)

- In a medium-size mixing bowl stir the turkey and Caesar salad dressing together until well mixed.
- Divide the lettuce evenly among four dinner plates.
- Top the lettuce with the turkey and salad dressing mixture.
- Sprinkle the cheese, croutons, and pepper on top of the salad.

Yield: 4 (entrée-size) salads

Calories: 220 (18% fat); Total Fat: 4g; Cholesterol: 69mg; Carbohydrate: 14g; Dietary Fiber: 4g; Protein: 29g; Sodium: 1166mg; Diabetic Exchanges: 1$^1/_2$ vegetable, $^1/_2$ other carbohydrate, 3$^1/_2$ very lean meat

Preparation time: 10 minutes or less

Menu Idea: A cup of soup along with some fat-free crackers would round this meal off perfectly. For lots of terrific soup recipes look in *Busy People's Slow Cooker Cookbook.*

Open-Faced Stuffed Steaks

For a high quality meal using leftover stuffing this steak is first class. To finish this meal all you need is a salad or green vegetable and you're set.

1¹/₂ pounds flank steak, cut 1 inch thick (or beef round or London Broil, all names for the same type beef) with all visible fat removed	1 cup leftover stuffing
	2 tablespoons light soy sauce
	1 teaspoon steak-seasoning blend
¹/₂ cup chopped onions, frozen or fresh	¹/₄ cup shredded reduced-fat Cheddar cheese

- Cut 4 ounces of the steak into ¼-inch pieces.
- Cut the remaining pound into four 4-ounce servings.
- Butterfly each 4-ounce steak by cutting three-fourths of the way through the middle of each steak horizontally.
- Put the diced pieces of steak into a large nonstick skillet with the onions and cook on high heat until the pieces are browned. This will only take a minute or two.
- Put the stuffing into a medium-size bowl. Heat the stuffing for a minute or two in a carousel microwave until the stuffing is fully heated.
- Add the cooked steak and onions to the stuffing and stir until well mixed. Cover to keep warm and set aside.
- Put the soy sauce into the hot skillet and immediately place all butterfly-cut steaks on top of the soy sauce. Cook each side of the steak on high heat for about 1 or 2 minutes.
- Remove the steaks and evenly sprinkle them with the steak seasoning.
- Evenly distribute the stuffing mixture among the steaks and press with your hands to form a mound on top of each of the steaks.
- Sprinkle 1 tablespoon cheese on top of each of the mounds of stuffing.
- Microwave each serving for 30 seconds or until the cheese is melted.
- Serve immediately with steak knives.

Note: I used turkey-flavored leftover stuffing and no one could tell because in this recipe the leftover stuffing picks up the flavors of the steak and onions. If you are using a leftover stuffing with chunks of poultry or sausage in it, remove the chunks first.

Yield: 4 servings

Calories: 340 (32% fat); Total Fat: 12g; Cholesterol: 68mg; Carbohydrate: 12g; Dietary Fiber: 1g; Protein: 43g; Sodium: 888mg; Diabetic Exchanges: 1 starch, 5 lean meat

Preparation time: 10 minutes
Cooking time: 5 minutes or less
Total time: 15 minutes or less

Menu Idea: To make a complete meal, serve the Romaine & Pear Tossed Salad on page 146 of *Busy People's Diabetic Cookbook*.

The Christmas Story

A nd it came to pass in those days that a decree went out from Caesar Augustus that all the world should be registered. This census first took place while Quirinius was governing Syria. So all went to be registered, everyone to his own city. Joseph also went up from Galilee, out of the city of Nazareth, into Judea, to the city of David, which is called Bethlehem, because he was of the house and lineage of David, to be registered with Mary, his betrothed wife, who was with child. So it was, that while they were there, the days were completed for her to be delivered. And she brought forth her firstborn Son, and wrapped Him in swaddling cloths, and laid Him in a manger, because there was no room for them in the inn. Now there were in the same country shepherds living out in the fields, keeping watch over their flock by night. And behold, an angel of the Lord stood before them, and the glory of the Lord shone around them, and they were greatly afraid. Then the angel said to them, "Do not be afraid, for behold, I bring you good tidings of great joy which will be to all people. "For there is born to you this day in the city of David a Savior, who is Christ

Continued on next page

Continued from previous page

the Lord. "And this will be the sign to you: You will find a Babe wrapped in swaddling cloths, lying in a manger." And suddenly there was with the angel a multitude of the heavenly host praising God and saying: "Glory to God in the highest, And on earth peace, goodwill toward men" So it was, when the angels had gone away from them into heaven, that the shepherds said to one another, "Let us now go to Bethlehem and see this thing that has come to pass, which the Lord has made known to us." And they came with haste and found Mary and Joseph, and the Babe lying in a manger. Now when they had seen Him, they made widely known the saying which was told them concerning this Child. And all those who heard it marveled at those things which were told them by the shepherds. But Mary kept all these things and pondered them in her heart. Then the shepherds returned, glorifying and praising God for all the things that they had heard and seen, as it was told them.

—Luke 2: 1–20

Turkey Potpie Casserole

I knew this recipe was a winner when the only thing I saw at our family meal was the top of my family members' heads.

2¹/₂ cups leftover cooked turkey, all skin and fat removed, cut into ¹/₂-inch pieces

1 (29-ounce) can home-style large-cut vegetables, drained (a combination of potatoes, carrots, celery, and onions)

1 (14.5-ounce) can green beans, drained

1 (14.5-ounce) can cut wax beans, drained (These are yellow beans and are found in vegetable aisle.)

2 (12-ounce) jars fat-free roasted turkey-flavored gravy

1 plus ¹/₄ teaspoons lemon pepper seasoning

5 (9 x 13-inch) sheets phyllo (fillo) dough

- Preheat the oven to 400 degrees.
- Spray a glass 9 x 13-inch casserole dish with nonfat cooking spray.
- In the prepared casserole dish stir together with a spatula the turkey, vegetables, green beans, wax beans, gravy, and 1 teaspoon lemon pepper seasoning until well mixed.
- Lay one sheet of the phyllo dough at a time on top of the casserole mixture. Spray each layer with nonfat cooking spray before placing the next sheet of phyllo dough on top. Repeat this step until all five sheets are used.
- Sprinkle the top of the potpie with the remaining ¼-teaspoon lemon pepper seasoning. With a sharp knife randomly cut thirty-six slits in the top through the layers of the phyllo dough. Cover with aluminum foil.
- Bake for 10 minutes.
- Remove the foil and bake an additional 10 minutes on the top shelf.
- Remove the potpie from the oven and let it sit a few minutes before serving. Cut into eight pieces with a sharp knife. Serve hot.

Note: You can substitute 1¼ cups leftover green bean casserole for the canned beans. Remove any fried onion. Simply place the green bean casserole in a strainer in the sink and rinse with water to remove the cream sauce.

Yield: 8 servings

Calories: 188 (4% fat); Total Fat: 1g; Cholesterol: 38mg; Carbohydrate: 26g; Dietary Fiber: 2g; Protein: 18g; Sodium: 1096mg; Diabetic Exchanges: 1 starch, 2 vegetable, 2 very lean meat

Preparation time: 10 minutes or less
Baking time: 20 minutes
Total time: 30 minutes or less

Menu Ideas: This is a complete meal all by itself, but a tossed green salad would also complete this meal nicely. For fantastic salad ideas try any of the following recipes found in *Busy People's Down-Home Cooking without the Down-Home Fat*: Creamy Cucumbers on page 50, Fresh Broccoli Salad on page 53, Slaw Salad on page 54, or the Tomato Zing Salad on page 52.

Tiny Turkey Turnovers

This is a great way to use leftover turkey.

I	cup finely chopped cooked turkey, all skin and fat removed	I	plus ¹/2 teaspoons lemon pepper seasoning
¹/2	cup fat-free cream cheese	I¹/2	plus I teaspoons dried parsley flakes
4	slices fat-free Swiss cheese, finely chopped (about ¹/2 cup)	13	(9 x 13-inch) sheets of phyllo (fillo) dough*

- Preheat the oven to 350 degrees.
- Spray two baking sheets with nonfat cooking spray.
- In a medium-size mixing bowl stir together the turkey, cream cheese, Swiss cheese, 1 teaspoon lemon pepper, and 1 teaspoon parsley flakes.
- Place a stack of phyllo dough onto a cutting board and with a very sharp knife cut the stack into three strips, making a total of thirty-nine strips 3 x 13 inches long.
- Using one strip phyllo dough at a time, put 1 teaspoon turkey filling at one end of a piece of the phyllo dough.
- Starting at the end of the strip of the phyllo dough with the teaspoon of turkey filling, fold one corner of the dough strip over the filling. This will make a triangle shape at the end of the strip. Continue folding the triangle all the way down the strip, around the turkey filling. Spray the turnover with nonfat cooking spray. Place the turnover seam side down on the prepared baking sheets. Continue until all of the turkey filling is used.
- Sprinkle the remaining ¹/2 teaspoon lemon pepper seasoning and the remaining 1¹/2 teaspoons parsley flakes evenly over all of the turnovers.
- Bake for 7 to 8 minutes or until the tops are lightly browned and crispy.
- Serve immediately.

Note: Phyllo dough is super easy to work with and is found in the dessert freezer aisle. It is very thin layers of pastry. It comes in either full sheets of 9 x 26 inches or half sheets of 9 x 13 inches. The 9 x 13-inch size is perfect for this recipe. If needed, full sheets can be cut in half.

Yield: 38 turnovers

Calories: 36 (0% fat); Total Fat: 0g; Cholesterol: 4mg; Carbohydrate: 5g; Dietary Fiber: 0g; Protein: 3g; Sodium: 85mg; Diabetic Exchanges: ½ starch

Preparation time: 15 minutes
Cooking time: 7 to 8 minutes
Total time: 23 minutes or less

Menu Ideas: These are fantastic with soups or salads for a complete meal. Try them with any one of these recipes in *Busy People's Low-Fat Cookbook*: Smokey Bean Soup on page 69, Sassy Slaw on page 91, or Spring Salad on page 103.

An Amazing Christmas Gift about God's Faithfulness

A s a little girl I could never understand the concept that God was faithful to us. I learned the truth of this concept in the late nineties. Friends of my husband and I had a horrific barn fire three days before Christmas and all ten of their horses burned to death. It was devastating. At that time in my life we didn't have a lot of money but really felt burdened to help our friends. We asked God to help us help them, and we agreed we would give to this family any gift we received above and beyond our normal Christmas gifts. The next day we unexpectedly received $250.00 from people who normally never gave us a Christmas gift. Because of these unexpected gifts we were able to *really* give to this distraught family. God is so awesome. He faithfully meets our needs.

Barbeque Turkey

For mini sandwiches this would be superb stuffed in the Onion Muffin Tops on page (162) of this book.

¹/₄ cup jellied cranberry sauce	2 cups (cut into I-inch chunks and
³/₄ cup barbeque sauce	shredded) turkey, all skin and fat removed

- In a medium-size, microwave-safe dish cook the cranberry sauce and barbeque sauce for 1 minute, stirring when it is complete.
- Add the turkey and stir. Microwave for 2 minutes and stir again.

Yield: 10 (¼-cup) servings

Calories: 85 (0% fat); Total Fat: 0g; Cholesterol: 24mg; Carbohydrate: 10g; Dietary Fiber: 0g; Protein: 8g; Sodium: 143mg; Diabetic Exchanges: ½ other carbohydrate, 1 very lean meat

Preparation time: 5 minutes or less
Cooking time: 3 minutes or less
Total time: 8 minutes or less

Menu Idea: This would be wonderful made as a sandwich and served with a cup of Corn Chowder on page 73 of *Busy People's Low-Fat Cookbook*.

Tom-the-Turkey Salad

Of course he's gonna say, "Eat more beef." This is a nice alternative to traditional high-fat turkey salad

1 cup firmly packed cooked (and cut into $^1/_2$-inch pieces) turkey, all skin and fat removed	1 tablespoon toasted and finely chopped sliced almonds
$^1/_3$ cup crushed pineapple (in its own juice), drained	$^1/_2$ teaspoon poppy seeds
1 tablespoon finely chopped dried cranberries	$^1/_3$ cup fat-free raspberry-pecan salad dressing
	Fresh chives (optional)

- Place the turkey, pineapple, dried cranberries, almonds, poppy seeds, and salad dressing in a medium bowl and stir until all the ingredients are mixed.
- Sprinkle with fresh chives if desired.
- Serve with low-fat, butter-flavored crackers.

Yield: 4 ($^1/_4$-cup) servings

(Crackers not included in analysis)
Calories: 97 (13% fat); Total Fat: 1g; Cholesterol: 30mg; Carbohydrate: 9g; Dietary Fiber: 0g; Protein: 11g; Sodium: 235mg; Diabetic Exchanges: $^1/_2$ fruit, 1$^1/_2$ very lean meat

Preparation time: 10 minutes

Menu Idea: Have a Tom-the-Turkey Salad/Sandwich and a cup of the World's Easiest Vegetable Soup on page 63 of *Busy People's Slow Cooker Cookbook.*

🝑 Ham & Green Bean Soup

I was pleasantly surprised at the wonderful flavor of this soup.

2	cups leftover green bean casserole	I	(12-ounce) jar fat-free, beef-flavored gravy
I	(15-ounce) can whole white potatoes, sliced, not drained	I	(14.5-ounce) Italian stewed tomatoes (with basil, garlic, and oregano), not drained
I	pound leftover ham, cut into tiny pieces with all fat removed		
		2	cups water

Slow Cooker Method:

■ Remove and discard any fried onions from the green bean casserole. Then put the casserole in a strainer. Rinse with water until all of the cream sauce is removed. It is okay if pieces of mushrooms remain. Place the rinsed green beans in a slow cooker.

■ Pour the water from the can of the potatoes into the slow cooker. Cut the potatoes into thin slices and put them into the slow cooker.

■ Add the ham, gravy, tomatoes, and water. Stir until well mixed.

■ Cover and cook on low for 4 to 5 hours.

Stove Top Method:

■ In a soup pan stir together the green beans, potatoes, ham, gravy, tomatoes, and water.

■ Cook over high heat for 10 minutes or until the mixture comes to a low boil.

■ Reduce the heat to medium and let simmer for 3 to 4 minutes. Serve hot.

Yield: 10 (1-cup) servings

Calories: 129 (20% Fat); Total Fat: 3g; Cholesterol: 29mg; Carbohydrate: 14g; Dietary Fiber: 2g; Protein: 11g; Sodium: 1078mg; Diabetic Exchanges: ½ starch, 1½ vegetable, 1 lean meat

⏲ **Preparation time:** 10 minutes or less
Cooking time: 4 to 5 hours or 14 minutes or less
Total time: 4 to 5 hours or 24 minutes or less

Menu Idea: Serve this satisfying delicious soup with the Tomato Biscuits on page 59 of *Busy People's Low-Fat Cookbook* for a complete meal your family will ask for again.

Index